T0255214

HISTORY OF COMPUTING AND EDUCATION 2 (HCE2)

IFIP – The International Federation for Information Processing

IFIP was founded in 1960 under the auspices of UNESCO, following the First World Computer Congress held in Paris the previous year. An umbrella organization for societies working in information processing, IFIP's aim is two-fold: to support information processing within its member countries and to encourage technology transfer to developing nations. As its mission statement clearly states,

> *IFIP's mission is to be the leading, truly international, apolitical organization which encourages and assists in the development, exploitation and application of information technology for the benefit of all people.*

IFIP is a non-profitmaking organization, run almost solely by 2500 volunteers. It operates through a number of technical committees, which organize events and publications. IFIP's events range from an international congress to local seminars, but the most important are:

• The IFIP World Computer Congress, held every second year;
• Open conferences;
• Working conferences.

The flagship event is the IFIP World Computer Congress, at which both invited and contributed papers are presented. Contributed papers are rigorously refereed and the rejection rate is high.

As with the Congress, participation in the open conferences is open to all and papers may be invited or submitted. Again, submitted papers are stringently refereed.

The working conferences are structured differently. They are usually run by a working group and attendance is small and by invitation only. Their purpose is to create an atmosphere conducive to innovation and development. Refereeing is less rigorous and papers are subjected to extensive group discussion.

Publications arising from IFIP events vary. The papers presented at the IFIP World Computer Congress and at open conferences are published as conference proceedings, while the results of the working conferences are often published as collections of selected and edited papers.

Any national society whose primary activity is in information may apply to become a full member of IFIP, although full membership is restricted to one society per country. Full members are entitled to vote at the annual General Assembly. National societies preferring a less committed involvement may apply for associate or corresponding membership. Associate members enjoy the same benefits as full members, but without voting rights. Corresponding members are not represented in IFIP bodies. Affiliated membership is open to non-national societies, and individual and honorary membership schemes are also offered.

HISTORY OF COMPUTING AND EDUCATION 2 (HCE2)

IFIP 19th World Computer Congress, WG 9.7,
TC 9: History of Computing, Proceedings of the
Second Conference on the History of Computing and
Education, August 21-24, 2006, Santiago, Chile

Edited by

John Impagliazzo
Hofstra University
New York, United States

 Springer

History of Computing and Education 2 (HCE2)

Edited by J. Impagliazzo

p. cm. (IFIP International Federation for Information Processing, a Springer Series in Computer Science)

ISSN: 1571-5736 / 1861-2288 (Internet)

ISBN: 13: 978-1-4419-4187-9   eISBN: 10: 0-387-34741-0
Printed on acid-free paper   eISBN: 13: 978-0-387-34741-7

Copyright © 2006 by International Federation for Information Processing.
Softcover reprint of the hardcover 1st edition 2006
All rights reserved. This work may not be translated or copied in whole or in part without the written permission of the publisher (Springer Science+Business Media, LLC, 233 Spring Street, New York, NY 10013, USA), except for brief excerpts in connection with reviews or scholarly analysis. Use in connection with any form of information storage and retrieval, electronic adaptation, computer software, or by similar or dissimilar methodology now known or hereafter developed is forbidden.
The use in this publication of trade names, trademarks, service marks and similar terms, even if they are not identified as such, is not to be taken as an expression of opinion as to whether or not they are subject to proprietary rights.

9 8 7 6 5 4 3 2 1
springer.com

Dedication

We dedicate this book

to the men and women who seek to preserve the legacy of the computing profession, particularly those associated with the education of future professionals in the computing field.

Contents

Invited Paper

Invited Panel

Refereed Papers

Preface

These proceedings derive from an international conference on the history of computing and education. This conference is the second of hopefully a series of conferences that will take place within the International Federation for Information Processing (IFIP) and hence, we describe it as the "Second IFIP Conference on the History of Computing and Education" or simply "History of Computing and Education 2" (HCE2). This volume consists of a collection of articles presented at the HCE2 conference held in association with the IFIP 2006 World Computer Congress in Santiago, Chile. Articles range from a wide variety of educational and computing perspectives and represent activities from five continents. The HCE2 conference represents a joint effort of the IFIP Working Group 9.7 on the History of Computing and the IFIP Technical Committee 3 on Education.

The HCE2 conference brings to light a broad spectrum of issues. It illustrates topics in computing as they occurred in the "early days" of computing whose ramifications or overtones remain with us today. Indeed, many of the early challenges remain part of our educational tapestry; most likely, many will evolve into future challenges. Therefore, these proceedings provide additional value to the reader as it will reflect in part the future development of computing and education to stimulate new ideas and models in educational development.

These proceedings provide a spectrum of interesting articles spanning many topics of historical interest. The invited paper by Deryn Watson describes a chronicle of the history of IFIP's TC3 over forty years. Its comprehensive detail promises to be a treasure for IFIP, TC3, and the educational community. The panel on the computing evolution in Spanish-speaking countries highlights the events leading to computing today in Spain and in Latin America. The panelists present their perspectives in these proceedings and they provide a record of interesting and interwoven accomplishments. In addition, a collection of four articles highlights the development of computing education in Argentina. These and other fascinating articles capture a historical perspective on the manner in which computing has affected the origins and progress of education in different parts of the world. They also preserve the computing legacies for future generations.

The HCE2 Program Committee expresses it gratitude to the organizers of the 2006 World Computer Congress for without their support, this conference would not be possible. We look forward to joining the presenters and attendees of the HCE2 conference and welcome all participants to this historic and interesting event.

John Impagliazzo

New York, 2006 May

Conference Organization

This conference

History of Computing and Education 2 (HCE2)

is a co-located conference organized under the auspices of the

IFIP World Computer Congress (WCC)

in Santiago, Chile

Mauricio Solar
WCC Congress Chair
<msolar@usach.cl>

Ramon Puigjaner
WCC International Program Committee Chair
<putxi@uib.es>

John Impagliazzo
HCE2 Program Committee Chair
<John.Impagliazzo@Hofstra.edu>

Program Committee

John Impagliazzo - Chair (United States)
Julián Aráoz (Venezuela)
Nicolas Babini (Argentina)
Cecilia Berdichevsky (Argentina)
Enrique Hinostroza (Chile)
Jan Lepeltak (Netherlands)
Nelson Maculan (Brazil)
Claudio Menezes (Uruguay)
Lena Olsson (Sweden)
José Pino (Chile)
Christina Preston (United Kingdom)
Arthur Tatnall (Australia)
Deryn Watson (United Kingdom)
Jan Wibe (Norway)
Cristina Zoltan (Spain)

Forty Years of Computers and Education
- A Roller-Coaster Relationship

Deryn Watson

Dept. of Education and Professional Studies,
King's College London, London SE1 9NN, UK <deryn.watson@kcl.ac.uk>

HCE2 Invited Paper

Abstract For forty years the relationship between computers and education has been engaged in a headlong journey, full of ups and downs, wild swerves to right and left, somehow both exhilarating and frightening, sometimes in tandem but at others barely still holding hands. The engine of the technologies keeps changing while the driver is sometimes a discipline, learners, or the teacher. The landscape passed along the way includes fleeting glimpses of beautiful but unconquerable mountains followed by attractive rivers with treacherous currents. The population is sometimes persuaded by innovators to come along for the ride, and then suddenly they embark on their own journey into an entirely different valley. The paper analyses this journey along the TC3 twin track of education with and about information and communication technologies, using evidence from its publications and debates, organisational structure and the influence of individuals. The presentation, from one who is neither a computer scientist nor mathematician, will aim to portray a particular perspective on this roller-coaster relationship.

1. Introduction

In essence, this paper is a history, specifically about the relationship between computers and education. I am choosing to characterise this historical journey. The decades of travel referred to in the title of this paper are the forty plus years since the establishing of the International Federation for Information Processing's (IFIP) Technical Committee 3 on Education in 1963, through to 2005. Because all history is more than a sequence of dates or facts – the story will be told by the identification

Please use the following format when citing this chapter:

Watson, D., 2006, in IFIP International Federation for Information Processing, Volume 215, History of Computing and Education 2 (HCE2), ed. J. Impagliazzo, (Boston: Springer), pp. 1–48.

of a number of key characteristics, structural, contextual and social that provide a shape to the nature of the journey. The thematic landscape passed along the way includes fleeting glimpses of beautiful but unconquerable mountains followed by attractive rivers with treacherous currents. Some enduring features however remain constant. Overall, this journey can be viewed as a process of innovation and change.

An exploration of the relationship between computers and education over this period is timely for a number of reasons: after forty years, 'folk' memory and knowledge about events and purposes in the early stages of any development fade; archival material may be sparse or relatively buried; and an understanding of history may help inform the future. But over-riding this is the sense that this has been exciting, heady time, during which, it can be argued, that Technical Committee 3 (TC3) has been a significant player. And the direction and speed of change in the information technologies and their relationship with education have been substantial. So I have chosen to characterise this as a roller-coaster relationship.

The evidential base for my research on the history of TC3 has been varied. I have gathered information on the structure and activities of Technical Committee 3, from its inception to its position with seven Working Groups and one Special Interest Group at the end of 2005 (Appendix 1). I have used information on its membership and its means of operation. I have evidence from minutes, but also informal notes and conversations during some meetings. And I have interviewed individuals who have been members of this structure. Analysis of structures provides indicators on why directions have shifted, and the significance of both the organisational context and influence of individuals in shaping events.

In addition there is a complete bibliography of publications for which TC3 and its various working groups have been responsible, mostly proceedings from conferences and working meetings, but also guidelines for curricula and 'good practice' (Appendix 2). The book titles themselves contribute to the charting of directions and are evidence of the interlinking between the activities of working groups and the substantial debates that have flourished, from teaching algorithms to computer scientists to an exploration of the school of the future. Papers in the official TC3 international journal, Education and Information Technologies, currently in its eleventh volume, supplement these debates.

One of the richest sources of evidence, however, for an analysis of the evolution of computers in education lies in the Proceedings of World Conferences on Computers in Education (WCCE), organised roughly every five years by the TC3. Eight such world conferences have been held, from the first in 1970 in Amsterdam, the Netherlands, to the eighth in 2005 in Stellenbosch, South Africa. The sections, papers and panel topics in these conferences reflect the concerns and views of the participants at the time and act as a unique record of debate and change (Appendix 3). The fact that they have been held at intervals enables shifts in the landscape to be noted that might otherwise be lost. From the first, WCCE has identified and addressed the dual concerns of our field; that is, education about computers, and using computers, or more recently, Information and Communications Technologies

(ICT), in education. It is to be expected that during a time-span of over forty years, the balance between these two would alter, and new topics emerge to reflect the changing attributes of the technology and the shifting perceptions about education.

Exploring this history provides challenges not so much because of the nature of the data available, but in finding an organisational modus vivendi. I have applied a style of ethnographic method; that is, I have probed or coded the range of evidence described above to identify themes, and then continually cross-referred between areas of data until I have been satisfied on their strength and validity. I have used this method for a number of reasons: I am familiar with it and it is often used in social science and educational research; it is based on the notion that individuals and structures can be probed for meaning through their written and spoken records; and it enables a variety of opinion and perceptions to emerge. Readers looking for a quantitative or statistical analysis will be disappointed.

Two features influence the story that emerges. The first is that no history can be 'definitive'; any history is but an interpretation of events and this one reflects my analysis of the data I have researched, and my selection of issues to probe. This means some themes may not be discussed, either because I do not feel I have a good enough 'handle' on them, or they are too large and deserve a separate analysis. Specifically this is the case with developing countries. And secondly it is also important to note that I am an insider ('informant') to this history. I presented my first paper at an IFIP TC3 conference at the third WCCE at Lausanne, 1981. I am currently chair of Working Group 3.1 (Informatics and ICT in secondary education) and thus a member of the executive committee of TC3, and editor-in chief of the journal Education and Information Technologies. Research insiders have access to information (such as notes, sometime contemporaneous, of issues at meetings, and informal as well as formal conversations) that is often unique. But they may not be as critical, or fail to see matters that a disinterested historian might consider significant. On the other hand, unlike many members of TC3, I have a humanities background, having studied geography and anthropology at University, and taught geography in schools before becoming involved with ICT in education through curriculum development and research. Although an elected member of the British Computer Society, one of the founding national member associations of IFIP, I am neither a mathematician nor computer scientist.

Analysis enables certain enduring themes such as teacher education to be identified, some such as debates on different programming languages have receded, and yet others such as Logo burst on the scene, briefly flourished and then disappeared. The growth and decline of topics and issues can be charted, from the initial dominance of higher education to the current broad scope of elementary through to higher and further education, and now embracing the community and lifelong learning agenda of the early 21st century. What trends could be, indeed were predicted, and what appear to have taken the community by surprise? What drives patterns of change – increasing technological sophistication, or a growing maturity of education and society in understanding what such technology can offer?

This paper will present a thematic analysis of these forty years, and also attempt a critique of the issues which surround the interaction between computers and the education process, and which might elucidate future debates.

2.   Technology and Educational Change

It is obvious that there have been substantial changes, both style and substance of computing power over the last forty years. This section will not include technical details, such as the shift from K to GB of memory, but focus on issues that affected the relationship with education. Six shifts are clear: the ever increasing in the level of computing power, a reduction of physical size, the development of graphical user interfaces, reduction in cost, and common software applications packages, and the growth of the internet and world wide web. All impact upon both the availability and nature of the technologies, with their consequential influence on education and society. I have identified three main time phases significant to education.

2.1   1963-1979

TC3 was established at a time when most computers were physically large - they took up substantial quantities of space. Huge cabinets in computer rooms or laboratories, with air-conditioning to ensure a relatively dust free environment, was the norm. They were expensive and located in universities, major businesses or establishments where automatic computation was a growing necessity. Their computing power was minute compared to today, but substantial compared with the world before computers, that is, of the manual calculator. Data had to be encoded into punched format (on either cards of tape) to reflect the 01 notation.

I first came across this world as a junior scientific officer in 1964 in the Royal Aircraft Establishment in Farnborough, UK. There, after manually recording the results of each wind tunnel trial, I would go to the computer rooms and enter the data by punching line after line of holes and blanks. It was tedious and prone to error, but it provided the aeronautical engineers with a means of fast processing data on air speed pressure and pressure on the shape of a plane as different angles. The computer however could not produce graphical results; I was introduced to the mysteries of using French Curves to manually plot the results.

Between 1963 and 1979, the demands for computers for businesses, local and national governments and agencies, and universities grew, as did the demand for individuals who understood the science of computers, data processing and programming. Equally, the computer industry grew to satisfy these demands. The computer remained a special fixed resource, but data entry shifted to automatic punch card or tape, then to terminals with a qwerty style, noisy keyboard, and finally to terminals that could be at a certain distance from the machine itself, connected by a cable. But for education at this time, this power remained in the hands of a few – computer science or mathematics departments in universities and a few schools.

Nevertheless, some software was being developed for use in departments other than mathematics in schools and higher education, specifically for instance science simulations and data processing. It is important to note that not all classes or lectures at that time were of the 'traditional chalk and talk' mode. Science laboratories had spearheaded a more active learning mode, as had for instance the use of geographical board games. Both these 'tools' facilitated more active discussion on classes. At this time, by a series of coincidences, I became involved in the Computers in the Curriculum project headed by Bob Lewis at Chelsea College, and remember working with geography teachers to develop a database of rain in Wales. Then in the later 70s, this landscape of remote but mostly unattainable mountain peaks changed dramatically.

2.2   1980-1989

The advent of silicon technology, 'the chip' was clearly a benchmark in the nature of computing power. By the start of the 1980s microcomputers were ubiquitous, although usually still in the hands of the specialist few. By the end of the decade, computing power was available for a range of disciplines and administration, had begun to penetrate elementary and vocational education, and been subject to wild swerves according to each new development. For instance, the flexibility of locating a stand-alone micro in any room – whether a university library, school classroom, or administrator's office, suddenly became curtailed with the growth of networks located in special rooms to increase the number of stations (terminals) with shared power and printer facilities. On the other hand, networks opened the vista for distance education, rapidly taken up for education by countries with remote populations such as the Inuit in Canada and outback in North Australia.

Alternative devices to keyboards were developed, floor turtles, robots and science laboratory controls and other peripherals emerged and the term multimedia emerged. With the development of the Apple Mackintosh, a benchmark of the graphical user interface was set; the need to program special applications led to specialist authoring languages, while general-purpose business applications for word processing, spreadsheets and data handling, such as Claris and Microsoft took hold. By the end of the decade, laptops were in evidence - I do still have a copy of an early information leaflet referring to a 'kneetop'.

Thus for all branches of education the availability and use of computing power became a possibility, mountains had been replaced by hills that could be scaled with relative ease. Governments began paying attention to fostering, and promoting the development of national computer industries geared to providing computers for business and micros for education. By the end of the decade, individual national machines with their own architecture and programming language only survived by becoming clones of major international companies with the ability to run a few standard application packages. The term computer science was often replaced by Informatics; the terms educational computing, computer assisted instruction and learning, and computer managed learning declined with the rise of the more general Information Technology; and computer or IT awareness moved to the centre ground.

It is not clear how much the world of TC3 anticipated the growth of standard application packages with the concomitant reduction of software development for specific disciplines and curricula purposes. Ironically after the gains of a decade of CAL, the growth of computer awareness for all led to a swerving away from the educational purpose of using computers for learning. Nevertheless, the eighties were an equally heady time for curriculum development, with attention to issues such as teacher style and interactivity in the classroom. As soon as micros with graphical interfaces arrived, the possibility for an incremental step for geography (and other humanities) became apparent, with the ability to turn the geographical board games into interactive simulations. One of the reasons some schools were in advance of using computers for learning, was because they could envisage it supporting the more open, discursive and active lessons that were becoming more frequent, and subject to much discussion at other educational fora. But these were not the norm. In universities interestingly, computers were used in laboratories for the processing and analysis of data, but they hardly penetrated the lecture or seminar room.

2.3   1990-2005

This period can be characterised by the flowering of global communications with the internet and world wide web, and finally digital mobility. The growth of satellite availability from specialist defence to generalist purposes provided a shift from local and national to international and indeed global networks. Previous networks replied upon telephonic cables; now the communications technologies began to impinge upon the perception of networks, and the nature and availability of information. The term computer was coined to reflect to its original calculation function. The term then changed to ICT to reflect the dominant the functions of information and communications; in turn this is now being replaced by digital technologies.

At first this affected more substantially business, administrative, and educational enterprises. But a change occurred that education is still grappling with, that of the penetration of computers into the social world. Some parents would have been using computers for work for a long time. Now with the further growth of the industry and subsequent reduction of price, personal computers (PCs) came within the reach of many households and students. Society was attracted in by the availability of global personal communication, accessibility of information, and substantial processing power through ubiquitous business applications of Microsoft.

In the developed world, computers have increasingly become a part of the equipment of a household, along with such items as a washing machine. And the commercial organisations of society have reacted swiftly; shopping, financial services, travel and entertainment. ICT also became common in all educational institutions, and also in community centre, further education college, and libraries. For those without personal access to a computer, libraries, community centres and an internet café is commonly available in urban streets.

The role and function of Information and Communication Technologies in schools is no longer specialist or unique; the challenge is to ensure that educational organisations use the technologies for the purpose of learning and teaching within this different inclusive environment. It is not clear how much TC3 can fully comprehend and explore this world without an influx of social scientists. Teachers, lecturers, administrators and students use the internet to communicate and the web to search for information. They use ICT to organise and manage their work. The real question is how much is it used in classrooms, lecture rooms, or online to teach and learn the concepts and disciplines that still lie at the heart of education, and to support process and styles of learning such as collaboration and debate?

So now the landscape of computing power has become the equivalent of a flat plain, with no difficult terrain of accessibility to negotiate. Flowing across this plain however is a wide river, which affects developing countries and those who are socially and economically deprived anywhere. Bridging this river, or overcoming the digital divide, is a cause of substantial concern that TC3 among others is seeking to address. However the ubiquity of the global digital technology has further issues worth noting here.

Because of the open nature of the global web, the river current is dangerous but which may not be apparent on the surface. And information of itself is not knowledge, but a means towards developing knowledge. And developing knowledge is the business of education – educare, to draw out knowledge and experience. Society needs education to grasp the complex issues about veracity, security, surveillance, legality and ethics now posed by global information networks.

The second issue to note had been the growth of mobile technologies, and particularly the use by the young. At the sixth WCCE in Birmingham, 1995, no mention was made of the growth of mobile phones. Yet by the late nineties the use of this technology already had a profound effect on the ready availability and form of communication. The young were the first to adopt the mobile (or cell phone) as an essential communication device; they use text messaging as often as voice and have developed a shorthand 4 speed. A new language of communication, incorporating graphical functions, has developed fast and is now penetrating formal structures. The educational world of language and communication specialists is studying this change, but it has as yet had little impact on topics debated inTC3.

And this is particularly important because this digital mobile world enables the incorporation of picture, music, film, and broadcast. This is in 2005 the current world of the young; it dominates their culture, interests, aspirations, and increasingly employment. This illustrates the new move to way beyond an information device. It is this digital culture that members of TC3 need to understand and embrace. And unlike previous waves of technology, it is not embedded in institutions and established professions where the power of understanding the technology and its use dominated. It has shifted to society; it is as if the population that has been persuaded by innovators to come along for the ride, then suddenly embarks on their own journey into an entirely different valley.

3.   Technical Committee 3 - Its Evolution and Structures

3.1   A new IFIP technical committee

In 1959, a conference was held in Paris on computers and computing, under the auspices of UNESCO. At that meeting, representatives of the main computer societies active at that time decided to explore ways of building on that conference. Subsequently, with the support of UNESCO, thirteen national computer associations agreed in 1960 to found an International Federation of Information Processing [1].

IFIP Council formally decided in 1962 to establish a new Technical Committee for Education (TC3). Richard Buckingham (UK) took over as chair for the establishment of TC3 in 1963. This early establishment of a Technical Committee for Education is historically significant, both as the first international committee on computers and education, and secondly that an organisation dedicated to computers and computing recognised in its earliest days, the fundamental role of education. It is true that the then prime concern was the growth of the training of professionals in data processing, both for educational institutions and the world of business and management. Nevertheless, many educationalists will have reason to thank IFIP for not calling their new Technical Committee 'Training'.

"It was inevitable that education should come to the fore early in the development of IFIP" avowed Buckingham [1]. In essence, he reports that in the early 1960s most educational efforts were focused on the use of computers for numerical computation, under the aegis of university mathematics departments, teaching programming and developing high-level languages. There was however little formal education concerned with information processing, a significant issue for business and administration.

The first formal meeting of TC3 was held in Paris, France in February 1964, followed in the same year by ones in Liblice, Czechoslovakia and Rome, Italy. By the end of that year, 14 members had been appointed, and a series of activities were planned to establish programmes for training and curriculum development in the science of information processing.

Three concerns characterised the early period in the 1960s, and laid the foundations for the development of the Working Groups of TC3. The first was a determination to engage with directly and support the needs of professionals in the field. This was characterised by the production of a series of guidelines for using computers in education that have continued at various intervals to this day. The second was to explore every avenue for collaboration with other groups, both national and within the fledgling IFIP, so as to draw on the early work of all to form an international corpus of understanding of issues and how to address them. Key individuals from new computing societies and organisations including Belgium, Denmark, France, Israel, Italy, Mexico, The Netherlands, Sweden, UK and the USA, led these activities. A third characteristic was the devising and running of training seminars for advanced data processing, with full accreditation and certification - the first in collaboration with the International Computing Centre in Rome, and the second with the IFIP Administrative Data Group.

Membership of TC3 therefore grew by the initiative of keen committed individuals from a number of countries, who spearheaded activities, which triggered a number of meetings. Many were employed in higher education, others in the computer hardware and software industry. In effect, these individuals formed a committed club of innovators, who were collecting information about activities and sharing developments between themselves and others at a series of meetings in their different countries. The initial membership of 14 grew to 23 by the early seventies. These individuals represented their national associations (which they themselves had often had a hand in establishing) that formed the bedrock of the subscribing membership of IFIP. The basis of membership of any Technical Committee is still this representation, although this has been modified in later years, the implications of which will be discussed later. And the practice of moving meetings to an ever-increasing circuit of locations has continued to this day. Apart from the personal joy at travelling to many diverse locations, such meetings are stimulating as they enable the exploration of the national activities at each location, and they can trigger new membership. On the other hand, there are substantial cost implications, which shall also be discussed later. For the purposes of this paper, the most significant of these meetings was the first World Conference on Computers in Education (WCCE) in Amsterdam, 1970. This conference was attended by many who were not then in the IFIP or TC3 'family', and provides by its scope and scale a benchmark for addressing the relationship between computers and education.

At the first formal meeting of TC3 in 1964 [1], the following aims were agreed:

a) to establish guidelines for comprehensive training programmes and curricula in the science of information processing, with special consideration for the needs of developing countries and to encourage the implementation of these programmes;

b) to generate material to acquaint the general public with the computer and its impact on various aspects of society;

c) to serve as a central clearing house for all educational material pertaining to the science of information processing.

Compare this with the current aims of TC3 in 2005 [2]:

- to provide an international forum for educators to discuss research and practice in;
  - teaching informatics
  - educational uses of communication and information technologies (ICDT;
- to establish models for informatics curricula, training programs and teaching methodologies;
- to consider the relationship of informatics and other curriculum areas;
- to promote on-going education of ICT professionals and those in the workforce whose employment involves the use of information and communication technologies;
- to examine the impact of information and communication technologies on the whole educational environment:
  -teaching and learning
  -administration and management of the educational enterprise
  -local, national and regional policy-making and collaboration

An understanding of the growth and expansion of these aims can be gleaned in part from analysing the intertwining of the organisational structure of TC3, its membership and activities, and in particular the Workings Groups.

3.2   The growth and activities of Working Groups

In an analysis similar to and entwined with that of technological change, the growth of Working Groups can be charted in the same three distinct phases.

3.2.1 The early period – 1966-1979

As the name suggests, Working Groups (WGs) are designed to take forward specific areas of interest within a Technical Committee. Working Group 3.1 was established in 1966 to reflect the question of how best to extend education about computers into secondary schools. Imaginatively, the remit considered the use of computers in all aspects of secondary education, and not simply the teaching of programming. Thus both Computer Assisted Instruction/Learning in the disciplines and teacher training were the dual concerns that remain to this day. Many of the members of this working group were nominated by national association members of the of the pioneering TC3 countries – Austria, Canada, France, Denmark, Israel, The Netherlands, Sweden, UK, US, and Yugoslavia. Others were 'known' about; at that time, a few individuals were pioneering using computers in schools. For instance, David Tinsley [3] reports that in around 1997/8 he was drawn in by Dick Buckingham to the schools committee of a new British Computer Society (founded 1967). There the over-riding concern was that "youngsters should be acquainted with the needs of industry and so understand computers and programming".

Through Dick, he was invited to join the new WG 3.1and attended his first working meeting in Paris in 1979. "The idea was simple really, the most sensible thing in the current climate of what's it all about was to sit down and write advice for schools. So that's what we did." He also suggested that under the chairmanship of Dick Buckingham, anyone who dared to publish anything (such as David Johnson in Minnesota or Hank Wolbers from the Netherlands) was perceived to have 'put their head' above the parapet, and would invited into the new working group.

This first working group met regularly between the late sixties to mid-seventies often in association with invitations to mount workshops on computer education for teachers in secondary education. Tinsley [3] remembers that at these meetings the members took the opportunity to work on writing the advisory guidelines. The first of these, Computer Education in secondary school – an outline guide for teachers [4] (known as the Red Book), was available at WCCE Amsterdam in 1970, with a revised version, the Blue Book, available in 1971 and subsequently translated into a number of languages. This developed with three further topic books, produced at a series of meetings funded by CERI (OECD), thus establishing the primacy of the notion of producing guidelines for the profession. All guidelines from WGs are noted in the Bibliography (Appendix2).

In the meantime, one of the three initial activities of TC3 noted earlier, that is the devising and running of professional training seminars in ADP, was devolved to a new Working Group 3.2, with the original title of Organising Educational Seminars. First came the expansion into seminars for Information Systems design, resulting in the publication of an international curriculum for information systems designers [5]. Later, to reflect the continuous concern for the nature of the curriculum for teaching computer science in universities, the name of WG 3.2 was changed to Informatics and ICT in Higher Education.

Bob Aiken [6] attended the first WCCE at the recommendation of his PhD supervisor, who was aware of the work ongoing with respect to the computer science curriculum. He welcomed the chance to visit Europe for personal reasons, but became "drawn into the debate – well arguments - between mathematicians and electrical engineers about the foundations of the science of computing" on both sides of the Atlantic. Having become a friend and colleague of Bernard Levrat, taking a sabbatical to work in Geneva, consolidated his commitment to IFIP, membership of WGs 3.1 and 3.2, national representative on TC3 and then GA.

Two further working groups were established in 1971. WG 3.3 was for Instructional Uses of Computers, which produced a further booklet on computers in learning and teaching. The remit of this working group however changed, in part because it was perceived to overlap with the existing groups, and was moved first to consider 'futures', especially with respect to new technologies, and now is identified as Research on Educational Applications of Information Technologies. And in a logical extension to the work of 3.2, but also to distinguish it from the higher education sector, WG 3.4 took on the more specific vocational education mantle, and is now called IT-Professional and Vocational Education in Information

Technology. Similar to the brief of 3.2, it is concerned with devising of curriculum and related accreditation. It is notable that in this early period, the emphasis on producing curricula and guidance for professionals in the workplace of the computing industry, business, universities and schools dominated the activities of these initial working groups.

Thus by 1979 and after 16 years, four working groups of TC3 had been established, and two world conferences (Amsterdam, The Netherlands 1970 and Marseilles, France, 1975) held. For these WCCEs, TC3 relied upon the efforts of the fledgeling WGs for their planning and execution. Guidelines and curricula for professionals had been published by WGs 3.1 and 3.2, and in addition WGs 3.1, 3.2 and 3.4 had each held their own first individual conferences from which 3 books were published.

3.2.2 An established pattern – 1980-1989

In the 1980s a substantial shift in activities occurred, best characterised by an increase in their number and scale and the consolidation of an establishing pattern. The third and fourth WCCEs were held in Lausanne, Switzerland in 1981 and Norfolk, Virginia USA in 1985. Two more working groups were set up, in 1983 WG 3.5 on Informatics in Elementary Education and in 1987 WG 3.6 on Distance Learning. Throughout the decade working groups held a number of conferences that dominated their energy and attracted new membership. In addition in the 1980s,TC3 through its WGs held two regional conferences, one in Japan (1986) and one in Europe that also coincided with celebrating 25 years of TC3 (1988). Two reasons appear to have triggered such regional conferences, which have so far not been repeated. The first was with WCCE 1985 in the USA, and WCCE 1990 in Australia, there was concern that the momentum of European involvement that characterised the first three WCCEs might be lost. Secondly, TC3, and indeed IFIP in general appeared to be having difficulty in attracting interest and membership from the Far East. There is in fact an ongoing discussion about whether IFIP is too 'Eurocentric'.

No guidelines were produced in the 1980s; no clear evidence explains this. Establishing guidelines and developing curricula were very much the raison d'etre of the first working groups [3]. In the 1980s, the focus shifted to mounting a series of international conferences to reflect the flowering of interest and activity in schools, further and higher education – and that of governments. Conferences reflected a different mutual relationship with the professional community. This was after all the first decade of micros, and the journey of exploration was fast, multi-facetted and optimistic. The WG conferences provided venues for the expanding university computer science departments, faculties of education and teacher training colleges, local and regional education boards, and government departments to explore the use this new, small and flexible resource, and discuss the issues that came with it. These might be open with an international call for papers, or working group conferences with attendance by invitation, and often limited to around 100. This latter style of conference have become an established feature; many consider them to be the ideal means of generating real debate, exploring change in perceptions, and a defining characteristic of working group membership.

Bernard Cornu [7] became involved in this period, being invited to attend the working conference on ICT and mathematics in secondary school, on behalf of ICME. So why did he continue and remain involved? "First the international context of IFIP – many, many different countries; then I wanted the topic computers in education, ICME was more about the didactics of mathematics; and of course I met good friends there....this is important , not a detail...it's a friendly way we work in IFIP."

In addition to classic paper and panel sessions, workshops were a substantial part of conference structure. They may have been on particular software designed to support the use of computers for subject learning, whether computer science, mathematics, or even occasionally for humanities and languages. And others might feature a particular programming language for computer science teaching. And a further feature of the three world conferences of 1981, 1985 and 1990 was the substantial exhibitions of hardware and software manufacturers, and the level of computer business sponsorship that underpinned these events. I attended my first IFIP event, at the suggestion of Bob Lewis, my project director, at WCCE 1981 in Lausanne – the scale of the programme and exhibition remain a vivid experience, despite the fact that I had been involved in software development for a number of years. I had no sense of the internal IFIP community however until my first WG 3.1 event the following year, at which firm friendships were formed; I became a member in 1990.

Thus by the end of the 1980s, 6 WGs had now been established, two WCCEs held, and 19 books published. Conference activity dominated agenda of the working groups

3.3   A shift in profile – 1990-2005

In the1990s, two further world conferences, the fifth and sixth WCCEs were held in Sydney, Australia in 1990, and Birmingham, UK in 1995. WG 3.7 on Information Technology and Educational Management was formed in 1996. And then into the new century the seventh and eighth WCCEs were held in Copenhagen, Denmark in 1991 and Stellenbosch, South Africa in 2005. The established pattern of WG conferences thrived, with 37 books produced. In addition, in 2005, a new Special Interest Group, was established on Lifelong learning (SIG LLL). An interesting development has been a revival of working meetings to produce Guidelines. These significantly have been funded by UNESCO and revived a relationship with the founding organisation. Involvement with UNESCO has led to two further activities. TC3 taken an active part of the UNESCO/IFIP world forum on IT for developing nations (WITFOR); two events, in Vilnius Lithuania 2003 and Botswana 2005 have been held. And TC3 was equally active, through UNESCO and the Swiss Academy of Technical Sciences in the United Nations World Symposium on the Information Society, Geneva 2004.

During conferences in the early 1990s, an additional element was developed to ensure the maximum interaction between all participants. Themed topical discussion (or focus) groups would be timetabled to meet regularly during the event. Attendees would select or be allocated to a focus group – and they would present the result of their deliberations to the collected conference in the last session, often with key recommendations. These reports and recommendations began to feature in the published books, and the style was adopted in both 1995 and 2001 world conferences, with well over a thousand participants all joining focus groups. This engendered a sense of inclusion; the collegiality generated amongst participants should not be underestimated. Post conference publication of the discussions meant that they were available to a wider readership. On the other hand no mechanism was in place, and it is still a challenge, to ensure that these debates and recommendations are communicated with policy-makers and practitioners.

3.3.1 Until 2005

At WCCE in Stellenbosch all participants at the event were invited to write down three key points they wished to communicate about 'what works' re ICT and education. Chairs of sessions also wrote three points down to reflect discussions following papers. Post conference these were collated to form a declaration by the IFIP Technical Committee community, entitled ICT in education – make it work. Its conclusions will be discussed later. This is known as The Stellenbosch Declaration- make it work [8], and has been distributed electronically to all the WCCE attendees with a request to distribute it further.

Unfortunately, in parallel, conference exhibitions and sponsorship has been in decline. It is possible to infer that the dominance of large multinational computer producers, the decline of national machines geared to local schools, and the reduction in investment in computer assisted learning that characterised the third technological phase has made the educational market less significant and relatively indistinguishable from that of society in general. The impact is substantial. First in the absence of the computer industry sponsorship, mounting conferences carries an increased financial concern for the host institution and TC3/WGs. Secondly, the overall financial climate in educational institutions makes it harder for individuals to get support to attend, particularly the young. Although IFIP does fund a small number bursaries for attendees from developing countries, this problem is affecting the ability of TC3/WG and Programme Chairs to mount events, in part because of the extra burden such financial pressure causes in addition to the already busy agenda of organisation.

Then another stream of conferences emerged. Since the early days of IFIP, the General Assembly (GA) has mounted a biennial World Computer Congress. These Congresses functioned as binding for the community of the enthusiastic committed pioneers in the development of the new Federation. Congresses maintained a bond during the expansion and rapid development of the constituent Technical Committees in the early period. Note that 9 of the 12 current Technical Committees were established between 1962 and 1976. Meeting at a biennial Congress helped keeping the original community together and sharing what were some substantial commonalities, such as software theory and practice and computer applications in technology. Only very occasionally was a paper presented at Congress on an educational topic. Indeed Peter Bollerslev [9] is of the opinion that TC3 became strong because "there was no competition from Congresses", which may also explain how TC3 was able to establish such a strong pattern of its own quinquennial WCCEs and sense of community.

In 1992 however, a substantial shift occurred. Congress was always designed around themes presented and organised by some of the TCs. TC3 was first invited to take part in WCC Madrid and was represented by Education and Society. Further thematic involvement of TC3 has occurred in every Congress since 1996. This involvement has been significant politically by raising the profile of TC3 and its educational themes within IFIP. Hitherto Education, though highly active within its own frame, had a lower profile overall within the GA. On the other hand, it has sometimes created a crowded events agenda, forcing members to make choices between attendance at working group events or WCC.

Another feature in these sixteen years was the number of times working groups collaborated to mount joint conferences, for example 3.1 and 3.5 on supporting change through teacher education, 3.1 and 3.2 on informatics teaching, cognition and social and ethical issues. Such joint events are increasing. There are practical advantages in association with the cost structures and organisation involved in mounting events. They have increased the sense of community between working groups, extending the collaboration developed during WCCE planning. But it also illustrates the relative arbitrariness of the particularities of the current working groups, that is the mix of sectors and activities, based on their historical development outlined above.

During this period, members of TC3 have discussed the strengths and limitations of the current WG structure. The debates have centred on crosscutting themes. Research is one example. WG 3.3 has had a chequered history and found it less easy to sustain a regular and coherent series of events. This is in part because research is a basis for many conference presentations and debates in the other working groups, and also because the group has had difficulty in sustaining a substantial membership of individuals who are often equally committed to reporting research in the contexts of other WG events. Other themes such as tele-learning illustrate the cross-cutting matrix whereby working groups operate, even though the structure of the seven groups may appear linear. Thus under the aegis of WG 3.6

Distance Learning, but sometimes independently as part of TC3, tele-learning/teaching conferences were mounted throughout the 1990s, and contributed to the revival of TC3 activity in Congresses. But of course tele-learning has changed in the last ten years to be associated with the impact of the web and e-learning; thus elearning is a now substantial feature across the WG events. Similarly, life-long learning embraces all elements of schooling, university and vocational education, as well as learning at a distance and learning in communities throughout life. On the other hand, WG 3.7 has operated very effectively since its inception as a relatively closed community, with its own biennial working conferences, with fewer cross-links. This suits the nature of the community. In effect WGs operate in a number of dimensions, but a matrix of activities, between the contexts and themes more truly reflect the way the structure and activities work in reality. Indeed, in more recent years, the WG chairs and TC officers have held an executive meeting before the formal AGM to discuss themes and plans of the WGs to ensure that this virtual matrix of connectivity operates as effectively as possible.

3.4   Other features

The section above has focussed on three time phases of structural development of the working groups and their main activities, writing guidelines and mounting conferences. There are however other features that I consider worth noting.

3.4.1 Camaraderie

A feature of the initial TC3 and its first two working groups is that initial membership was basically a group of committed individuals with common interests in this new field. The meetings in the first period were mainly internal working events of often no more than 10-12 people where the members produced guidelines, and planned the first two world conferences. Such intensive activity clearly fostered a camaraderie; the sense of a collaborative team, with common interests and concerns is an enduring trait of the TC3 working groups that is frequently mentioned, both formally and informally by its members. As Tinsley [3] said "really we were just a group of friends – but a powerhouse too". The sense of a working collective of individuals from many different contexts and countries has not only underpinned the growth of activities since the start, but enduring friendships have developed. When asked how they continued to be involved after their first contact, Tinsley [3], Aiken [6], Bollerslev [9] and Cornu [7] all commented on the friendship embedded within the community. Each returned to this point, ensuring that I took it seriously. Aiken [6] called it a "nice confluence of the professional and personal aspects" of life. This certainly reflects my experience as a member. Meetings are relaxed and we always socialise in the evenings. My children grew up with a range of visiting 'friends for IFIP' passing through. Indeed the fact that all interviewed agreed to a telephone interview with me was in part because we are friends and colleagues, but it also meant I could understand their tone and reflect on the meaning they were imparting. In addition, I could not simply ask questions about their views, but also explore my tentative analysis with them, which drew out further opinion.

One means whereby this camaraderie has continued is because, as can be seen from a scrutiny of working group chairs and book editorship, the initial group of individuals were active in establishing all the subsequent working groups. So the style of operating, and the social agenda, was perpetuated. In the same way, the strategies for organising a conference and producing proceedings have been passed on to newer members from the pioneers. It is only in the last few years that TC3 has felt the need to capture such information in guidelines for members' use.

3.4.2 Membership

Another feature of working groups is that members did not have to be affiliated or part of their national association, but have been invited to take part on the basis of their activity and personal interest. Indeed, they may be from a country that has no formal affiliation with IFIP. TC3 working groups rarely have more than a few members from any one country, as care is taken to ensure country 'blocks' do not form. The way an individual interacts and works with the community at an event is a major point towards nomination. This way both the international and working nature of the community has been maintained. A further feature of working groups is that many members have relatively little to do with TC3. They see themselves as active in support of the practitioner and professional community. Thus David Tinsley [3] was interested in having working meetings with outcomes, not being a committee member.

Members of TC3 represent the educational interest of IFIP national member organisations, and thus the structure of IFIP and the General Assembly. There is substantial overlap as the some individuals are members of both, as national members representatives on TC3 and members of working groups. For example, Peter Bollerslev [9], having met members of WG3.1 at the OECD seminars in Paris in 1971/2, attended the second WCCE in Marseilles, and was invited to join WG 3.1 while attending a conference organised in Lancaster by Bob Lewis. (1977) He says that there "he met Uli Bosler [from Germany] there, and found they got on well and could collaborate, so... that was it". This reflects the similar comments by Tinsley – this was an active group where working and friendship mattered. Then the following year, the Danish Computer Society asked him to be their representative on TC3. In essence, TC3 is the formal committee with responsibilities for the activities it working groups undertake, while also reporting to GA on its undertakings. Johnson [10] notes TC chairs also hold a unique position in the structure between the GA and working groups.

This hierarchical pattern existed until the last period, and manifested itself in an interesting way. Working group chairs were not formal members of TC3 unless they happened to be national representatives. They were invited to attend TC3 AGMs, but traditionally sat at the rear of the room, and only took part when asked a specific point. Not only has this been specifically reported to me by Peter Bollerslev [9], but I happened to experience it myself, when attending a TC meeting in the 1980's on behalf of a colleague who was a national member.

This pattern changed in the early 1990's; working group chairs became full members of TC3 and encouraged to take full part in discussions. By the end of that decade, an executive had been formed specifically of the main officers and working group chairs to plan the forward agenda for activities. This seems to be wholly appropriate as after all it was the working groups who were responsible for devising and organising these activities. It has been intriguing for me to realise during the course of this research that a remarkably similar pattern of structure operated at the General Assembly level. GA consists of national member association representatives who embody of the federal structure and responsibilities to the whole. Chairs of the Technical Committees were invited to attend, but had no formal constitutional role. Indeed, Bollerslev [9] has informed me that they even sat at a separate table removed from the main body, and had little part in discussion. And yet it was their activities through the working groups that made the federation function. In the early 1990s, by a combination of strong leadership of TC chairs [9] and equally strong leadership by the IFIP President [10], the rules were changed and Technical Committee chairs became active full participants of the GA. Indeed the members also form a Technical Committee, and as a collective provide a powerful voice within the whole [9, 10].

This has had interesting consequences. The first has already been noted. It is clear that the timing of the invitation for TC3 to take part in Congress in 1992 was no accident. It was part of a political shift in the roles of TC chairs within GA. It has been clear that some WG chairs dislike their pattern of events, already reported to TC3 and GA, being disrupted by the intervention of WCCs. It is equally clear no TC chair would wish to dilute their influence by refusing to contribute to WCCs. This conundrum was actually debated in TC3 AGM in 2003 in Pori, Finland with the President of IFIP, Klaus Brunstein – who was there to attend the TC3 fortieth birthday celebrations. Johnson [10] suggests that the role of Congress is also under discussion in GA. One issue for TC3 is that WCCs on the whole are structured around a series of mini conferences that are virtually stand-alone. Therefore, there is no particular benefit that distinguishes a WCC from other TC3 events. Indeed, I remember my enormous disappointment at the Madrid 1992 Congress when the education stream and that of TC9 for social and ethical issues ran in parallel rather than being entwined.

A greater intertwining of the relationships between the various stakeholders in the Federation is obviously beneficial. One anomaly remains; the direct links between active members of a working group and the national member organisation may be few – yet the former is central to continuing activities while the latter pays the IFIP fee. Thus, the actual workings tread a careful informal path to ensure that formal relationships remain intact. For instance, as a chair of WG 3.1 and member of TC3; I was aware that there was an IFIP strategy working party, but had seen no report. When interviewing Johnson, [10] it was apparent that some of the issues I was seeking clarity about for this paper were in a draft document of this working party. Good happenstance. Johnson says that "one of the issues under discussion is the links, existing or broken, between the various stakeholders and structures of the organisation". He also reports a desire by the working party to ensure that "a permissive structure" should reflect what is essentially a permissive group of member organisations.

Equally significant is the relationship between IFIP and other international organisations such as UNESCO. Here Bollerslev [9] asserts that the strengthening relationship between IFIP and UNESCO in the last period has benefited IFIP by raising its profile. This has been apparent both in the work with TC9 on WITFOR and also the UN World Summit on the Information Society. Peter Bollerslev [9], being at the same time a member of WG 3,1, TC3, GA and a former President of IFIP, has interesting reflections on the complications of the relationships between the different structures and activities within the Federation. I know he was particularly pleasured that Aicha Bqah Diaqllo of UNESCO addressed the seventh WCCE in Copenhagn in 2001. He thinks that it is now the time to try to formalise more closely the relationship between IFIP and UNESCO, as it was IFIP's founding sponsor in 1960. It has also been reported in GA minutes following the 2003 AGM that this was desirable and I believe it has the attention of the President Klaus Brunnstein. Bernard Cornu [7], of WG 3.1 and TC3, who is also a UNESCO representative of France, thinks that UNESCO could use IFIP more as a group of ICT experts with connections at the policy and practitioner levels.

One last question. How does TC3 maintain it relations with the practitioner community? On the whole they not come to international conferences unless specifically encouraged or sponsored. They may then however be drawn into the community as their career progresses. But it will mainly be through individual contacts. The majority of active members and attendees at events are academics or managers and policy makers in the field. The task for TC3 is to find a means, preferably both electronic and personal to connect more strongly with policy makers and practitioners so that the themes we discuss reach as wide an audience as possible, and they in turn need to influence our debates.

It would appear that the combined efforts of individuals, some with notable leadership skills, and the style of operating as an active community of practice which characterises the nature of Technical Committee 3 and its working groups. These would seem to be the critical factors that have enabled it to thrive and change over forty years and to become one of the most important TCs in IFIP today. However I remind readers that this is an insider perspective.

4.   The Main Debates

4.1   A word on data

It was not possible to do any sensible numerical analysis with regard the WCCEs and their publications (Appendix 3), for the following reasons. Each conference selected from submitted papers for presentation on merit. In some conference proceedings, all papers presented were included in the proceedings. In others, a further selection was made from presentations for inclusion. Thus no inference can be made from the different number of papers from each event. Out of curiosity, I counted 65 countries that have been represented by publications from the eight world conferences (Appendix 3). And while you might expect certain English speaking countries to dominate, such as the USA, UK and Australia, others (measured by papers at 6, 7, or 8 WCCEs) have provided consistent presence throughout, notably Brazil, China, Denmark, France, Italy, Japan, The Netherlands, Norway, Sweden, and Switzerland. The range of countries may not represent all attendees, but attendance information is not in any archive. But this range does reinforce the actuality of an international community, and at the same time in part refute the assumption that it is a Eurocentric organisation.

It is a shame that actual attendance data is not available, as there is a general 'feeling' in the community that attendance in general is not holding up, and that from some regions in particularly North America, is on the wane. Aiken [6] supports this, suggesting that it is caused by the growth of other specialist communities that embrace ICT in education. There can be no doubt about the growth of such communities; in one 5 day period in February 2006 I received notification of eleven different such events. Aiken [6] considers that TC3 will have to work hard to ensure that its constituency is not reduced by the attractions of other organisations offering similar debates, in events closer to home and therefore less costly.

Two other matters caught my attention. When reading the 1970 papers, I noted a few female names. I then searched as far as I was able for the number of woman who wrote, or co-authored papers in the conferences. This count is crude because many authors only provide initials for their forenames. Nevertheless, I have recorded it, as the expansion from 6 to 46 reminds us of issues associated with equality over this time. I was also delighted to be reminded of interesting geopolitical changes that have occurred. Thus, the reunification of Germany, the handing back of Hong Kong, the separation of Czechoslovakia and the break up of the USSR all emerged from perusal of the country affiliation of authors.

4.2 Themes

Perusal of the titles of TC3 publications (Appendix 2) indicates the spread and shift of interests. Thus from Large information systems to the virtual campus via Interactive multimedia in university education; from Computer assisted learning: scope progress and limits, to Quality education @ a distance, and Lifelong learning in the digital age. A clearer picture of thematic development can be provided first considering the following.

In 1988, TC3 published a book, a selected compilation, celebrating 25 years of TC3 publishing [11] organised in the following sections:

> The history of TC3
> The impact on Society
> Developing Countries
> Information Technology Literacy
> Computers in support of learning
> The impact of computers on the curriculum
> The role of programming
> Teacher Education
> The provision of hardware resources
> Computer science curriculum

Compare this with the preamble to the 2005 The Stellenbosch Declaration - ICT in education; make it work [8]

Having reflected on many aspects of Education, and the influence of ICT on education, we recommend that stakeholders and decision-makers in ICT in education focus on six major areas that will shape a beneficial use of ICT in education.

> • Digital solidarity
> • Learners and lifelong learning
> • Decision-making strategies
> • Networking
> • Research
> • Teachers

For each of these 6 areas we formulate recommendations and we propose a set of possible actions in order to put the recommendations in place. These actions address three main levels

> L1 Societal Level
> L2 Learning and teaching level
> L3 Technological and infrastructure level

An understanding of these shifts in foci may be provided by an analysis of the themes that have occupied this community. Taking the main source of the proceedings of the eight world conferences [12, 13, 14, 15, 16, 17, 18, 19], I am highlighting only some areas to illustrate to characteristics of the journeys undertaken. Perusal of other slices indicated by the contents lists of WCCE proceedings, such as distance education, developing countries, elearning or national policies would be equally valid

Computer science, programming, and data processing dominated the papers in the early period, including those in the section entitled use of computers in education, which is in fact mainly about choices of programming language and the structure of computer science courses. Some interesting thoughts emerged. Programming was considered the second literacy, and Ershov [14] claimed made that it would enhance the intellectual power of mankind. All children should be expected to take a course in programming. Indeed Charp [12] starkly stated that all educators must be concerned about computers, must learn about them, and must teach about them. By 1988, however Hebenstreit [11] provides a different perspective on the assumptions that programming teaches people to think logically, formulate solutions and handle detail with care. He says that the truth is that we should like future programmers to have these qualities, but that experience has shown us that the teaching of programming, even intensively, has been unable to develop those qualities for people who did not already have them beforehand. But a substantial interest remains in the computer science curriculum, the role of programming and information literacy courses. Many papers [12,13] replicated their whole course structures and acted as a collective information base where none previously existed. One of the problems underlying the first developments of a computer science curriculum was the competing claims of the electrical engineering perspective and the mathematics perspective. Overall the work at this time reflected the need to establish the science of information and ensure students and professionals have a thorough grounding in its principles and methodologies. A number of branches emerged from this theme.

The computer science curriculum has developed from the reproduction of the timetable for a three years undergraduate course as a means to identify the disputed core components of the nature of computer science, to a debate about the inherent concepts underlying computer science, or Informatics, and whether these concepts are best learnt theoretically or through an examination of their application. This suggests there has been a substantial shift in the articulation on the conceptual of nature of Informatics, in which the role of algorithms has played a part. The role of programming appears to have taken two further branches. One route combined with software development and debates about software production and design. As authoring languages and tools emerged, this stream is appears to have progressed towards object oriented modelling, html, XML and virtuality.

Another route programming took led to Logo [20], the development of a programming language with associated claims that the learning of 'turtle' geometry and programming protocols together were tools for cognitive development of young children. This received substantial attention at the time, but subsequent research into its use in the classroom indicated that the there some major flaws in this proposition; young children were often not yet at the stage of cognitive development to cope with a notion of recursion, they also did not take to these tools without intervention of their teachers, who were themselves not necessarily familiar with the language, and who often later recorded little conviction that this was really helping with mathematical understanding. After a spate of interest fostered by some hype for over a decade, it suddenly disappeared. Nevertheless Cornu [7] on Logo thinks "it was an important step for the teaching of mathematics as it was a time when you could not use the computer in a deep way without programming or a style of programming to think about what an algorithm is". But he considers that this was but a phase, as "we now have sophisticated tools for mathematics, with the capacity to experiment things." In the similar way to Logo, artificial intelligence in education flourished then died when it became apparent that it was an exercise in programming logic that used educational exercises as a mere context for the experiments, and ones that bore little relationship to real learning tasks. But it is equally valid to propose that they lost significance because the nature of technological developments with applications to suit for instance learning in mathematics and science. Indeed, Bentley suggested in 1990 [16] that the use of a computer as communicating device creates a more powerful educational tool than its functions as a delivery mechanism.

A final comment on the computer science and programming papers is that in the earlier years and especially in higher education, they exposed a poor understanding of the nature of educational thinking about teaching and learning. It was some time before the didactics of instruction were replaced by a more active problem solving style of learning activity was employed. In 2005, Cornu [7] noted that there continues a debate in Informatics about the whether we should teach it, or simply ensure we can use it.

The rise of Logo did however have one notable effect, that is increasingly serious attention was paid to the theories of learning and how they may be supported by ICT. This attention to learning theory was not new; previous attention had been paid to active learning and constructivism. For instance, Bewley, Holznagel and Klassen [12] proposed a cognitive development rationale to underpin the instructional use of computer simulations. A shift in perspective emerged however that instead of learning from the use of software, students learned with it, and the computer was referred to as a 'mindtool' [21] in its own right. Applications became categorised by the nature of constructive learning they enabled. Thus for instance applications could be categorised as semantic organisers, dynamic modelling tools and knowledge construction tools. Such tools would represent cognitive scaffolds, engaging learners in critical thinking. Active, constructive, internal and authentic learning theories provided fertile grounds to analyse the potential of the new medium not simply to support learning, but even led to suggestions that applications could possibly reorganise how students think. More attention was paid to this than the actual subject concepts and knowledge as the contexts for learning. This focus on the nature of learning shifted attention towards individual learning, self-directed learning and independent learning.

Problems have arisen as attempts to confirm the efficacy of such an approach. Further results often neither isolate the specific effects of a package, nor confirm that that any effect was sustainable. Attention has returned to the situation in which such learning occurs, in essence the context of both the problem being considered, whether mathematical or geographical, and also the role of the teaching and fellow students in the totality of the learning environment. As Erling [16] stated with respect to elementary school, it is essential that pupils are given real tasks. Situated cognition, collaborative learning, and activity theory have increasingly entered the language to support the use of ICT for learning. Despite many studies undertaken it is not clear what learning gains can be explicitly associated with using ICT, and such lack of clarity remains problematic. The first is that an increasing number of voices are emerging probing the nature of the research undertaken. Broderick, as early as 1970 [12], suggested that the study of the effectiveness of simulation in the classroom is usually difficult to conduct in a scientific manner. And with respect to learning, Cox and Marshall [19] state clearly that despite a plethora of studies on the effects of ICT in education, methodological problems mean that results are not reliable, and those which are tend to be inconclusive. They report that the most robust evidence of ICT use to enhance students' learning comes from studies that focussed only on specific uses of ICT. As Leiblum noted [14] there have been many disappointments due partially to unfulfilled expectations about the development of learning theories to support the medium. And the most recent challenge has been an exploration of the nature of student learning and collaboration online. Studies by Stacey [18] on issues such as the development and maintenance of a social presence online, by Furr and Ragsdale [18] on incidental learning and learner frustration with desk top video conferencing, and Yip [18] on the way students, favour web-based learning but still fail to use the system's full potential for problem based learning – all suggest the exploration of learning with, by or though the technology remains problematic. And how will we explore mobile learning, MP3 systems and broadcasting?

Throughout the forty years teacher education for the use of the computer has been a consistent theme. Teachers have been directed to courses to learn basic programming in order to be able to write their own software packages, provided with an armoury of subject specific software packages, and encouraged to undertake computer awareness/literacy courses. But with respect to awareness courses Ragsdale [22] noted that knowledge of IT skills do not mean that these skills are always applied. Indeed acquiring IT tool skills may be relatively easy, but gaining wisdom to use them effectively is not. General-purpose applications are current, though often designed for business practices, but still the actual use of computers in classrooms to support the curriculum has remained disappointing, even by new teachers who have used ICT in their training. Teachers have been categorised as traditional, conservative, barriers to innovation and reluctant to change, and some teacher education initiatives have been designed on this premise.

Yet, Jones Preece and Wood [15] recommended that teacher education should be based on a question raising technique – so that a balance was found between introducing and discussing educational perspectives (theory) and building on teachers' own experiences (practice). Teachers are returning to the centre stage in the agenda with an acknowledgement that they are both the key to the educational enterprise, and thus to educational change. Thus, a dichotomy is apparent whereby teachers are perceived as both the problem and the key to the solution. Recent studies are acknowledging that the using ICT can be part of the personal and professional expertise and judgement of the teachers, but only when it is embraced within the complex pedagogic model that acknowledges subject expertise, experience of teaching, understanding of learning, and the organisational context. Teachers can be represented as communities of practice. And throughout sits the conundrum that using ICT to support existing professional understanding, knowledge and expertise could reinforce practices and styles that have been fixed and the opposite of intentions. As Argues pointed out [11] the educational advantages of the new information technology can be turned into disadvantages if it is not used according to an explicit and well defined educational philosophy. For this to happen, he asserts that our schools must be turned from 'auditories' of isolated listeners into laboratories of active collaboration. And Knezek and Christensen [18], reporting on a range of studies undertaken over a ten-year period, confirm that the highest stage of integration involves a change in perception of teaching with technology rather than additional training or resources. But they also report that in almost all studies research is far from conclusive.

There have been a number of sociological studies on the identification of stages in the process of innovation in education, and in particular of planned innovation during times of curriculum innovation or changes in government policy. Some take a top-down management approach; others focus on the role of a change agent as a catalyst within the innovation process. And the anthropologist Katz [23], as early as 1961, discussed the social itinerary of technical change. Using studies of technology change in medicine and farming, he advocated the notion of studying the process of diffusion by tracing a) the movement of a given new practice, b) over time, c) through specific channels of communication and d) within a social structure. Using such method provided the opportunity to understand the social characteristics of innovators, how they adopt the change, and the strong interpersonal influence in the diffusion process within communities of practice.

And research, such as that done by Gross et al [24] indicated that there was no resistance to planned change, on the part of teachers. On the contrary, they were receptive to educational innovation, but the strategies for implementation were deficient in two respects – failure to identify and bring into the open various difficulties teachers were liable to encounter in their implementation effects, and failure to establish and use feedback mechanisms to uncover barriers that arose during the period of attempted implementation. Some more recent papers

[17,18,19] use the notion of affordances, activity and transformation theories as means to explain and explore how teachers may negotiate organisational barriers.

Indeed the implementation of organisational change in education is central to our concerns. Kozma [25] reports from the substantial SITES2 study of 174 cases across the world that a number of the positive messages about what can happen are true – but these depend on a complex set of variables being a necessary pre-condition. In particular, coordinated strategies for change and more models of technology intensive learning are needed. He indicates that all forms of societal institutions even schools are altering slowly but radically. Yet he asserts we are already inhabiting a profoundly interconnected, knowledge based, global market place. A further conundrum is posed when he argues that the complexity of this innovation has been seriously underestimated. It is clear from this study, and a seeming increasing consensus in 2005 [19] noted by Cornu [7] that the role of pedagogy is a third critical variable.

It is clear that publications from the eight WCCEs reflect a community of innovators, who are confident about the value of information and communication technologies and who spend much time espousing the possibilities and opportunities for education. Statements about the efficacy of learning a particular programme, or curricula design for training IT professionals have been gradually superceded by reports of how an application or training programme has actually been used and the apparent effects. Sometimes these effects or outcomes are measured; on occasion unexpected issues are reported. But on the whole this is a community committed to the innovation and concerned to explore how to get it used. They are convinced change will happen.

Many would say this is a problem, suggesting that unabased enthusiasm of authors such as Papert [20] and Gates [26] has presented an imagery or new positive change and renewal for learning. This presents confused notions of a technocentric society [27, 28, 29]. Evaluation studies by Cuban [30] suggest that unreflective and unabashed enthusiasm about the necessarily transformative nature of new information technologies is both naïve and historically unfounded. He has written that in the battle between classrooms and computers, the classroom wins. Indeed Miller and Olson [31] have pointed out that "the history of innovation in education should teach us to be cautious about predictions associated with new technologies. However, there is something about computers that negate this caution. Whenever computers are discussed, words such as revolution, powerful ideas, microworlds, and student empowerment occur frequently".

And so after forty years of endeavour, perhaps it is less surprising that we see from a number of national and international reports that the classic curve of innovation has still not progressed beyond the initial stages of the classic S curve of innovation diffusion [23]. There is no doubt that change is happening in our environment, but the change is mainly the rapid advances of the technology, thus change in the shape, character and attributes of the innovation itself. Indeed Baron and Bruillard [19] suggest that one of the problems is that educational technology appears to be under a curse of cyclical unfinished business. And I propose that this cycle could be characterised as a headlong journey from the didactics of certainty to an the uncertainty of complexity.

There are for me some black holes in the themes explored at WCCEs. In subject terms, where is an exploration of creativity? In the Arts, there is a whole new world supported by the technology, from new computer generated installations to the impact of graphical design perceptions, concepts and capabilities. Vast new applications dominate the world of students and practitioners in this area. Similarly, the digital world has had a profound effect on music and film, its creation, its production and influence in society. The young use the technology in the home, in schools and university departments and digital music and film studios are a feature of new employment. Finally where are the papers and discussions on the creative change to language, both in form and style, introduced by the technology and now a feature if society?

It is in part not surprising that creative subject disciplines have not featured – the community of TC3 has been founded on, and to some extent still substantially reflects the disciplines of mathematics and science. But there is a danger that TC3 could become fossilised, fixed by the science of information. It has already become obvious that we must engage with and incorporate expertise from the social sciences. After all education is defined as a social science and professionals within social science bring a different style and set of ontologies to bear. Understanding communities and communication, the fears and role of stakeholders, the influence of decision-makers and politics, the power of position and knowledge lie at the heart of many sociologists working within education. After producing the Strellenbosch declaration, Cornu [7] suggests "that future conferences must include the social dimension". The significant topics of security, surveillance, ethics and legality must play a part in the educational scenarios of the future; at the societal level these are major concerns in association with the digital world. We have started to touch on these topics in TC3 but fresh perspectives from others would seem to be pressing.

5. Reflections

I have no intention to summarize or repeat argument here. This paper could be unpicked to form a SWOT (strength, weaknesses, opportunities, costs) analysis of TC3. But I will leave that to others. My intention has been, ever the geographer, to explore rather than conclude, as there are always further places to go. Indeed I could describe in greater detail the landscape of the last forty plus years, to include where analogous deserts and ice, weather systems, or modes of transport from canals and railways, to motorways and Concorde. Instead, I will simply record my expectation that the next forty years will be as full of excitement, change, dichotomies and the unexpected as the first.

References

[1]   Buckingham, R.A. TC3 – The first ten years. In Zemanek, H. (ed.) A quarter century of IFIP. (North Holland, Amsterdam, 1986)
[2]   IFIP IFIP Bulletin No 36 (IFIP Secretariat, Austria, 2006)
[3]   Tinsley, David Interview 11th April 2006
[4]   WG 3.1 Computer Education for teachers in Secondary Schools: Outline guide "the Blue book" (1971), Aims and Objectives in teacher training(1972), Elements of information and information processing (1976). Analysis of algorithms (1977). WG 3.1 IFIP, Geneva.
[5]   Brittain, J.N.G. (ed.) An international curriculum for information system designers (WG 3.2 IFIP, Geneva, 1974)
[6]   Aiken, Robert Interview (6th April 2006)
[7]   Cornu, Bernard Interview (12th April 2006)
[8]   TC3 The Stellenbosch Declaration (WCCE 2006), www.ifip.or.ac/
[9]   Bollerslev, Peter Interview (8th April 2006)
[10] Johnson, Roger Interview (10th April 2006)
[11] Lewis, R. and Tagg, E.D. (eds.) Informatics and Education: An anthology of 25 years of TC3 publications (North Holland: Amsterdam, 1988).
[12] Scheepmaker, B. (ed.) 1st IFIP World Conference on Computer Education (IFIP: Amsterdam, 1970).
[13] Lecarme, O. and Lewis, R. (eds.) Computers in Education; 2nd IFIP World Conference on Computers in Education. (North Holland/American Elsevier: Amsterdam/New York, 1975)
[14] Lewis, R. and Tagg, E.D. (eds.) Computers in Education; Proceedings of 3rd IFIP World Conference on Computers in Education – WCCE 81 (North Holland: Amsterdam, 1981).
[15] Duncan, K. and Harris, D. (eds.) Proceedings 4th IFIP World Conference on Computers in Education – WCCE 85 (North Holland: Amsterdam, 1985)
[16] McDougall, A. and Dowling, C. (eds.) Computers in Education, 5th IFIP World Conference on Computers in Education - WCCE 90 (Elsevier Science, Amsterdam, 1990).
[17] Tinsley, D. and van Weert, T.J. (eds.) Liberating the Learner, 6th IFIP World Conference on Computers in Education - WCCE 95 (Chapman and Hall: London, 1995).
[18] Watson, D. and Andersen, J. (eds.) Networking the Learner: Computers in Education. 7th IFIP World Conference on Computers in Education – WCCE 2001 (Kluwer Academic: Boston, 2002).
[19] 8th IFIP World Conference on Computers in Education - WCCE 2005. (University of Stellenbosch, South Africa. CD DTT2103 Document Transformation Technologies, South Africa, 2005).
[20] Papert, S. Mindstorms: children, computers and powerful ideas (Harvester Press, Brighton, UK, 1980)
[21] Jonassen, D. H. Computers as mindtools for schools: engaging critical thinking (Prentice Hall, Ohio, 2000)
[22] Ragsdale, R. G. Permissable computing in education: values, assumptions and needs (Praeger Press, New York, 1988).
[23] Katz, E. The social itinerary of technical change: two studies on the diffusion of innovation. Human Organization XX (2) (The Society for Applied Anthropology, 1961).
[24] Gross, N., Giacquinta, J.B. and Berstein, M. Implementing Organisational Innovations: a sociological analysis of planned educational change (Basic Books, New York, 1971)

[25] Kozma, R. (ed.) Technology, innovation and educational change: a global perspective (International Society for Technology in Education, Oregan, 2003)

[26] Gates, B. The road ahead. (Viking, London, 1996)

[27] Mackenzie, D. and Wajcman, J. (eds.) The social shaping of technology (Open University Press, Milton Keynes, 1985).

[28] Turkle, S. Life on the screen: Indentity in the age if the internet (Weidenfeld and Nicholson, London, 1996)

[29] Finnegan, R., Salaman, G. and Thompson, K. (eds.) Information Technology: social issues (Hodder and Stoughton, London, 1991)

[30] Cuban, L. Oversold and underused; computers in the classroom (Harvard University Press, Cambridge, Mass., 2001)

[31] Miller, L. and Olson, J. Putting the computer in its place: a study of teaching with technology. Journal of Curriculum Studies 26 (2) p121 (1994)

Appendix 1
Technical Committee 3

Technical Committee 3
Established 1963

Chairs

Neils Ivar Bech	1962 initiating chair
Richard A.Buckingham	1963-1972
D. Henk Wolbers	1972-1978
Jacques Hebenstreit	1979-1984
Wilfred Brauer	1985-1990
Peter Bollerslev	1991-1996
Brian Samways	1997-2002
Jan Wibe	2003-

The seven working groups of Technical Committee 3 as of December 2005, following 43rd AGM, Stellenbosch 2005.

WG 3.1
Informatics and ICT in secondary education
established. 1966

Chairs

William F. Atchison	1966-1977
Frank. B. Lovis	1978-1983
Peter Bollerslev	1984-1989
Tom van Weert	1990-1994
Bernard Cornu	1995-2000
Deryn Watson	2001-

WG 3.2

Informatics and ICT in higher education
established 1968 as Organising Educational Seminars.
Re-named late 1970s.

Chairs

Richard A. Buckingham	1968-1979
Not recorded	1980-1982
William F. Atchison	1983-1989
Bernard Levrat	1990-1995
A. Joe Turner	2002-2005
John Hughes	2006-

WG 3.3

Research on education applications of information technologies
eststablished1971, as Instructional Uses of Computers
re-est. and re-named 1988

Chairs

Sylvia Charp	1971-1979
Robert E. Lewis	1980-1994
Betty Collis	1995-1996
John Tiffin	1997
Jari Multisilta	1998-2001
Niki E. Davies	2002-2004
Paul Nicholson	2005-

WG 3.4

IT-Professional and vocational education in information technology
Established 1971

Chairs

A. Berger	1971-1977
Patrick G. Raymont	1978-1984
Ben Zion Barta	1985-1994
Peter Juliff	1995-1998
Mikko Ruohonen	1999-2004
Barrie Thompson	2005-

WG 3.5

Informatics in elementary education
established 1983

Chairs

Frank. B. Lovis	1984-1989
Erling Schmidt	1990-1995
Anton Knierzinger	1996-2000
Sindre Rosvik	2001-

WG 3.6

Distance learning
established 1987

Chairs

G.Kovacs	1987-1992
Jan Wibe	1993-1999
Gordon Davies	2000-2005
Elizabeth Stacey	2006-

WG 3.7

Information Technology in educational management
Established 1996

Chairs

Ben Zion Barta	1996-1998
Alex Fung	1999-2004
Adrie Visscher	2005-

Special Interest Group on Lifelong Learning
Established 2005

Convenors
    Brian Samways and Tom van Weert

Appendix 2
Bibliography for TC3

Books
- in date order

Scheepmaker, B. (ed.) 1st IFIP World Conference on Computer Education (IFIP: Amsterdam, 1970).

Lecarme, O. and Lewis, R. (eds.) Computers in Education; 2nd IFIP World Conference on Computers in Education. (North Holland/American Elsevier: Amsterdam/New York, 1975)

Buckingham, R.A. (ed.) Education and large Informatics Systems (North Holland, Amsterdam, 1977)

Johnson, D.C. and Tinsley, J.D. (eds.) Informatics and mathematics in secondary schools: impacts and relationships (North Holland, Amsterdam, 1978)

Jackson, H.L.W. and Wiechers, G. (eds.) Post-secondary and vocational education in data processing – tomorrow's needs for computing education and training (North Holland, Amsterdam, 1979)

Lewis, R. and Tagg, E.D. (eds.) Computers in Education; Proceedings of 3rd IFIP World Conference on Computers in Education – WCCE 81 (North Holland: Amsterdam, 1981).

Lewis, R. and Tagg, E.D. (eds.) Computer assisted learning: scope, progress and limits (North Holland, Amsterdam, 1980)

Tagg, E. D. (ed.) Microcomputers in secondary education (North Holland, Amsterdam, 1980)

Jackson, H.L.W. (ed.) Teaching Informatics courses – Guidelines for trainers and educationalists (North Holland, Amsterdam, 1982)

Lewis, R. and Tagg, E.D. (eds.) Involving micros in education (North Holland, Amsterdam, 1982)

Lovis. F. and Tagg, E.D. (eds.) Informatics education for all students at university level (North Holland, Amsterdam, 1983)

Atchison, W. F., Brauer, W., Buckingham, R.A. and Heibenstreit, J. (eds.) A modular curriculum in computer science (IFIP, Geneva, 1984)

Lovis, F. and Tagg, E.D. (eds.) Informatics and teacher education (North Holland, Amsterdam, 1984)

Tinsley, J.D. and Tagg, E.D. (eds.) Informatics in elementary education (North Holland, Amsterdam, 1984)

Barta. B.Z. and Roab, B.H. (eds.) The impact of Informatics on vocational and continuing education (North Holland, Amsterdam, 1985)

Briefs, U. and Tagg, E.D. (eds.) Education for the system designer/user cooperation (North Holland, Amsterdam, 1985)

Duncan, K. and Harris, D. (eds.) Proceedings 4th IFIP World Conference on Computers in Education – WCCE 85 (North Holland: Amsterdam, 1985).

Griffiths, M. and Tagg, E.D. (eds.) The role of programming in teaching Informatic (North Holland, Amsterdam, 1985)

Levrat, B. Tagg, E.D. and Lovis, F.B. (eds.) The computer in the home: its challenge to education (Elsevier Science, Amsterdam, 1987)

Lewis, R. and Tagg, E.D. (eds.) A computer for each student (Elsevier Science, Amsterdam, 1987)

Lovis, F. and Johnson, D.C. (eds.) Informatics and the teaching of mathematics (Elsevier Science, Amsterdam, 1987)

Moriguti, S., Ohtsuki, S. and Furugori, T. (eds.) Microcomputers in secondary education (Elsevier Science, Amsterdam, 1987)

Ercoli, O. and Lewis, R. (eds.) Artificial intelligence tools in education (Elsevier Science, Amsterdam, 1988)

Lovis, F. (ed.) Remote education and informatics: teleteaching (Elsevier Science, Amsterdam, 1988)

Lovis, F. and Tagg, E.D. (eds.) Computers in Education – ECCE 88 (Elsevier Science, Amsterdam, 1988)

Wills, S. and Lewis, R. (eds.) Micro Plus: educational peripherals (Elsevier Science, North Holland, 1988)

Tinsley, J. D. and van Weert, T.J. (eds.) Educational software at the secondary level (Elsevier Science, Amsterdam, 1989)

Barta, B.Z., Fourel, L., Raymont, R and Lovis, F. (eds.) Methodologies of training data processing professionals and advanced end users (Elsevier Science, Amsterdam, 1990)

McDougall, A. and Dowling, C. (eds.) Computers in Education, 5th IFIP World Conference on Computers in Education - WCCE 90 (Elsevier Science, Amsterdam, 1990).

Bara, B.Z. and Haugen, J. (eds.) Training: from computer aided design to computer integrated enterprise (Elsevier Science, Amsterdam, 1991).

Lewis, R. and Otsuki, S. (eds.) Advanced research on computers in education (Elsevier Science, Amsterdam, 1991)

Aiken, R.M. (ed.) Education and Society (North Holland, Amsterdam, 1992)

Barta, B. Z., Goh, A. and Lin, L (eds.) Professional development in Information Technology Professionals (Elsevier Science, Amsterdam, 1992)

Samways, B. and van Weert, T.J. (eds.) The impacts of informatics on the organisation of education (Elsevier Science, Amsterdam, 1992)

Barta, B. Z., Ecclestone, J. and Hambusch, R. (eds.) Computer mediated education of Information Technology (Elsevier Science, Amsterdam 1993)

Barta, B.Z., Hung, S.L. and Cox, K. R. (eds.) Software Engineering education (Elsevier Science, Amsterdam, 1993)

Collis, B. Moonen, J. and Stanchev, I. (special issue eds) Exploring the nature of research in computer-related applications in education. Computers and Education, **21** (1&2) (Elsevier Science, Amsterdam, 1993)

Davies, G. and Samways, B. (eds.) Tele-teaching 93 (Elsevier Science, Amsterdam, 1993)

Johnson, D.C. and Samways, B. Informatics and changes in learning (North Holland, Amsterdam, 1993)

Lovis, F. (special issue ed.) Teaching advanced subjects in Informatics. Education and Computing 7 (1&2) (Elsevier Science, 1993)

Barta, B.Z., Gev, Y. and Telem, M. (eds.) Information Technology in educational management (Chapman and Hall, London, 1994)

Beattie, K., McNaught. C. and Wills, S. (eds) Interactive Multimedia in university education (Elsevier Science, Amsterdam, 1994)

Franklin, S.D. Stubberud, A.P. and Wiedmann, L.P. (eds.) University education uses of visualisation in scientific computing (Elsevier Science, Amsterdam, 1994)

Lewis, R. and Mendelsohn, P. (eds.) Lessons from learning (North Holland, Amsterdam, 1994)

Wright, J. and Benzie, D. (eds.) Exploring a new partnership with educational technology. (North Holland, Amsterdam, 1994)

Barta, B.Z., Telem, M and Gev, Y. (eds) Information Technology in educational management. (Chapman and Hall, London, 1995)

Collis, B. and Davies, G. (eds.) Innovating adult learning with innovative technologies (Chapman and Hall, London, 1995).

Lee, M., Barta, B.Z. and Juliff, P. (eds.) Software quality and productivity – theory, practice, education and training (Chapman and Hall, London, 1995)

Tinsley, J.D. and Watson, D. (eds.) Integrating Information Technology into education (Chapman and Hall, London, 1995)

Watson, D. and Andersen, J. (eds.) Networking the Learner: Computers in Education. 7th IFIP World Conference on Computers in Education – WCCE 2001 (Kluwer Academic: Boston, 2002).

Tinsley, D. and van Weert, T.J. (eds.) Liberating the Learner, 6th IFIP World Conference on Computers in Education - WCCE 95 (Chapman and Hall: London, 1995).

Katz, Y, Millin, D. and Offir, B. (eds.) The impact of Information Technology: from practice to curriculum (Chapman and Hall, London, 1996)

Barta, B.Z., Tatnell, A. and Juliff, P. (eds.) The place of information technology in management and business education (Chapman and Hall, London, 1997)

Dariva, D. and Stanchev, I. (eds.) Human Computer interaction and educational tools (NCP, 1997)

Franklin, S.D. and Strenski, E. (eds.) Building university electronic educational environments (Kluwer Academic, Boston 1997)

Fung, A.C.W., Visscher, A.J., Barta, B.Z. and Teather, D.C.B. (eds.) Information Technology in educational management for the schools of the future (Chapman and Hall, London, 1997)

Johnson, D.C. and Tinsley,J.D. (eds.) Informatics and mathematics in secondary schools (Chapman and Hall, London, 1997)

Passey, D. and Samways, B. (eds.) Information Technology, supporting change through teacher education (Chapman and Hall, London, 1997)

Bottino, R., Dowling, C. and Fernandez Valmayor, A. (special issue eds.) Human computer interaction and educational tools: theory into practice. Education and Information Technologies. 3 (3/4) (Kluwer Academic, 1998)

Davies, G. (ed.) Teleteaching 98 – distance learning, training and education (Kluwer Academic, Boston, 1998)

Fulmer, C.L., Barta,B.Z. and Nolan, P. (eds.) The integration of information for educational management (NCP, 1998)

Marshall.G. and Ruohonen, M. (eds.) Capacity building for IT in education in developing countries (Chapman and Hall, London, 1998)

Mulder, F. and van Weert, T. (eds.) Informatics in higher education (Chapman and Hall, London, 1998)

Verdejo, M.F. and Davies, G. (eds.) The virtual campus (Kluwer Academic, Boston, 1998)

Juliff, P. Kado, T. and Barta, B.Z. (eds.) Educating professionals for network-centric organisations (Kluwer Academic, Boston, 1999)

Tinsley, J.D. and Johnson, D.C. (eds.) Information and Communication Technologies in school mathematics (Kluwer Academic, Boston, 1999)

Watson, D.M. and Downes, T. (eds.) Communication and networking in education; learning in a networked society (Kluwer Academic, Boston, 2000)

Nolan, C.J.P., Fung, A.C.W. and Brown, M. (eds.) Pathways to institutional improvement with information technology in educational management (Kluwer Academic, Boston, 2001)

Taylor, H. and Hogenbirk, P. (eds.) Information Technologies in education, Quality Education @ a distance: the school of the future (Kluwer Academic, Boston, 2001)

Passey, D. and Kendall, M. (eds.) TelELearning, the challenge of the third millennium (Kluwer Academic, Boston, 2002)

Cassel, L. and Rees, R. A. (eds.) Informatics curricula and teaching methods (Kluwer Academic, Boston, 2003)

Davies, G. and Stacey, E. (eds.) Quality education @ a distance (Kluwer Academic, Boston, 2003)

Dowling, C. and Lai, K-L. (eds.) Information and Communication Technology and the teacher of the future (Kluwer Academic, Boston, 2003)

Marshall, G. And Katz, Y. (eds.) Learning, Home and Community: ICT for early and elementary education (Kluwer Academic, Boston, 2003)

Selwood,l I.D., Fung, A.C.W. and O'Mahoney, C.D. (eds.) Management of education in the information age (Kluwer Academic, Boston, 2003)

van Weert, T. J. and Munro, R.K. (eds.) Informatics and the digital society (Kluwer Academic, Boston, 2003)

Courtiat, J-P. and Villemar, T. (eds.) Technology enhanced learning (Springer, Boston, 2004)

Impagliazzo, J. and Lee, J.A.N. (eds.) History of Computing in Education (Springer, Boston, 2004)

Nicholson, P., Thompson, B., Ruohonen, M. and Multisilta, J. (eds.) E-training strategies for professional organisations (Kluwer Academic, Boston, 2004).

Tatnall, A., Osario, J. and Visscher, A. (eds.) IT and educational management in the knowledge society (Springer, Boston, 2004)

van Weert, T. J. and Kendall, M. (eds.) Lifelong learning in the digital age (Kluwer Academic, Boston, 2004)

Somekh, B. (special issue ed.) Learning for the twenty-first century: what really matters? Education and Information Technologies **10** (3) (Kluwer Academic, 2005)

van Weert, T. (ed.) Education and the Knowledge Society WFEO/IFIP at the UN 2004 World Summit on the Information Society, Geneva Switzerland. (Kluwer Academic, Boston, 2005)

van Weert, T. and Tatnall, A. (eds.) Information and Communication Technologies and real life learning (Springer, Boston, 2005)

8th IFIP World Conference on Computers in Education - WCCE 2005. (University of Stellenbosch, South Africa. CD DTT2103 Document Transformation Technologies, South Africa, 2005).

Reports, Guidelines and Journal
- in date order

WG 3.1 Computer Education for teachers in Secondary Schools:
-   Outline guide " the Blue book" (1971),
-   Aims and Objectives in teacher training(1972),
-   Elements of information and information processing (1976)
-   Analysis of algorithms (1977). WG 3.1 IFIP, Geneva.

Brittain, J.N.G. (ed.) An international curriculum for information system designers (WG 3.2 IFIP, Geneva, 1974)

Taylor, H.G., Aiken, R.M. and van Weert, T.J. Informatics education in secondary schools. Guidelines of good practice, IFIP WG 3.1 (IFIP, Geneva, 1992)

Ruiz I Tarrago, F.R. Integration of Information Technology into Secondary Education: main issues and perspectives. IFIP WG 3.1 Guidelines of good practice (IFIP, Geneva, 1993)

Tinsley, J.D. and van Weert, T.J. (eds.) A modular Informatics curriculum for secondary schools. IFIP 3.1 (UNESCO/IFIP, Paris, 1994)

IFIP WG 3.2 (1994) A modular curriculum in computer science. UNESCO/IFIP Paris.

Tinsley, J.D. Tele-learning in secondary education. Guidelines for good practice, IFIP WG 3.1/3.6 (IFIP, Geneva, 1994)

Knierzinger, A., Rosvik, S. and Schmit, E. (edsElementary ICT curriculum for teacher training. IFIP WG3.5 (UNESCO Paris, 2001)

Anderson, J. and van Weert, T. J. (eds.) Information and Communication Technology in education: a curriculum for schools and programme for teacher development (UNESCO/IFIP, Paris, 2002)

TC3 The Stellenbosch Declaration (WCCE 2006)
www.ifip.or.ac/

Education and Information Technologies Volumes **1** to **10** (Springer, Boston, US, 1996-2005)

Appendix 3
World Conferences on Computers in Education

1st WCCE – Amsterdam, The Netherlands 1970

Total - 148 papers, from 23 countries
6 women among authors

Papers typed.

Section headings, substantial number of papers per section.

I Education about computers

Computer education in secondary schools: Teacher training
National schemes for computer education and governmental responses
The place of computer and informatics sciences in higher education
Education (Data Processing) and Management
National and international efforts to develop computer education
The planning and execution of programs for computer specialists in Universities
Professional training (programmers and systems analysts

II Use of computers in education

Strategies for development and presentation of computer based learning exercises
Practice of computer based learning
Languages for education
Simulation

2nd WCCE – Marseilles, France 1975

Total – 179 papers from 33 countries
13 women among authors

".... produced typed on special paper for off-set printing" Lecarme and Lewis (eds.)

Sections reflect session order

Education and management
Computers and Physics education I
Reports on CMI (computer managed instruction) projects

Teaching programming I

National and international planning for Informatics Education I

Curricula for management education

Computers and Physics education II

Computer managed learning: case studies

Computer education in developing countries

National and international planning for Informatics Education II

Large scale experiences in computer assisted instruction

Computer education for all teachers

Computer aided teaching of programming

Computer education in developing countries: case studies

Informatics in universities I

Informatics in secondary schools I

Theoretical aspects of computer assisted instruction (CAI) I

UNESCO involvement in the use of computers in developing countries.

Computer aided evaluation of students work

Informatics in Universities II

Informatics in secondary schools II

Theoretical aspects of CAI II

How can we transfer experience on computer education from
    developed countries to developing countries?

On teaching computer application for commerce, industry and administration

The use of computers in university science teaching

Teaching school mathematics I

Making CAI economical

Directions of research in developing countries

Informatics in the learning process

Teaching humanities at school

Special applications of CAI: Medical sciences

Teaching operations research

Teaching advanced concepts of - Informatics learning with data bases

Computers in Education – hardware resources

Informatics systems for management

Applied mathematics

Science teaching in schools

Teaching school mathematics II

Special applications of CAI: Language applications

Education for management II – using gaming and simulation in management and
    social science education

Computer assisted test construction

Management of education

Computer literacy I

Computers and fine Arts

Economics teaching

Teaching mathematical concepts

Software resources for computers in education

Computer literacy

Computers and the teaching of engineering science I

Guidelines for the training teachers for secondary schools

Models for CAI

Economics and Social Sciences

Computers and the teaching of engineering science II

Exchange of material in CAI I

The impact on society of computers in education

Which programming languages for an introductory course on informatics

Computers in the teaching of engineering science III

Exchange of material in CAI II

Change of the role and behaviour of teachers and students when
        involved with CAI – 1 paper

Teaching Programming II – 1 paper

3rd WCCE – Lausanne, Switzerland 1981

Camera-ready copy, produced by mix of golf ball and other typewriters.

Total - 114 papers from 30 countries

9 women among authors

6 general sections, and then grouped according to the sessions of the conference.

1. Information and various disciplines
        Social and environment issues
        Teaching programming
        Informatics and Science I
        Informatics and Science II
        Informatics and Language
        Informatics and engineering design
        Informatics and mathematics I
        Information and mathematics II
        Informatics and Art/Design
        Informatics and Music
        Informatics and Medicine

2. Computer assisted learning and other direct uses of the computer in education
      CAL systems
      Improving CAL
      Language skills through CAL
      CAL in schools

3. The impact of new technologies
      Audio-visual developments
      Special applications in computer aided education
      Microcomputer systems
      Education and Professional People

4. Social impacts including changing role of teachers
      Education for the disabled and disadvantaged I
      Education for the disabled and disadvantaged II
      Education for techniques
      Education for an Informatics Society I
      Education for an Informatics Society II

5. National policies and models for computer education with special reference to the needs of developing countries
      National policies in developing countries I
      National policies in developing countries II
      National policies in secondary education
      National policies in university education

6. Aims, policies and curricula for informatics education
      Informatics in secondary education I
      Informatics in secondary education II\
      Teacher training in Informatics
      Topics in computer science teaching
      Advanced techniques in Informatics teaching
      Mathematics in computer science curricula
      Experiences in computer science teaching

4th WCCE – Norfolk, Virginia, USA 1985

Camera-ready copy, produced by mix of golf ball and other typewriters.

Total - 226 papers, from 30 countries
33 women among authors

Sections are session themes in order

Across the curriculum
Design and development of CAL
Pedagogical tools and techniques
Mathematics, science and engineering education
Humanities
New teach, high tech, and using tech
Computer languages, problem solving and programming
LOGO
Graphics
Course and curricula recommendations
Computer literacy
Non-traditional education
Teacher training
Issues and ethics
National systems and policies
Non-curricula aspects of computing and education
Computers and research
Future of computing and education

5th WCCE – Sydney, Australia 2000

Camera-ready copy, produced by mix of golf ball and other typewriters.

Total – 143 papers from 29 countries
36 women among authors

Large sections – which reflect the working group titles

Informatics education at secondary level
Informatics education at the university level
Research on educational applications of information technologies
Vocational training and education
Informatics in education

Rainbow Stream elementary

Also 3 Mini conferences held within

Computers in education – national perspectives
CBT 90
Teleteaching 90
PEG 90 (Prolog in Education Group)

6th WCCE – Birmingham, UK 1995
First with subtitle: **Liberating the learner**

Note, here only six WGs are recorded – Distance 3.6, has re-absorbed Tele-teaching

Produced in Word - copy was sent to publisher in electronic format;
          includes a list of keywords
Was also available also as a CD.

Total – 104 papers, from 30 countries
24 women among authors

The sections follow the main conference themes

Artificial intelligence
Costing (one paper)
Developing Countries
Distance learning
Equity issues (2 papers)
Evaluation (2 papers)
Flexible learning
Implications
Informatics as study topic
Information Technology
Infrastructure
Integration
Knowledge as a resource (1 paper)
Learner centred learning
Methodologies
National Policies
Resources
Social Issues
Software

Teacher education
Tutoring (2 papers)
Visions (1 paper)

7th WCCE – Copenhagen, Denmark 2001
subtitle **Networking the learner**

Produced in Word sent to publisher in electronic format; includes list of keywords.

Total - 84 papers from 22 countries
37 women among authors

Open and distance learning
ICT in learning
New pedagogic ideas
Teaching maths
Teaching computer science
Forms of assessment
Management and resource
Teacher education
National initiatives

Also
13 professional groups discussion reports
12 panel reports

8th WCCE – Stellenbosch, South Africa 2005
subtitle: **What works?**

Total – 165 papers, from 25 countries
46 women authors/joint authors

Output not a book, but CD of papers

Sections organise by session

Pre-service teacher education
The future of lifelong learning
HE: distance education
Collaboration and interaction
Management of learning

Learning environments
In-service teacher education
LLL: dealing with special students
HE theory and practice
What works in the classroom?
Analysis of what is successful
Enhancing interaction between students
E-communities and learning theory
Learning with networks
HE: ICT is everywhere
Information, learning and thinking
Teacher education: Theory and practice
Broadband, virtual experts and XML
E-inclusion
LLL: ICT and the learner
HE: creativity and learning
Teaching and learning with ICT
Case studies in using ICT in teacher education
Digital learning resources
HE: what can we learn from history
Online learning environments
LLL: the way ahead
HE: professional training
Technology enhanced learning for the future
National and local approaches
Research and formative assessment
Computer science and the setting of standards
HE: on-line learning
Technology and learning activities
National success stories
Tools for tutoring
Informatics, computer toys and drop-out rate
Disseminating ICT skills in higher ed
Learning materials and pedagogic practices
Quality and values
Capturing the opportunities now available
Teaching modelling
E-learning in higher ed
Examples of teachers learning
Culture and learning
Collaboration and learning
Courses in programming
National and local policies

The professional development of teachers
Content policy
Research and collaborative learning
Important influences in our school
Professional competence
Net-learning for teachers
Management and partnership

Note: 65 countries have been represented by the publications from these eight conferences.

Algeria, Argentina, Australia, Austria, Belarus, Belgium, Botswana, Brazil, Bulgaria, Canada, Chile, China, Czechoslovakia, Denmark, Egypt, Ethiopia, Finland, France, Germany (both GFR and GDR before unification), Greece, Hong Kong (before reunification), Hungary, India, Iran, Ireland, Israel, Italy, Jamaica, Japan, Kenya, Kuwait, Lithuania, Malaysia, Mexico, the Netherlands, New Zealand, Nigeria, Norway, Oman, Paraguay, Peru, Philippines, Poland, Portugal, Romania, Singapore, Slovak Republic, Slovakia, Slovenia, South Africa, Spain, Sri Lanka, Sweden, Switzerland, Taiwan, Tanzania, Turkey, United Kingdom, United States, United Soviet Socialist Republic, Venezuela, Yugoslavia, Zimbabwe.

Evolution of Computing in Spanish-Speaking Countries
- A Panel Presentation

John Impagliazzo, Julián Aráoz, Benjamín Barán,
José Contreras, Ana Pont Sanjuan, Ramon Puigjaner

Abstract. Two decades ago, people used computers as an information resource for many fields. These fields include library information, climatic information, medicine, transportation schedules, banking, and other areas. The use of international networks at that time enabled people to communicate globally in a rapid and accurate fashion not only to experts, but to the public also. In regions such as South and Central America, however, the uses of information resources were not as widespread as they were in developed countries. Indeed, estimates showed that Latin America contained two percent of the world's informatics equipment. At that time, computers appeared in commercial and governmental agencies as well as universities that used global networks such as the internet, BITNET, FidoNet, and other similar networks.

In the mid-1980s, of course, the world wide web was only a dream and the individual use of computers was almost non-existent. The emergence of web-based technology in the 1990s caused a worldwide transformation in the use of computers and their applications, particularly in Latin America. Their natural associations with Spain and Portugal and their strong desire to be at the forefront of informatics changes, Latin American countries developed a new resurgence – a small renaissance – thrusting many of these countries into a modern technical society with accelerated growth and educational promise.

This panel attempts to emphasize the progress of computing in representative Spanish-speaking countries and to celebrate the computing achievements made there. The distinguished panelists will bring forward ways in which computing had emerged and the way the computing evolution affected computing education in the regions. The summaries of their dialogue follow.

Julián Arturo Aráoz Durand

Some South America Experiences: I will comment the evolution of the informatics curricula in some countries of Latin America, as I saw it. I participated

Please use the following format when citing this chapter:

Impagliazzo, J., Aráoz, J., Barán, B., Contreras, J., Sanjuan, A.P., Puigjaner, R., 2006, in IFIP International Federation for Information Processing, Volume 215, History of Computing and Education 2 (HCE2), ed. J. Impagliazzo, (Boston: Springer), pp. 49–57.

in curricula design, from 1965, in Argentina, Venezuela, Uruguay, Nicaragua, and Cuba directly and in forum discussions for Latin-America computing education at UNESCO and CLEI. My focus is on undergraduate studies.

Since 1962, the University of Buenos Aires (UBA) offered the "Computador Científico" program. The curriculum I studied had much mathematics and several courses about computer use. We had several courses of analysis, algebra, and geometry; from applied mathematics: probability, statistics, numerical calculus, and operations research; from computer use: programming, data processing, simulation, and computer seminar. Our professors were either mathematician or engineers working for computers companies like IBM or NCR for the computer courses, which meant that they had a very narrow knowledge of the emerging computer science.

In December 1964, three of us became graduate students. While studying, we were working as programmers and analysts; hence, we were the first people that had a broad view of the area. Our first task was to design and propose a new and more extended pensum than the one we had at UBA. However, neither the Science Faculty nor the Engineering Faculty accepted our proposition. Nevertheless, this pensum was used as a basis for the one used in 1967 at Central University of Venezuela to create the first degree in computer science. Here we incorporate a solid mathematical background more suitable for computer science, including finite math with logic, structured and linear algebra, and graphs among others and more theoretical and structured computer science.

We always kept these principles over the years and used this philosophy at Central University of Venezuela: 1967 and 1974; Simon Bolivar University, Caracas: 1976; University of Guyana, Venezuela: 1983; Latin American School of Computer Science ESLAI, Buenos Aires: 1985; among others.

As time went by, more changes were due to computer science development, like the new areas that appeared in the 1970s such as software engineering, analysis of algorithms, and networks. The schema was based upon solid mathematics that was adequate for an informatics emphasis in basic computer theory, specialization areas, and graduate projects. The core we propose was logic and algebraic structures required for the programming courses, which were independent of programming languages. The emphasis was on algorithm analysis and data structures. Advanced courses included subjects as operating systems, comparative study of programming Languages, data bases, and networks; a software engineering design workshop (as in architecture) and limited time final projects were also part of the curriculum. I believe that this paradigm is still valid for an informatics curricula design today.

Benjamín Barán

Evolution of Computing in Latin America: From the 1970s to Our Days: There was a substantial worldwide excitement in the computer field in the early

1970s but few organized regional activities had been done in Latin America, mainly because only a few universities offered specific careers in computer science or engineering. The first visionaries had realized that a regional organization was needed to develop the Latin American region exploiting the opportunities that computer meant for the well-being of its people. Thus, the Catholic University of Valparaiso – Chile organized the first Latin-American Panel in Informatics in January of 1974 based on two previous experiences organizing smaller Chilean panels by professors Amillara Morales and Aldo Migliaro in 1972 and 1973.

The success of the first Latin-American Panel encouraged the organization of an annual Latin-American Panel with computer exposition, known at that time as *Panel/Expodata* where researchers, professors, and professionals of South America met to present their work and to discuss how to develop the computer field in the region. By 1979, the number of universities and research centers interested in computers had increased considerably to more than one hundred. It was clear that the region needed a formal Latin American organization and a Latin-America Center on Informatics Studies - CLEI (*Centro Latinoamericano de Estudios en Informática*) was established during *Panel/Expodata 1979* in Caracas – Venezuela, with Colombian Victor Yockteng as its president and Chilean Aldo Migliaro as its first Executive Secretary.

The 1980s was the decade of computer consolidation in Latin America. Most Latin America traditional universities incorporated computer programs and research centers began to publish their work. The number of institutions interested in a regional collaboration through institutions as CLEI increased rapidly given the availability of personal computers (PCs) at several companies and most universities and research centers. The Latin America Conference was organized every year in a different country to encourage computer utilization in the whole region, with increasing success in Chile, Venezuela, Uruguay, Brazil, Argentina, Peru, and Colombia.

In the 1990s, the interest in computers continued and internet became the main phenomena of the field, facilitating interaction between LA professionals and the realization of workshops, conferences as well as research projects and networks. By that time, most LA universities had computer programs and research began to be significant, especially in Brazil (with almost 50% of LA scientific publications), Mexico, Chile, Argentina, and Venezuela. The Latin-America Conference became larger with an average presence of around one thousand computer professionals and students of several countries around the world, including a remarkable participation of Europe and the United States of America.

The new millennium found a promising Latin-America computer field with hundreds of LA researchers around the world, CLEI as a consolidated LA center with an itinerant LA conference visiting most countries of the region, a large amount of universities interested in informatics and investing in computer resources, at least, at a level the economy permits. Several LA countries have begun to export software and systems and the figures for the field had begun to become considerable in several LA economies.

The future seems very hopeful with a larger number of young students interested in computers as well as increasing postgraduate's opportunities in master and doctorate programs. Research networks sprout constantly, especially with Europe and the U.S. companies requiring an even larger number of specialized computer professionals. Software assembly and exportation is already a reality that may help improve the quality of life in the LA region.

José Lino Contreras V

Perspectives from Chile: Since late 1950s, computing at universities has played an important role in the development of the computer and informatics society in Chile. With precarious data processing centers at the beginning and modern computer sciences and informatics academic departments later, computing at Chilean universities has always played an outstanding role in the building of the computing society in Chile.

During the 1950s and 1960s, the Chilean Economic Development Agency, CORFO, promoted the creation of some intensive technology based enterprises such as the national telecommunication company, ENTEL, the Chile's national television company, TVN, and EMCO, a computing services company aimed to promote and develop the use of computers at the public sector. CORFO also provided research and technical support to industry, all of what demanded for better-qualified professionals in the computing area. By introducing computers in the late 1950s, EMCO was one of the main driving forces that promoted computers use in Chili.

Some state owned universities, such as Universidad de Chile and Universidad Tecnica del Estado, also worked close to EMCO in computing, from the beginning. One of the most relevant projects of EMCO was Synco, also known as Sybersyn, a National Information System aimed to integrate information coming from more than 700 state companies placed along the country. Started in 1970, Sybersyn was a project conceived and led by Staford Beer, one of the fathers of cybernetics, who based the conception of the project on his "viable system model" as the central paradigm. The idea was to implement an online, integrated information system allowing real time data to flow from the ongoing activities of the state companies, to a central office, where decision makers would have the relevant information needed to make decisions about production and economic activities. This was one of the most advanced cybernetic projects at the time and produced a big influence in some prestigious people such as Fernando Flores (The Coordinator) and Raúl Espejo. The project ended with the military coup in 1973 and practically disappeared from the Chilean memory.

Later on, under the military regime, the Chilean internal revenue system and the central intelligence agency developed some of the most advanced computerized information systems in the world. From the university side, advances in computing research took place during the 1970s and the 1980s and new Computer and Information Systems careers were created. During the 1970s, computer programming and System Analysis were careers offered at some universities. Later on, at the beginning of the 1980s, Civil Informatics Engineers and Computing Civil Engineers (twelve-month engineer curricula) were offered by universities starting a very rich educational offering on computing. Nowadays, being the Chilean society one of the most IT developed societies of Latin America, more than thirty universities offer computing and informatics engineer careers with ten or more semesters. The university computing educational activities and research have been continuously shaping the modern computing society in Chile.

Ana Pont Sanjuan
The Effect of the Computing Evolution upon Computing Education: This presentation focuses on the evolution of computers during the past thirty years and how this fact has affected the contents and the methodology used in computer curricula at the universities in Spain. Despite the majority of aspects we can point out that are common and general in all the countries, we will give details about the Spanish universities curricula.

The evolution of computing has supplied more powerful and friendly computers and environments but also much more complex and much more difficult to teach. This has affected the computer and network architecture courses as well as the programming languages used, causing big problems to the teaching staff and interesting controversies not only about the contents that must be included in the curricula, but also about the time needed to teach them and the appropriate methodology. We present a short summary of these problems and discussions and illustrate with examples their effect in the evolution of teaching computing in our universities.

Computer Architecture Courses: When teaching topics in computer organization and architecture, we find more complex and powerful processors and devices each year (or sometimes each half a year). Since the working principles of a CPU are an important part of the basis of a computer organization course, the teaching staff is continuously dealing with the problem simplicity versus highly topical, when choosing a processor example to illustrate their classes. This fact also affects the choice of the assembly language selected for this purpose.

Twenty-five years ago, an important discussion among the teaching staff in the Spanish universities was the choice of using the Intel 8085/8088 microprocessors (or the Motorola family) as example of CPU or a processor like the PDP-8 or 11. The defenders of the first option argued that this family of microprocessors was widely used in low cost computers and systems and, consequently easily found in real life. In addition, the lab equipment based on these microprocessors was (at that moment) cheaper than systems based on PDP processors. On the other hand, the defenders of the PDP family argued that the internal architecture and assembly language of these processors were easier to understand and use by the students than the Intel family of microprocessors.

This controversy continued in the Spanish universities during many years creating two currents of opinion that have been maintained up until few years ago. However, in the last years the argument of reality versus simplicity has grown stronger and has added new elements to take into account when designing computer curricula. This fact affects even more strongly the design of lab sessions because in those cases the choice is more complex. On the one hand, we must decide between simpler and theoretical systems or real systems with all their powerful, possibilities and complexity and, on the other simplified simulators for educational purposes or current commercial tools

Currently an important number of Spanish universities have chosen the use of MIPS RX000 family processors for teaching examples in computer curricula. This family of RISC processors can easily illustrate how a simple CPU works taking the R2000 as processor basis. Important improvements in the architecture like pipelining, superscalar issues, or cache hierarchy can be easily added in this basic processor and be illustrated with more powerful members of the family, as for example the R10000 microprocessor. This trend is also supported by the existence of free access educational simulators that permit the design lab sessions to deal with assembly language programs, I/O systems, and cache memories. Obviously, there are still defenders of the use of real systems that do not share this extended option.

Programming Courses: Similar circumstances appear when dealing with teaching programming. We can summarize a simplified vision of the problem in the selection of the programming language to teach. In this case, the evolution of the computers has led to (a) the constant emergence of new and specific programming languages, (b) the evolution of programming models, from a structured programming to a more specific models like the declarative programming, passing through an object oriented model, and (c) the need of exploiting the improvements of the processor architecture, like the use of threads of parallelism.

According to these facts, the most common programming languages selected in the Spanish universities from their beginnings until now have been: Fortran, Pascal/Turbo Pascal, C, C++, and Java. During many years, the universities in Spain also reflected the controversy between the use of Pascal or C for teaching purposes like happened in the majority of universities around the world. In these polemical decisions, the pressure of the student's point of view has not been negligible. They always would like to learn the most recent and widely used language, as for instance Visual Basic, without considering any other educational reason.

When teaching programming the selection of the most appropriate language must be made according the following facts. (1) The capability of evolving from a simple models to a more complex ones, being useful in the first programming courses and in more specifics ones. (2) The learning ability for offering solid basis that permit the students quickly learn the new and different languages that they will find in his/her professional life. Currently, in the Spanish universities we can find two well-defined groups according to the language/model chosen C or JAVA.

New Concepts and Dilemmas: With the computer evolution, new concepts appear or increase the leading role in computer curricula. Networks and computer communications, operating systems or databases are, currently, important subjects for our students. Web related concepts from its infrastructure, site design and maintenance, multimedia services and applications are the most recent examples.

However, each year we find more concepts, applications, services, and methodologies to teach, increasing the workload of the teaching staff and of our students. Since the available time (number of credits) for the courses is still the same or even less than at the beginning of the computer science, teachers must make the difficult decision of skipping a part of the subject when giving a course. However, what shall one select? Generally, new concepts derive from previous ones. Some of us can give in temptation of skipping the basic concepts. However, this can negatively affect the learning process making it more difficult for our students to understand or adapt to new concepts that will appear during their professional life. The question of fundamentals versus applications or functionalities still lures.

Conclusions: In this presentation, we have given some examples of how computer evolution has affected the design of computer curricula, conditioning the examples used, the lab courses offered, and the methodology employed. Many questions about designing the best curricula and which is the most appropriate methodology to explain concepts that are continuously changing or appearing are still open and will remain open during many years because the evolution of computers and technology still continue.

Ramon Puigjaner

From Early Times to Recent Times of Computers and Computer Education in Spain: Computers arrived to Spain in the late fifties and early sixties, mainly introduced by IBM and big companies. At university level, just the Universidad Complutense de Madrid had an automatic computation speciality with some courses on the basic computer architecture and on programming, common to the curricula in mathematics and physics. The industrial engineering schools had a course on computers that mainly explained the basic von Neumann architecture and the Fortran language. Historic machines of that time were an IBM 1620 at the Industrial Engineering School of Barcelona and an IBM 7090 in the computer centre of the Universidad Complutense de Madrid.

In the mid 1960s, IBM introduced the IBM 360 series and Bull merged with the computer division of GE introduced the GE400 series. In the late 1960s, the

UNIVAC appeared in the Spanish market quite strongly with the 1100 and 9000 series.

In March 1969, the Ministry of Education created the Instituto de Informatica, a strange organization, without any contact with the university and provided a strange curriculum where the students earned a different title after each one of the five years of studies. This Institute created a delegation in Donostia in 1971 and in 1972, the Universitat Autònoma de Barcelona created a Department of Informatics in its Faculty of Sciences. This Faculty was obliged to follow the same curriculum of the Instituto de Informática.

In 1974, the Spanish Ministry of Education considered that Informatics should be included in the university studies. A commission was created to study how to pass the Instituto de Informática to the university. Several universities fought with this commission to get the computer studies. Finally, by the end of 1975, it was decided that three Faculties of Informatics had to be created: Barcelona (in the Universitat Politècnica de Catalunya), Donostia (in the Euskal Herriko Unibertsitatea) and Madrid (in the Universidad Politécnica de Madrid), and that the previous institutions giving informatics studies had to stop to teach informatics. This was true in Madrid and Donostia because the Instituto de Informática and its delegation were incorporated at the corresponding universities and their denomination had changed. In Barcelona, the situation was more complicated because it was necessary to pass studies from one university to another (unbelievable in Spain at that time). Finally, both universities kept their studies. The new Faculties started to work in October 1977 with a five-year curriculum that, for the first time in Spain, was different for each university. In addition, in the Faculty of Barcelona the classical curriculum structure of courses per academic year was broken and the curriculum was organized by courses with their corresponding pre-requisites in such a way that the student was able to organize his/her own curriculum choosing courses among those offered by the Faculty but respecting some compulsory courses.

Around 1980, a new three-year study in informatics was created that started in Madrid and Valencia. Since then the number of universities that created studies in informatics has been growing and currently there are more than eighty.

Two important changes have occurred since that time. (1) The general revision of the official titles started in the late 1980s and finished in the early 1990s that transformed the "License in Informatics" into the "Engineer in Informatics". The three-year curriculum transformed into two three years leading to the "Technical Engineer in System Informatics" and the "Technical Engineer in Management Informatics" (literal translation), also known as the "Technical Engineer in Computer Systems" and the "Technical Engineer in Information Systems" (free translation). (2) In 1995, they initiated periodical meetings of the people responsible in each university of teaching informatics. This assembly has had and is having a strong influence in the current changes introduced in Spain that reflects the European Higher Education Space.

From the marketing and technological viewpoints, the main changes experienced as found in many other countries in the world, are as follows. (a) The introduction of mini- and micro-computers in the late 1970s started the changes in the computer market. (b) The introduction of personal computers by mid eighties, with the decreasing importance of the mainframes and the increasing importance of distributed computing, and the transformation of computers from specific use by qualified people to a wide use element able to be bought at supermarkets. (c) The spread use of communication networks in mid nineties and the popular use of Internet as usual communication mean.

What will the future be?

Contact Information

John Impagliazzo
Professor of Computer Science
Hofstra University
Hempstead, New York 11549 USA
<John.Impagliazzo@Hofstra.edu>
Also Chair, IFIP Working Group 9.7 on the
History of Computing

Julián Arturo Aráoz Durand
Professor of Statistics and Operation Research
Universitat Politècnica de Catalunya
Edifici C5, 2 Planta, Campus Nord
08034 Barcelona, España
<julian.araoz@upc.edu>
Also at Universidad Simón Bolívar
Caracas, Venezuela

Benjamín Barán
Professor, Centro Nacional de Computación
Universidad Nacional de Asunción
Campus de San Lorenzo, Paraguay
<bbaran@cnc.una.py>, http://www.cnc.una.py
Also, President of Centro Latinoamericano de
Estudios en Informática (CLEI)

José Lino Contreras V
Professor, Departamento de Informática
Universidad Técnica Federico Santa María
Av. España 1680 Valparaíso, Chile
<jose.contreras@usm.cl>
http://utfsm.cl

Ana Pont Sanjuan
Professor, Departamento de Informàtica de
Sistemes i Computadors
Universitat Politècnica de València
Camí de Vera s/n, 46022 València, España
<apont@disca.upv.es>

Ramon Puigjaner
Professor, Departamento de Ciencies
Matematiques i Informatica
Universitat de les Illes Balears
07122 Palma, España
<putxi@uib.es>

Great Expectations

*The computerization of research and educational literature
in Swedish university libraries 1960-1980*

Lena Olsson

Stockholm Institute of Education, <Lena.Olsson@lhs.se>

Abstract: Searching for information in databases or on the world wide web to enhance our knowledge has become an everyday task. The internet is a major source of information for education. When we want to make new material available in digital form, we examine how contents can be made searchable by the creation and attachment of metadata. We now have expectations that most educational material, literature and research will be described and to a great extent also readable as full-text in digital form. For the benefit of future university research and teaching the digital global university library is a prevailing image. The work of organizing and representing information with metadata and make it searchable and usable for education and research started already in the 1960's. A vision of the global library was presented during the same period originating from the Library of Congress in Washington DC.(Library of Congress,1963)[1] Some of the expectations, discussions and choices which took place during this period can be recognized as having meaning for processes 20-40 years later.

1. Information Overflow – A Problem for Research Libraries in the 1960's

Research and university education had become important issues in society after the WW 2. Researchers started to compete for positions by increasing their publishing. University libraries all over the world faced the problem of coping with an escalating growth of scientific and educational publications and thus storing and handling big collections and make research literature physically accessible. (de

---

[1] Library of Congress, Automation and the Library of Congress,1963

Please use the following format when citing this chapter:

Olsson, L., 2006, in IFIP International Federation for Information Processing, Volume 215, History of Computing and Education 2 (HCE2), ed. J. Impagliazzo, (Boston: Springer), pp. 59–65.

Solla Price, 1962.)[2] The cost of cataloguing and managing the collections were rising out of proportion. Swedish university libraries had, during the 1950's started a process of modernization with the help of available office technology, typewriters, copying techniques and microfilm. When the computer arrived, it provided a promising solution to the handling of bibliographic data and the administration of the growing collections. Mastering the information overload became a main task for librarians. The information explosion was used as an argument to introduce the new technology.

There were two lines of computerization for application in libraries. One aimed at automating and computerizing routines such as cataloguing, circulation of loans and interlibrary lending through networking between libraries. Another was aimed at information retrieval which was made possible by the introduction of bibliographical databases such as Medline and Chemical abstracts. Originally bibliographic databases were developed by NASA as a means of competing with scientific information in the cold war of the 1950's – 1960's.

2.   Libraries and Their Professional Differences

What is a library? A library shall provide physical access to literature of various forms of publication and provide intellectual access to the contents of literature. (Shera, J.,1966)[3] Various scientific disciplines differ and used to differ even more in their research methods and publication practises. This has implications for how librarians were handling literature collections as well as managing and retrieving bibliographic data. The targeted literature for computing in the university libraries was on one hand, monographs that represented the main big collections of humanities and social sciences. Journals and research reports were on the other hand at the core of the medical, science and technology literature at the special libraries. A monograph could be classified and catalogued as a piece and put on a shelf as a physical artifact; a journal article could be indexed but was part of a larger package. These differences inspired different professional practices.

At the turn of the century a new professional group, the documentalists, had argued for a new concept, concerning bibliographic description, documentation which was aimed at retrieving information out of journals and research reports.(Shera, J.1953;)[4] Information retrieval for the benefit of the user was of more interest to them than describing a monograph as an item which was part of a bigger collection.   Since these practices also were represented by different libraries/librarians it affected how university libraries/librarians and special libraries/librarians expected the computerization to solve their respective problems.

[2] De Solla Price, D., Science since Babylon. New Haven, 1962

[3] Shera, J., Documentation and the organization of knowledge, London, 1966

[4] Shera,J., A review of present state of librarianship in Bradford, ed, Documentation;

We shall se how their various practices and expectations influenced the development of the system.

3.   Expectations on Technology

Already during the 1960's computer technology was introduced as a means of modernizing some of the problems in research libraries. Library of Congress published 1963 a visionary ten-year plan for rationalizing all library work by one integrated system (Library of Congress, 1963)[5] A standard format was established, MAchine Readable Catalog, MARC.

The Swedish Royal library had the task of organizing a union catalogue for Swedish research libraries. There were problems with back logs and an increasing number of libraries participating in the union catalogue as well as demands from most research libraries for more personnel to handle collections. This was the cause of looking to automation for solutions and thus establishing a committee for ADP 1964 that worked until 1969. The proposals from the committee were aimed at automating the union catalogue by using principles for shared cataloguing. A standard MARC format entry of bibliographic data was to be executed by one participating library and was then to be copied by other participating libraries. This could be extended to an international cooperation of libraries, thus creating a global catalogue.

These suggestions were criticized by a well known documentalist, Björn Tell, who meant that the technology should be used not as a way of rationalizing internal routines but be used as a means of support for decision making and qualitative development directed towards the researchers not the librarians. (Tell, B., 1966)

4.   A Vision of the Modern Library

Normally the computerization processes were designed to automate single routines, often starting with the circulation of books. But there was a more interesting option to the Swedish Agency for Administrative Development (SAFAD) and the systems designer Mr Lindberg. SAFAD got the commission to examine the feasibility of a library information network for university libraries. The civil servants from SAFAD were interested in finding a way of rationalizing the libraries with the latest technology as well as implementing bureaucratic reform. Long term planning, mainframe computers and strong belief in radical change inspired the system development plan. The ultimate solution to library automation was to create the totally integrated system, which would be achieved by applying a total systems

[5] Library of Congress, *Automation and the library of Congress*, 1963

approach. By this approach it was planned that an organization and its various functions should be computerized to work as an interacting whole, which meant that work processes and information flow would be facilitated and easy to control. The concept of a totally integrated library system was introduced in visionary terms as the Library Information System, LIBRIS (Statskontoret, 1972)[6].

The original plan for LIBRIS had utopian features such as a lack of historical perspective i.e. not growing out of a familiar reality, an assumption of universal consensus of values or institutional arrangements, being characterized by social harmony which helps maintain stability, following recurrent patterns and and being isolated in time and space from other parts of the world.(Boguslaw,R.1965)[7] Thus the development of the system was planned according to given standards without much consideration to context.

5. Developing of a National Library System

LIBRIS developed through three phases: the design phase, 1970-1973; the implementation phase 1974-1979; the use phase 1980 and onwards. The first phase was dominated by the promotion of the totally integrated system accompanied by the rational planning ideology of SAFAD, responsible for systems development and with an interest to rationalize and implement bureaucratic reform of the research libraries. Through LIBRIS the librarians at various libraries would be able to perform all functions, acquisition, cataloguing, circulation of books as well as communicate with international databases. A master plan was set up and the project would start with the cataloguing routine. Mr. Lindberg, the systems designer was able to enroll head librarians and cataloguers in the implementation. The new online technology gave the librarians and their librarians immediate contact with the central database and they could process shared cataloguing which means that a book could be catalogued at one library and then copied at all the other libraries which purchased the same item. This was a major effort of rationalization: less personnel would be able to perform the same duties.

But LIBRIS did not advance according to the master plan. During the implementation phase, the practical efforts of establishing common rules and methods undermined the initial vision of a total system. The cataloguers who struggled at accomplishing the perfect catalogue were able to enforce their standards of alphabetical representation to a level far exceeding normal computional praxis. In fact they argued that all different alphabets should be represented. They succeeded however in forcing the developers to a full Swedish representation, which we very often do not have today! Other problems arose due to the choice of hardware; LIBRIS ran on a Saab machine D22. Saab had replaced IBM in several

---

[6] Statskontoret, LIBRIS, ett informationssystem för bibliotek, 1972. p.14

[7] Boguslaw,R., The new utopians, A study of system design and social change,. 1965

national applications. Computer problems were frequent and opening hours were too short. The diffusion of LIBRIS was slow.

6. Technological Development as Processes and Conflicts

As opposed to following a rational plan, technological development can, as be understood as a conglomerate of developmental phases, of constellation of actors, problematic situations and conflicts. (Rammert, W.1992)[8] The development of LIBRIS can be seen as various processes which led to the diminishing of a national totally integrated information system to a mere union catalogue. During the design phase, the technology was envisioned as open, potent and capable of developing into a fully computerized library: During the implementation phase, technological flexibility was narrowed to a cataloguing system in the form of a bibliographic utility.

The general idea of LIBRIS invited the actors to various interpretations of what the system could accomplish. According to their various interests different actors attributed different meanings and goals to the system and had different reasons for taking part in and supporting LIBRIS:

- The university librarians wished to keep their autonomy. They were on the other hand enthusiastic about the modernity and status, which LIBRIS represented.
- At the Royal Library, the librarians wished to use LIBRIS as a central function and to rationalize the production of the union catalogue.
- The documentalists wanted to shape LIBRIS according to the norms of their standard UNISIST, which suited their professional purposes.
- The SAFAD systems designers wished to develop an advanced technological project as well as succeeding in implementing bureaucratic reform.

The researchers, the real users of the system, were invisible actors who probably would have had other ambitions if they had been engaged in the process. The development of LIBRIS can thus be understood by the processes in which actors took part to further their interests. Some processes were connected; others were not. The various interests of the actors extended into various conflicts. They developed between:

- the librarians (in general) and SAFAD. The conflict emanated from different institutional practices and from their different roles; from SAFAD being the reformers and the librarians the ones being reformed; conflicts arose from the parties having different competences and from their lack of insightful communication.

[8] Rammert, W., Research on the regeneration and development of technology in M. Dierkes &Hoffman, eds. New technology on the outset. Frankfurt 1992

- LIBRIS as technological project and LIBRIS as bureaucratic reform: The goals of these activities collided on the one hand and encompassed each other on the other hand. The bureaucratic reform aimed at a coherent organization where as the technological project envisioned using and developing advanced technology. The technological vision inspired the cataloguers to make sophisticated demands, thus undermining the plans for efficiency outlined in the bureaucratic reform.
- Traditionalists and radicals among the library professionals: The heart of the conflict concerned the role of technology. Technology could serve as a means of transforming the library into something qualitatively new, by enhancing the possibilities for action and accomplishing new kinds of services or technology could improve the existing routines and functions of the library by substitution, making them faster or better but mainly maintaining the original routine or method. An example is use of the MARC standard format by the traditionalists. The new MARC-format used for computerized catalogues contained the same information as the traditional catalogue card. A traditional technological style was preserved. A radical alternative would have been to use the indexing format of the documentation databases thus violating the traditional norm but gaining new possibilities of retrieval.

The cataloguers became the winners and the losers of the system. Their routine was originally the main target of rationalization. They managed however to make use of the possibilities and promises of the design phase to enforce their professional norms and rules. The catalogue remained during the whole project period the main task for computerization. In the long run, however, cataloguers diminished in number due to the frequent use of standardized routines and copy cataloguing.

The actors' various interpretations of the LIBRIS system; the various conflicts; the enforcement of professional norms and the institutionalization of practices; inadequate resources and computer incapability, interacted in shaping the system and limiting the alternatives. Finally, the system came to a temporary closure. This was obtained when the remaining alternative, the union catalogue, was agreed upon. The role of closure in technical development can be understood as a punctuated evolution as described by Wiebe Bijker (1990):

> "the combination of stabilization and closure processes makes it understandable that technical change is a continuous process although not occuring at equal rates at every point in time — it's like a punctuated evolution"[9].

Temporary closure occurred when alternatives other than the union catalogue were pushed aside. This depended not only on the strategies or lack of activity from the actors but also because a totally integrated library system could not be achieved within the established institutional framework.

---

[9] Bijker, Wiebe, The social construction of Technology, Den Haag, 1990, p.97

7. Conclusions

LIBRIS inspired and laid the foundations of library computing during the 1980s. A whole generation of librarians gained computing experience through LIBRIS. LIBRIS can be seen as a cooperative effort and a joint development task. LIBRIS is still developing as the Swedish national library system. The influence of technology on the actors and on library activities, did not originate from the inherent capacity of the technology itself, but the technology presented a circumstance for organizational change, cooperation and learning.

Through the computerization of research libraries, research and educational literature became available on a broader basis. The visibility and use of university collections increased which was valuable for education and research. This development can also be seen as a step towards the virtualization of libraries. We are in fact today approaching the vision of Library of Congress of the global library in the 1960's. There is still however a need for further standardization and cooperation if we are going to accomplish the global digital library.

There are other challenges as well. Today information and literature searches are performed on the internet and on the world wide web. We face problems with how to make critical reviews of sources presented on the web. This is an important quality issue. Open access publication of research and educational material creates a need for new solutions for indexing and coordination

Endnote

In this paper findings from my doctoral dissertation Olsson, L., The computerized library – machine dreams of the 1970's, 1995, have been concentrated and further elaborated. The dissertation has only been published in Swedish.

Nineteen Sixties History of Data Base Management

T. William Olle

T.William Olle Associates, Walton on Thames, Surrey, UK
<BillOlle@aol.com>

Abstract: Data base management evolved during the sixties and seventies. The evolution period was protracted. Many driving forces impacted the evolution and it is the aim of this paper to analyze these driving forces (some technical and some political) and to discuss the impact of each. The driving forces are identified as follows: higher level languages, generalization of software, non-procedural approach, program maintenance, recognition of different levels of data definition, direct access storage, and relational theory.

1. Introduction and Terminology

The origins of the term "data base" and subsequently "database" go back a long way. The first sighting of the term was its use in 1963 by the System Development Corporation who sponsored a symposium with the title "Development and Management of a Computer-centered Data Base" [1]. The term "data base" was picked up by the contributors to the symposium in the titles of their papers. The defense industry in the USA was a major development force in those days.

The term "data base management" was a natural derivative from the juxtaposition of "data base" and "management". The terms "database" and "data base" have subsequently both been in widespread use. However, the latter is preferred in this paper.

At the time (namely 1963), the primary storage medium for data was magnetic tape. Early work on data processing focused on the optimization of the processing associated with magnetic tapes and on the required sequential processing through a file of data. The term "data base" was at the time and indeed still should be related to the term "file" in the following way. A data base is a collection of inter-related

Please use the following format when citing this chapter:

Olle, T.W., 2006, in IFIP International Federation for Information Processing, Volume 215, History of Computing and Education 2 (HCE2), ed. J. Impagliazzo, (Boston: Springer), pp. 67–75.

files. Many authors confuse the two by using the term "data base" to refer to a "file".

2. Higher Level Languages - COBOL

At the time the concept of "data base management" was beginning to emerge, programming languages for commercial application were rather more advanced. The initial developments were based on a series of earlier languages and systems. The US Department of Defense had used its influence to bring about the development of a common language for business oriented applications. This common language was COBOL - Common Business Oriented Language – the first version of which was available in 1960 [2]. This early COBOL had no facilities for, and indeed awareness of, database management. However, it is useful to note some of COBOL's ideas had an impact on the development of data base management.

COBOL recognized the importance of separating the definition of the data from the definition of the procedures to be performed on that data. These concepts were provided in the Data Division and in the Procedure Division of COBOL. In the FORTRAN language, which was developed largely for scientific and engineering applications, the two definition processes were intermingled.

COBOL also offered what seems (with hindsight) to be a primitive way of structuring data. One could define files, record types, groups and data items. A file could have one or more record types. Each record type could have one or more items and zero or more groups. Each group could be either a fixed group (basically a naming convention) or a repeating group which allowed a group of data items to occur a number of times up to a prescribed maximum. These conventions allowed for the definition of different kinds of hierarchical structure, which could be represented on the widely used magnetic tape files of the time.

COBOL was above all a procedural programming language. It was a considerable advance on machine language programming available on the earliest machines and indeed on Symbolic Assembly Language, which was specified in 1957.

The terms "procedural" and "non-procedural" were often interpreted as follows. "Procedural" said "what" and "how", "Non-procedural" said "what" but not "how". These two concepts are not "black" and "white" but rather represent a spectrum of capability. COBOL represented a useful progression along this spectrum from the procedural to the non-procedural – but further progression was needed.

3. Generalization

In January 1959, William C. McGee of IBM published a paper with the title "Generalization: the key to successful data processing" [3]. This paper emphasized the idea that any computer program should be designed to address, not just one simple application, but a set of necessarily inter-related applications. Given the open interpretation in any business context of the term "application", it is perhaps more appropriate to think in terms "small" and "large".

However, the message is clear. It is inefficient and indeed time consuming to design several small applications, each with its own program, rather than one larger application in which the processes to be performed are generalized and the data which they reference is "integrated". The complex trade-off between pre-design and post-integration is still with us today. In the era before higher-level languages, the balance towards the latter must have been less telling. McGee's seminal paper clearly foresaw the emergence of data base management.

4. Disc Memory – IBM Ramac

The first computer to include a disc drive was introduced by IBM in September 1956 [4]. The computer was the IBM RAMAC and the disc drive was called the "IBM 350 disk drive". It had a capacity of five million 7-bit characters that translates to 4.8 megabytes in contemporary terms.

Despite this early introduction, IBM did not seem to push the new facility. This may have been because the capacity of the disk was modest and the cost high compared to the already widely used magnetic tapes. Even the first magnetic tapes on the Univac machine had a capacity of 1.4 megabytes and it was possible to have several such magnetic tape units on a single machine.

Another reason for the slow uptake of disc memory might well have been the uncertainty of how to make effective use of these devices.

5. Bachman and Dodd

Charles W. Bachman is widely recognized as a pioneer in the field of data base management. One of his papers [5] bears witness to the basis for this recognition. In October 1964, C.W. Bachman and S.B. Williams published this paper [5} in the Proceedings of the Fall Joint Computer Conference. It was entitled "A general purpose programming system for random access memories". The term "random access memory" was in early use to refer to what subsequently and more accurately became designated as "direct access memory" on the basis that the accesses to the data were certainly not random (or should not be).

In comparison to the sequential accesses to data necessary with magnetic tape storage, direct access memory certainly provided an extra dimension to the processing. The Bachman and Williams work certainly provided a means of exploiting this extra dimension. Bachman's approach was called "Integrated Data Store" and was developed in one of General Electric's divisions in which Bachman was employed.

Bachman subsequently claimed that the choice at the time of the more British term "store" was preferred to the American "memory" was quite deliberate. "Integrated Data Memory" certainly lacked something!

Also in the early sixties, George Dodd, of General Motors Research Laboratory, developed an approach to handling data, which was somewhat similar to Charles Bachman's. This was published the Proceedings of the Fall Joint Computer conference in 1966 [6] and entitled "APL - a language for associative data handling in PL/1". (This use of the acronym APL had nothing to do with Iverson's APL).

The two approaches had in common their departure from the hierarchical structures predicated on the sequential processing of magnetic tape files. The two approaches were both based on the less restrictive and more flexible network structures. In mathematics terms, the structuring facility could most accurately be described as a directed acyclic graph structure. This is based on the fact that circularity was not permitted in the structures.

6.   Program Maintenance

Another driving force in the evolution of data base management systems was the realization that was creeping in concerning the cost of corrective maintenance on computer programs already in use.

Many companies went into computerized data processing with great enthusiasm first time round. Computers were a major advance on the electro-mechanical accounting equipment, which they replaced. Speed and flexibility were both achievable.

However, after the early programs had been in use for some time, it was found necessary to make changes to the code. While this was certainly easier if the code had been written using a higher level language, it was realized that, if more than one program was using the same file, any change to that file to support a new business requirement would have a knock-on effect on other programs using the same file but which otherwise did not really need to be modified.

This problem began to hit US industry in the mid-sixties. There was a need to redesign and reprogram application systems and hopefully not repeat the earlier mistakes of the first generation systems. The search for a "silver bullet" frequently found a home in the emerging database world.

7. COBOL List Processing Task Force

The development of COBOL discussed above and Bachman's IDS were two sets of ideas that had to be brought together. In 1965, COBOL was already gaining considerable momentum and the host organization, CODASYL (Conference on Data Systems Languages), had supported further work after the first draft of 1960.

It was in 1965 that one of the major non DOD non computer manufacturer protagonists, namely US Steel, proposed that the COBOL Language Committee of CODASYL should to create a Task Force (clearly a military term) to investigate the extension of the COBOL Language to incorporate the kind of facilities which Bachman had proposed in his IDS work. The "task force" was initially named the List Processing Task Force."

It should be noted that the term "data base" was already in use in 1965, but not in the COBOL Committee and not in the IDS work. Hence the term "list processing" which was in more widespread use at that time, thanks to the work of MacCarthy, in artificial intelligence (which was mostly Fortran based) [7].

Both Charles Bachman and George Dodd were involved on the early work of this List Processing Task Force. It was not until May 1967 at a meeting in Minneapolis (attended by the present author) that the meeting decided that the term "list processing" gave the wrong impression to practitioners and that the term "data base" would create less confusion. The Department of Defense oriented term "task force" was also replaced by the less emotive tem "Task Group" to generate the better-known term "Data Base Task Group". There is little doubt that this decision lead to the widespread acceptance of the term "data base". Given the emphasis, already in those early days, on "management" in all its forms, the term "data base management" was part of the package.

8. CODASYL Data Base Task Group

The CODASYL DBTG was a very hard working group between 1967 and 1971 holding meetings every two months. The first report to the parent committee (the CODASL COBOL Language Committee) was submitted in December 1968, followed by a second more complete report in October 1969. The final report was published in January 1973 entitled "Proposal for a data base facility in COBOL".[8]

The DBTG work introduced some ideas that were not in IDS or APL. The view that a data base was something central to an organization's data processing had emerged. The data base could be accessed by several programs which were written in COBOL and possibly in other languages. IBM was beginning to promote PL/I at the time and the DBTG felt that it was meaningful (and possibly also political) to support this multiple programming language thinking.

This evolved into the notion of a programming language independent schema and to the concept of a set of programming language schemas. (The term "schemata" was favoured by some language purists).

For reasons only a committee can conceive, much of the IDS terminology was changed. For example, IDS terminology referred to "chains" formed by two (or possibly more) record types, one of which was referred to as a master and the others as trailers. The IDS term chain was deemed to connote a specific representation of data in storage and the term "set type" was coined to depict this construct. A set type may have an owner and a member.

The work of the DBTG had a major impact. Implementations were produced by various vendors excluding IBM who initially were committed to an old style hierarchical system IMS that had been developed in the late.

Most international companies developed implementations of the DBTG proposals. These included ICL, Phillips Electrologica, CII, DataSaab and Hitachi. However, the implementation produced by an IBM customer, namely BF Goodrich and known as IDMS was taken over by a new company started by John Cullinane. Cullinane did rather well from their sales of IDMS to IBM customers. The early mastermind behind IDMS was Richard F. Schubert (indeed a descendant of his famous namesake). Dick Schubert had also been an active member of the DBTG.

Tribute must be paid to the two persons who served as chairman of the DBTG during most of its existence. The initial chair was Warren Simmonds of US Steel mentioned earlier. When he resigned because of other commitments, his responsibilities were taken over by Appollon Metaxides who was employed by the Bell Telephone Laboratory in Holmdel New Jersey.

9.   CODASYL Systems Committee Publications

In the years from 1962 when Bachman published his initial paper on IDS, interest in what came to be called "data base management systems" burgeoned. Numerous systems emerged bearing the acronym DBMS – data base management system. In 1964, the CODASYL Systems Committee, a sibling committee of the CODASYL COBOL Language Committee (parent of the DBTG), turned its attention to these systems.

It was clear that several systems were becoming available reflecting various factors identified in this paper as contributing to the idea of database. In addition to the COBOL Language Committee, CODASYL had also created a committee with responsibility for taking a more long-term view. The CODASYL Systems Committee had been in existence since the formation of the CODASYL organization in 1959

In 1966, the Systems Committee started to analyze "generalized data base management systems". The term "generalized" was added in order to emphasize that the systems being analyzed were each applicable to any kind of application area for which a data base could be defined. Such a system is different from a "tailored" system, which was defined for a specific application.

The Systems Committee published two reports in 1968 and 1971. The first report comprised 400 pages and was entitled "Survey of Generalized Data Base Management Systems" [9] and presented a survey of each of nine systems available at the time. The aim of the survey was quoted as being "to find a common basis for describing generalized data base management systems, to demonstrate its usability, and to make this information available for further theoretical and developmental work within CODASYL". The aim was not to assess evaluate any system. The reason for avoiding comparative evaluation was that any kind of collective and objective evaluation at the time by persons (many of whom were involved with one of the systems analyzed) would have proved impossible.

Following on publication of this survey, the CODASYL Systems Committee immediately started work on a more detailed analysis of generalized data base management systems. The 1971 report of over 500 pages was entitled "Feature Analysis of Generalized Data Base Management Systems" [10]. Several of the systems analyzed in this second report had been treated in the earlier report. These included IBM's Generalized Information System (GIS), GE/Honeywell's Integrated Data Store (IDS), Informatics Mark IV, System Development Corporation's Time-Shared Data Management System (TDMS) and Western Electric's System Control-1 (SC-1). The Feature Analysis also included an analysis of the CODASYL DBTG's Proposal [8].

During the seventies, it can safely be claimed that the three reports [8,9,10] added considerably to the understanding of what data base management was all about and helped to promote acceptance of the concepts and hopefully clarify some aspects of the confusion which prevailed about the systems being promoted.

10. Logical Data Structure and Storage Structure

One of the aspects of data base management, which caused confusion, was what is here identified as the level of data definition. In simple terms, the level of data definition refers to the extent to which a definition of the data in a given DBMS referred to the degree to which a DBMS represented the stored aspects of the data structure.

A definition of the logical perception of the data could be referred to the "logical data structure". A definition how the data structure was perceived to be represented in storage was referred to as the "storage structure".

A DBMS could possibly not any contain facilities for defining the storage structure. This meant that the system had an essentially unique way of representing the data in storage, but the person defining the data (and ipso facto the person using the data) had no means of controlling or influencing this definition.

Alternatively, a DBMS could provide both a logical data definition and a storage definition. This, it would be argued, allowed the system to be "tuned" hence providing a more computer efficient system. The other argument was that the storage definition was not something that the user needed to both about when defining a process to access the data.

It should be pointed out that at the time much of the development work already described in this paper was being undertaken, computer hardware efficiency was a major issue for larger applications, that is to say larger data bases. The trade-off between hardware efficiency and people efficiency had already been moving towards the latter. However, in 1971, it was still a little premature to assert that compute time should be regarded as an inexpensive resource.

11. Relational Approach

In June 1970, the late Ted Codd published his seminal paper entitled "A relational model of stored data for large shared data banks" [11]. This paper did not build on earlier work in the data base field, but rather on some theoretical work in pure mathematics concerning relational calculus.

It developed its own set of terminology – relations, tuples, attributes and referential constraints were used to refer to concepts already well established as record types, records, data items and set types. Of the four terms in each of these two terminology set, the last one of the four is the one which was clearly an improvement on its predecessor.

The relational approach triggered more research work into data base management than any other published paper in the field of computer science. While data base management at that time had been largely of interest to practitioners involved in commercial applications, the academic world was now attracted to the whole issue of the "best" data base approach – in whatever way the "best" might be interpreted!

12. Debates on Data Base Management

During the early seventies, there were numerous debates held at technical conferences all over the world on the relative merits of various data base approaches. Interest focused on the CODASYL DBTG proposals for which commercially available implementations were being promoted, on the relational proposals, Cincom's TOTAL and IBM's Integrated Management System (IMS), a German system called ADDABAS.

Both TOTAL and IMS were aggressively promoted during the seventies. The CODASYL DBTG proposals were implemented by practically every computer manufacturer except IBM. The main implementation for the IBM 360 hardware was Cullinane's Integrated Data Management System.

13. Database Standardization

It is important to recall that the CODASYL work discussed earlier in this paper was never seen as a standardization effort. The CODASYL organization (now defunct) had established its roll in connection with COBOL in the mid-sixties as "pre-standardization) with full awareness that national organizations such as AFNOR, ANSI and BSI had responsibility for defining and approving standards.

As the world became smaller (in a certain sense) the role of the International Standards Organization became more significant. The database work was one of the areas where the major thrust of standardization took place in an international context.

The history of data base standardization is as extensive as the nineteen sixties history of data base management presented in this paper. Although many papers and articles have been written on this topic, an update remains a topic for a subsequent paper.

References

[1] "Development and Management of a Computer-centered Data Base" 1964. Published by System Development Corporation as TM-2624/100/00.
[2] COBOL - Common Business Oriented Language 1960.
[3] "Generalization: the key to successful data processing" Published in January 1969 in Communication of the ACM.
[4] "IBM 350 disk drive" 1956. http://www.cedmagic.com/history/ibm-305-ramac.html
[5] C.W. Bachman, S.B.Williams "A general purpose programming system for random access memories". Proceedings of Fall Joint Computer Conference, October 1964 Volume 26 Pp 411 – 422.
[6] G.G.Dodd "APL - a language for associative data handling in PL/1". Proceedings of Fall Joint Computer conference 1966. Vol 29 pp 677- 684.
[7] http://encyclopedia.thefreedictionary.com/Lisp
[8] "Proposal for a data base facility in COBOL". CODASYL Database Task Group. January 1973.
[9] "Survey of Generalized Data Base management Systems" Published 1968. CODASYL Systems Committee
[10] "Feature Analysis of Generalized Data Base Management Systems" Published 1971. CODASYL Systems Committee
[11] E.F. Codd. "A relational model of data for large shared data banks", Communications of ACM. Vol 13 No 6. Pp 377 – 387 (June 1970)

A Creative Approach to Educational Computing
Key incidents in a typical life cycle

Christina Preston

MirandaNet Academy, Bath Spa University, www.mirandanet.ac.uk
<Christina@mirandanet.ac.uk>

Abstract: This auto-ethnographical narrative traces the history of an educational computing professional. Christina Preston describes her experience of computers began in the 1950s as her father was a computer professional. After graduating, she developed her skills as a journalist and short story writer for women's magazines at the same time as teaching English, Drama and Media studies in London secondary school. Her late introduction to computers through her own children was typical of UK teachers in the early nineteen eighties who suddenly found that they were expected to train in Information Technology and to teach the subject as part of the curriculum although this had not been included in their teacher training. Christina Preston is now the chair of the international industrial and government funded MirandaNet Fellowship, which is a community of practice for teachers, advisors, teacher educators, software designers and ICT policy makers. In this ethnographical study she uses her women's magazine writing skills to recreate her own experiences in a way that will help advisers and teacher educators to understand how the history of many teachers who are middle aged in 2006 has affected their attitude to computers and their willingness to use them in classrooms. Critical incidents include her introduction to mainframes as a child, her own children's experiences, her first ICT training, the first lesson she give and her authorship of educational software. The unexpected death of her daughter opens her mind to the potential of computers in democratic participation and active citizenship between local, regional and national community.

1. Computers and Revolution

I will introduce myself as the narrator of this story about an educational computing and world wide web (www) professional which now spans three decades and two centuries. As Ms. Average Classroom Teacher, I shall trace the pattern of computers in my life, experiences of teaching, thoughts about effective educational

Please use the following format when citing this chapter:

Preston, C., 2006, in IFIP International Federation for Information Processing, Volume 215, History of Computing and Education 2 (HCE2), ed. J. Impagliazzo, (Boston: Springer), pp. 77–91.

software and some ideas about where computing might go in the future in the future. But most of all I want to warn you not to be complacent because computers have had so little effect on the average teacher's practice in the last fifty years. Exponential advances in the nineties will take you by surprise.

My story is about creative educational computing. Some academics still argue the case that computers, the Silicon Idols[1], encourage mechanistic thinking. This view is based on lack of knowledge about the best use of computers in learning and teaching today.

> "This potential of computers for interactivity or participation in a
> work of art or reference is giving writers what artists and musicians
> have enjoyed for some time - a new creative medium."[2]

In my opinion, those teachers who refuse to understand the potential, run the risk of disenfranchising their students from important liberties of expression.

The exponential growth of educational computing and the internet in the twentieth century has to be acknowledged. In his preface to my book on computers and literacy,[3] Professor Gunther Kress warns us that it is impossible to overstate the enormity of changes in literacy and literacy practices wrought by developments in electronic technologies. This revolution, he maintains is more far-reaching, and more fundamental than Gutenberg's invention of the printing press. Gutenburg did not disturb what was understood about written language: its formality; its impersonality; its objectiveness and 'timelessness'; its grammatical complexities; its hierarchical mode of organisation. But technology is now challenging these notions - for instance, the geographic separation and temporal co-presence of two people interacting via electronic mail.

This challenge of the new communications media also has a deeply subversive potential in relation to language. While Gutenberg's revolution made language in its written form more central, the current revolution is taking us both backwards and forwards into a new era of iconic forms of communication, backwards and forwards into hieroglyphics. The emphasis is on the visual. In a new multi-modal, multi-media form of text, what is happening is a fundamental challenge to the hitherto unchallenged cultural centrality of written language.

In some ways we are returning to a medieval manuscript, early print culture where books were rare, copying was current, authorship was not important, reading aloud, listening were the main forms of information distribution, and varied international orthography was acceptable. As the power of the book as an information authority is weakened our society is adding to these medieval conventions: the death of copyright, collaborative composition and changeable texts.[4] Indeed this revolution is central to what we learn and teach in our schools.

---

[1] Micheal Shallis *The Silcon Idol*. Oxford University Press ISBN 0-19-286032-1 (1984)

[2] Jane Dorner *Writing on Disk* John Taylor publications 0707 265908 (1992)

[3] C. Preston *Apple to Zap Handbook of Literacy for Learners of all Ages* (July 1994) Apple Publications

[4] Chandler and Marcus - *Education and Computers*, Harrap (1989)

Only the commitment of people like us will ensure that the computer is used as creative and empowering catalyst for the betterment of life not an excuse for the reduction of all human activity to the binary system: yes or no, black or white, male or female. Life is irreducible as we all sense, feel, intimate - and the best computer practice *can* reflect these facts of life.

2. Computers and Ms Average

So how did it all start? My first encounter with computers was in the fifties. I can see in this incident the excitement of a young learner.

The imperious ringing of the telephone broke into my sleep at two in the morning. A throbbing taxi squatted in the road. Hanging from the window, I saw my father, his pin-striped pajamas replaced by his pin-striped suit, dashing out into the night like Dr. Findlay Black bowler firmly on. The patient was the bank computer. Down again!

The mysterious deletion of a couple of million pounds was the staple diet of breakfast conversation - computer fraud and security issues for our late, late, supper when he came home. The computer seemed a voracious night and day devourer and regurgitator of information requiring constant attention, devotion and coaxing to perform.

My father's bank was in Threadneedle Street in the City of London. Every Christmas the children of bank employees were invited to a spectacular party. Travelling through the grey and empty City streets on a Saturday was exciting in our new party dresses and our hair frizzled by curling tongs. The windowless buildings dwarfed us as we struggled up the marble steps. The Xmas party always lived up to expectations: the biggest tree, the most avuncular Father Xmas, the most sumptuous presents and the wobbliest jelly.

But there was a greater excitement in store one year. My father took my sister and I up in one of the lifts; "To see the computers." In an antechamber, we pulled white gauze hats over our hair like operatives in a food factory. White plastic overshoes and stiff overalls signalled that dust and dandruff were the enemy.

Secret codes were punched into the door panel. Inside the room that was about 20 feet by 20 feet there were ten tin boxes the size of wardrobes. Through the window on their chests I could see giant brown tape reels whirling round.. These mainframe computers looked rather like the old reel-to-reel tape recorders that had eaten from the wrong side of the mushroom like Alice - and grown. There was a hallowed silence. So this was the operations sanctum to which my father, the high priest, was called night and day.

In the sixties and early seventies my adolescence and teacher training days were blissfully free of 'computer awareness'. This has not changed much for student teachers today. I have been keeping the figures for some years. Although BT and the Institute of Education can now assume that mature students will have some computing knowledge[5], the large majority of initial teacher training institutions only have time for one or two days on computers in the year. This absence of general information is not yet counterbalanced by a wider use in subject areas. As schools take over the full responsibility for teacher training it will be even harder to organise some degree of consistency in computer awareness. Let me remind you, nevertheless, that we remain world leaders in telematics in education in this country, with the possible exception of Holland. We also have the highest concentration of computers in the classroom with the exception of Iceland - but that's another story.

The personal computer revolution found me in the early eighties when we bought a Spectrum 48K for our growing children, a girl and a boy. Games for children seemed to be the purpose of a home computer. I never actually touched the keyboard. On the first day of purchase, we took it with great pride to show my father who had recently retired from Citibank. Usually an obliging man, we were surprised when he refused, point-blank, to plug the little computer into his television.

"How many K does it have?" he said, eyeing it warily, 48"? You remember the dust-proof data-processing centre I ran when you were still at school? You remember all those life sized boxes?" Of course I did. "Well in that entire room there was 30K of memory - and you're not putting 48K through my television set!"

In the seventies we thought we were past all that. Computers were so much more reliable and user friendly. My children invested in a joystick so that they could kill little yellow people, the Green Berets or furry monsters with more efficiency. They jet-setted with Willy and skied with Horace. They went in for karate, kick boxing and diving with the Red Arrows. I began to wish they would return to the television.

In the early eighties my son's school held jumble sales and 'bring and buys' to purchase some ICL computers. My daughter's school held a parents' evening for us to admire and use the new 'Pets'. The young enthusiastic female head of the maths department extolled the virtues of women in the computer world and we, parents, were impressed. My daughter brought home printouts of drawings and games programmed herself. She began to leave the house early so that she could join her computer teacher at 8.00 a.m. - the only space for her year in the computer suite. This stopped suddenly - the young and enthusiastic teacher had developed morning sickness - the Pets were abandoned. Good computer teachers were thin on the ground in girls schools.

---

[5] Mellar and Jackson- *IT and entrants to teacher training* Journal of Computer Assisted Learning September(1993)
Preston *The BT Model* - 1994 in progress

3. My First Training

Reviewing this incident I realized that the quality of the teacher is paramount regardless of whether computers are used as a resource or not. Computers do not appear to replace teachers.

By this time, at the large south London comprehensive where I taught English and Drama, there were computers only in the maths department. So I was surprised to receive an invitation to a 2-day computer course at Kingston in May 1985 run by a body called The Microelectronics Programme (MEP). I was curious - how could computers have anything to do with English or Drama?

Jean Beck, now a director at the National Council of Education Technology, was in those days a down-to-earth advisor with MEP. Librarians have been a great unsung influence on the development of computer use in schools. According to my research, Software in Schools[6], librarians have led the way in CD-ROM and communications services. On this first morning, Jean Beck gave us a brief run down on computer devices in the High Street. She even told me that I would soon be getting my money from a hole in the wall. "Well," I thought, "a pleasant woman, but deluded".

The English heads of department on the MEP course were not very impressed by the couple of spelling programs, a multi-choice questionnaire on Hamlet and a rather explicit version of Hangman selected by a programming advisor. These titles were typical of educational programs written by teachers learning how to program in Basic. The content of these programs was just a useful vehicle for justifying the programming exercise. These programs did have a place in establishing educational aspects of software but I would only recommend professional development today. Not that this debars teachers from the consultation process.

The next day on the course Jean Beck introduced us to Bob Moy, the designer of 'Developing Tray'[7] and an ILEA advisor/teacher. Bob was a teacher and a half. He introduced us to his program as if we were his class. There were thirty of us and one computer used as an electronic blackboard. This was a program that we could see was based on learning theory. The computer was adding to the learning process in a way that could not be replicated by conventional methods. We were faced with a blank screen. We knew that there was a passage of writing to be discovered but we had no idea what it was. We could buy or predict letters and punctuation. The computer would enter our predictions and tell us the score.

Bob kept us in suspense. He pretended absolute ignorance of what the passage really said. And we believed him. We couldn't leave the puzzle alone; the text was perplexing and obscure: some poetry? It was worth investigation. We refused to cheat. We were learning about language structure and styles from the bottom up. At

---

[6] Harris and Preston *Software in schools* - NFER/NCET (1993)From NFER, The Mere, Slough, Berks.

[7] Bob Moy *Devtray* and *Allwrite* Software published by ILECC, the Inner London Education Computing Centre. Closed down by Hammersmith Education Authority in March 1994

lunch time we all refused to leave for the pub. Sandwiches were ordered and we continued on our quest for meaning throughout the afternoon.

Devtray has remained an important program for English teachers for a decade. I have seen it used badly and well over the years. I have seen children merely guessing and I have seen them actively devising reading strategies. It is typical of the kind of teaching tool that depends on the teachers' ability to use resources well.

4.   Computers in the Curriculum

This teaching experience is typical of the way in which many teachers find themselves introduced to computer teaching, ill prepared.

It was something of a surprise the next September to find 'IT' in four slots on my timetable.

> "What is IT?" I asked the curriculum deputy.
> "Information technology" he said patiently. "You are teaching
>   IT to two first year classes this year."
> "Why me?"
> "Because English teachers communicate well and because you
>   had a two day MEP course on computers in May."
> "Two days!" I squealed.
> "Well it's two days more than anyone else teaching information
>   technology this term."

Remember at this point in time I had still never touched a keyboard. I'm surprised I did not make more fuss but I was too ignorant to know what I was agreeing to.

Actually, the first term was easy as the computers had not arrived. We taught the bemused classes from earnest, newly-minted Croydon information technology books.[8] We looked at traditional and modern methods of storing information and tried to see how much information was important to our lives. We interpreted road signs, maps and timetables and learnt about using the computer for information retrieval, creating quizzes and learning to word process. It all seemed very relevant and I just wished I had more training than the experience of life in this field.

When the £75,000 grant from the Manpower Services Commission finally was secured for a computer suite, it was a difficult pill to swallow. I didn't resent the money spent on computers - I thought it essential. But the roof of my classroom leaked and I had no lights or curtains in the drama studio. Therefore, I did hope if the cake was small, the arts would not starve altogether.

---

[8]   Trisha Strong and Paul McGee *The Information Technology Project* MEP and Addison and Wesley ISDN 0 201 1550 9 (1984)

When the Research machines network of 186 computers was installed, I was promised training. We would be kept a week ahead of the students, we were assured. But, oh dear, the week we were to start turned out to be the first week of industrial action on the matter of directed time. No training for me after all.

Never mind. The director of computing studies had stuffed a word processing manual in my overloaded pigeonhole with a note pinned to it, which said, "Teach this for the first six weeks". He had also left instructions for turning the network on. Luckily, one of the boys in my class seemed competent in operating the system. I let him get on with it. For me, every plunge into the computer room felt like driving a different car out of the staff car park each night. I had no opportunity to use a computer between the sessions with the pupils and they were not at all keen to let me have a whole keyboard to myself.

The night before the first class, I sat up late copying commands from the manual onto flashcards. The package was Word: tiny white letters on a black screen - remember- and a menu at the bottom that had impenetrable American commands like 'transfer'. We diligently typed, saved and printed.

> "I'm bored, Miss," said one of my charges after about two weeks
> of word processing procedures.
> "So am I" I confessed. "What do you suggest?"
> They huddled together in conference.
> "Why don't we use these computers to do some proper English?"
> one ventured.
> "Yes, let's get back to writing about Chernobyl," said another.
> "That matters."
> "We could use these machines to publish a sort of newspaper
> about the tragedy."
> "Or a magazine. We could write letters about nuclear accident."
> "Yes, they won't know the letters are from children if we use
> these computers. They might listen to us."

So we did learn the niceties of word-processing as we needed them, compelled by the need to communicate in the most professional way possible. We were learning at our own pace. Experts were emerging who were able to move the others on - new techniques spread like wild fire - soon we could all change fonts and sizes - check spelling - centre and justifyThis early experience of computers in the classroom was formative. I have never since been persuaded to 'teach' word processing skills. In contrast, I have found that a publication purpose is a great spur to learning in context.

In that computing laboratory with the pupils, my teaching style changed for ever as well. I was used to commanding a class from the front like a keynote speaker - I could tell a good tale to keep them in their seats. But the cables had been laid round the edge of the room. Computer installation teams knew no better. As a random consequence, the children had their backs to me and they were totally absorbed, on task, committed - they did not need me. It was a tough moment of truth.

We allowed the technicians to dictate the room layout until Deryn Watson[9], pointed out that teaching methodology should take priority over technical convenience in the general scheme of things. Nowadays an IT manager will take far more care over computer groupings. Some schools have designed computer rooms with mushroom workstations, cabling coming through the centre of the mushroom. What makes the difference now, of course, is the laptops which do not dominate a small classroom and are portable enough for field trips.

But faced by the pupils' backs in that south London computer lab, I reoriented myself and became facilitator and a learner. It was an exciting opportunity to explore the mechanics of good writing. After I had overcome the initial terror at teaching a subject I was not trained in, I discovered students empowered and enthused by working at their own pace. Each student was engaged in purposeful activity and I was free to sort out the real intellectual obstacles. The machine reinforcement freed me to give more individual attention to pupils who were self-motivated. Reorganising text and correction were easier on the screen. Publication opportunities made pupils more concerned about accuracy: a group of girls nearly come to blows over a full stop. This was the kind of commitment in the classroom we were all searching for in the run up to the new GCSE courses.

5.   Designing Educational Software

The best boost to my teaching skills was the opportunity to design software. Just after Christmas in the first academic year of teaching computers, an invitation from BT arrived asking me to join a team of teachers to design educational software at King's College, London University. This was to involve me in an eighteen-month project that published an adventure game, SCOOP, and a newsroom simulation, NEWSNET, teaching information technology in the classroom by practical methods. But when the invitation first arrived I simply saw it as an opportunity to keep ahead of students who were, at the time, teaching me.

My one-day secondment to Computers in the Curriculum at King's College was a whirlwind of activity on top of four days teaching without a free period. But I began, at last, to learn in depth about educational computing. The full-time associateship, sponsored by Croydon LEA the next year, was a welcome opportunity to use my co-ordination of the 'SCOOP' and 'NEWSNET' design group as a reflective experience.

[9] Deryn Watson *Developing CAL: Computers in the Curriculum* Harper ISBN 0 06 318382-X (1987)

This major collaboration between industry and education began in 1985. The Computers in the Curriculum project, based at the Centre for Educational Studies, King's College, London University, worked with the BT Education Service on a software project that was planned to coincide with the DTI three year £3.5 million scheme to encourage schools to buy software. This project which was intended to widen the choice for schools cost £200,000 and resulted in six titles in science, technology, information technology and English.[10]

Teachers from Croydon and Leeds were invited to propose ideas for software that were relevant to classroom needs and teaching demands. These groups were to work with telematics specialists in designing, specifying, developing the software. Group co-ordinators were seconded from their schools for one day a week. Other teachers would be bought in to trial the material in the classrooms. Co-ordinating the players was no small feat. The team numbered 46 people: programming teams, industrialist and educators[11]

Leeds LEA had identified the need for telecommunications software for use in physics. The teachers who joined this group were, by chance, all male science teachers. Their shared subject gave them a united purpose and a clear understanding of what their subject required: signal transmission, pulse code modulation and picture manipulation for sixth forms.

Croydon LEA already had a track record in developing materials to teach the new subject information technology. The project, therefore, attracted teachers across a range of subject specialisms and included both men and women. As information technology was such a new subject and no-one in the group had the security of a formal training, it took us much longer to identify the subject matter that was appropriate.

What we were sure about was that we wanted to harness the motivation and concentration we had seen in children in computer games. Eventually, using the theme of investigative journalism, we created an adventure game called Scoop and an international newsroom simulation called Newsnet..

In Scoop the student took the role of a journalist using on line information retrieval, fax, radio pagers to investigate a recluse millionaire and tell his story. Yes, not millionairess - I realise we missed a trick but Croydon teachers were unversed in equal opportunities in the days when Croydon was a Tory flagship. The theme of our second program, Newsnet, daughter of Scoop, indicates how much our own understanding of international journalism and IT had improved. Each terminal represented a different country. The simulation was based on headlines for a simulated week. The more the journalists collaborated on electronic mail and the more detail they uncovered in the databases, the nearer the truth they moved.

[10] *BT Educational Resources Catalogue* BT Education Services, BT Centre, 81 Newgate Street. London, EC1A 7AJ 0800 622302 (1994)

[11] *C. Preston Computer Assisted Learning from the Coordinator's Perspective* Centre for Educational Studies, Kings College, London University (1989)

I wrote an investigative novel into these three databases.   Slick Cut, an international jet-setting criminal, oiled through the data under a range of pseudonyms, putting his relatives in positions of power all over the world. As the student journalists uncovered information about his nefarious dealing the extent of his criminal operation became clearer. Eventually the pupil journalists would realise that the man who had rigged all kinds of activities internationally, was the same man who had bought the paper mills in Sweden that supplied the paper to the International Gazette group and the factory in South America that supplied the computer chips. Just a little more digging and delving and they would discover that, yesterday, Slick Cut bought the International Gazette Group. So what could they say about their owner?

To be able to give students the experience of the pressures of ownership on writing was for me the highest level of learning that Newsnet could achieve. But the computing skills they were learning were also not inconsiderable. Newsnet was the first educational integrated package. The user worked in an environment that linked three databases, desktop publishing, electronic mail, word processing and a networked wire service like Reuters. It was also the first educational program to use the communications facilities of a network as well. As a result of the Newsnet design I have just been out in Chile developing a system of collaborative rural newspapers based on those ideas of eight years ago.[12]

Scoop was also technically innovative. The design emulated Microsoft windows on the BBC microcomputer and was the biggest program ever designed for the BBC with twenty-five picture locations.

This innovative style owes most to the programmer, Phil Wood. He had decided to use Assembler because Scoop promised to be so big. Assembler was a low-level language closest to the binary code that involved him in coding long series of numbers. There was no prototyping or subroutines in those days in educational computing. If the teacher designers did not like the interface he had taken a month to write he would have to start all over again. One number in the new sequence wrong and the program would not function. One day we arrived to find that he had programmed a story line left lying around from our meeting the month before. He showed me that he had nearly reached the page turn. "Why do you do this section, Phil?" I asked. "Because it was there," came the reply. I turned the page and showed him the other side. "But Phil, this story line has no ending! We've rewritten the whole thing now!" He had to start again.

The coding for Scoop took Phil eighteen months to complete. Using a HyperCard prototyping shell it would take about a fortnight today. The teachers donated nine months 'spare' time to the project. Political views have changed and teachers would no longer be prepared to give this commitment unpaid. However, there are now new strategies used in Project Miranda work to make the best of

---

[12]   C. Preston *Surfing the Net*, a multimedia interactive network for Chilean schools (1994) Paper in Progress

teachers' relevant experience without overloading their time. Professional development rewards are the key.

After two years, Scoop had sold ten times more than any comparable educational package. This commercial success was because BT supported a marketing and dissemination programme, which allowed me to train teachers in information technology all over the country using Scoop as an illustration and a tool. Scoop has since been adapted by the Dutch government POCO project to use with a series of television programmes and national training workshops.

Commercial success in educational software is difficult because the school base in this country is so small. Much of the commercial material has American roots and displays the technical virtuosity of programming teams rather than interesting content. In the commercial world programmers intent on displaying their programming pyrotechnics will grab any little furry animal and any kind of Holy Grail to use as pegs. I have put out an SOS: "Where are Shakespeares Of Software?" to my colleagues in the Society of Authors and the Guild of Writers do not insist on getting involved. Authors are beginning to respond. Authors and artists should develop more confidence in their collaborative role. When Phil, Wood the Scoop programmer, landed a programming job in industry at three times the salary, he took me out to lunch. We had had some really heated discussions at times about what Scoop and Newsnet ought to do, so I was particularly pleased that there seemed to be no hard feelings. "Far from it," he said. "You insisted on achieving the educational aims and objectives of the programs in complete disregard of what I thought the computer would do. You made me stretch and bend the rules. In fact, I was given this job because I had taken the BBC B further than anyone thought it could go - so thanks for the push!"

This priority given to educational good practice above technical expediency was the most important philosophy I learnt from the Educational Computing Unit at King's College, London University, which was directed by Dr. Margaret Cox. Most teachers' progression is rather behind that of their students. In the Computers in the Curriculum department at King's College, I was seen as the below average teacher test-bed. "If she can use it so can a chimpanzee with a sock over its head" was the general view of my computer competence. Richard Millward of Small Talk fame was especially patient with me. I called him in one day in the conviction that my computer had taken leave of its senses. I had been shouting at it for half an hour already because, since I had changed the position of the keyboard, the screen filled with gibberish every time I typed. Richard summed up the problem as delicately as he could. "If women of your ample build" he explained. "Lean too far over the keyboard, gobbledy-gook will result!"

After my work with BT at Kings College, going back to Croydon as an advisor in 1987 was something of a shock. Although I had designed for 8-bit machines, at Kings College I had not used them. I was using an Apple machine, which was already greatly in advance of the 8-bit computers. I couldn't believe that primary school teachers were expected to get the hang of these illogical beasts. A blinking cursor on a black screen is a threat I will never forget. And when someone whispered that the code for formatting a disc on a 186 was a: b:/s I suffered the same sense of incredulity as when a boy in the playground told me about the mechanics of sex. "Why bother?", I thought,." I mean did you ever hear such an unlikely and inelegant waste of time?

This was not the only shock I had. Our daughter, who was sixteen, caught a virus that attacked her heart muscle. She had all the care that the national health and medical technology could give her including a new heart. But three months from the diagnosis she had died.

6.   Special Needs and Computers

I do not need to describe the pain. You can imagine I am sure. But you may like to consider the role of the computer in my life in those first two years. When I could not sleep, when the pain was too much I would put my head into the computer. I could write or develop ideas with a total concentration that gave some relief from the suffering. There is a danger, of course, that inadequate students may find the sense of control they derive from playing a computer game preferable to the life they lead. Why should they ever leave the friendly shores of the screen where they are in control? My experience taught me to respect the way in which they are dealing with difficult feelings.

This kind of concentration can be used for good as well as ill. Yes, the pornographic possibilities of virtual reality are worrying[13] but what about the terminally ill patient who can go to the theatre or walk through a sunny wood without leaving their bed? And what about the trainee surgeon who can practise on virtual patients instead of killing a few real ones on the way to perfection? We have to be alive to the potential of virtual reality and seize the chance....or else?

As a result of my experiences I believe that we must learn to use computers as teaching and learning tools. Broadband and the World Wide Web now provide extended opportunities for learning and teaching at a distance when the lines are more widely installed. More informal and accessible video conferencing and the transmission of multimedia materials, simultaneous exchange of text, graphics and speech make lecturing and collaborative work across any distance more effective.

I have also found that the computer is becoming a tool that is indispensable for the most disadvantaged. Stephen Hawking, the great physicist, could not write or speak without his system nor operate his 'smart house'. Chris Nolan won the Whitbread prize for his novel Under the Eye of the Clock. Not a prize for fiction written by the severely disabled, but an international prize in which his word-processed novel won on its own merits.

---

[13] Mark Sealey Educational Computing and Technology March 1994

My greatest insight into the enabling power of the computer was when I was running the Computer Assisted Reading project in Croydon Local Education Authority. One reluctant reader maintained that there was a conspiracy by other pupils and teachers to pretend that the black squiggles on book pages meant something. When we supplied a computer for her she wanted to tell a story. A friend showed her how to key in the first word - THERE.

She stared at it on the screen.

"Print it out please", she said.
I was busy.
"Shouldn't you write some more before we print?" I suggested.
"Print it out please", she insisted.

The girl went to her exercise book and pointed to an unintelligible squiggle. The girl said, "That 'There' printed is the same word as my written 'there', isn't it?" Her teacher described the look of revelation on the girl's face as the kind of expression that keeps a teacher going for another half term. In fact, the sort of expression that blesses a teacher's vocation.

The explanation for the girl's joy was her new understanding. Her handwriting was so uncontrolled that she had never been able to make the connection between printed book and exercise book before. Interacting with the keyboard made all the difference to her perception of words. She became a normal reader.

There are many good moments like this in my early history of using computers. I saw Gujerati children in Tower Hamlets burst into tears of pride when they saw their own writing on the screen for the first time using ILECC's Allwrite; other children with special needs clamouring to have their work put on the wall because it looked as good as all the other children's work. Mapuche Indians in Chile have never had a written language. Translating their culture onto a multimedia network is not only preserving it: their self-esteem has risen, they are using their language in school which had embarrassed them before. They are recording old traditions on the network and creating new words for a new world in the oral and pictorial networked dictionary.

7. Surfing the Net

And what about the Internet in education – the World Wide Web which was first hyped as the Superhighway? What is interesting is that from the first I found that on the Internet everyone communicated as an equal. And information was available internationally to people who had previously been disenfranchised. For example, the academic community never reveal sources. But I was impressed that eye witness accounts of the Beijing Tiennamen Square massacre were spread around the

world in 24 hours. In addition, in the Balkan Wars messages like this cry from
Vukovar in Yugoslavia under siege were affecting.

APEL ZA VUKOVAR IZ VUKOVARA!!!!!!!!!

How can I start a story of death and desire to live?
How can I describe millions of feelings in plain words?
How can I concentrate when a packet of death explodes nearby
     every few minutes?
How can I ask for help from someone whose face I cannot even
     imagine?
How can I ask in the name of thousands of people, and whom
     can I ask, when all the appeals and cries for help to stop this
     insane bloodshed have been unanswered?

Some of the twenty million users worldwide answered and passed this poem on.
This lack of editorial control on the Internet is, for most users, the most important
feature. Opportunities for research are increasing as well. The service represents
learning at its most anarchic and individual. On the other hand, it appears that still
ninety per cent of users are actually male, white and middle class. Any doubt is
because some female users sign on as men to avoid sexual harassment.
Nevertheless, despite uncertain gender, internet users are growing by at least five
per cent a month. The Internet has become an element of popular culture new
learning methodology is emerging.

'The only really new metaphor is internet. I've spent the last six
months with my head in cyber space. I tell you that Internet is
different. It's a paradigm shift, a new world.'[14]

Whether this was the expectation of the US federal government which started
this phenomenon is doubtful, but it has great draw for the users if only because it
can insulate from the uncontrollable elements of human life on the planet. 'There is
no weather on the Internet'.[15]

Electronic communications products raise international issues. This amorphous,
unedited service available on BT networks represents a challenge to government,
education and industry. The Internet is a challenge to some company cultures that
are hierarchical and authoritarian. There are strong demands in America and in
Britain for more control of the service especially government rights to read
messages in order to intercept the activities of international crime and doubtful

[14] David Brown *Surfing the net* ICTE Conference address March 1994 the Institute of Education,
     London   University.
[15] Douglas Adams *Media* The Guardian September 1992

entertainment industries. But only rich nations can be corrupted: the developing world is disenfranchised from this information service by poverty, gender and poor telecommunications infrastructure.

Where does education stand in the debate? Some academics welcome the opportunity to 'surf the net' unhindered. Some teachers may prefer to have some control over the interface used by the students in their charge. The debate will rage on.

8. Telling Old Stories in New Ways

And who was the Miranda who gives her name to the MirandaNet Fellowship? She is not an acronym. The Fellowship was founded in memory of the spirit of our daughter, Corinna – a new Renaissance woman – already making digital learning contacts around the world. But the namesake is the daughter of Prospero in the Tempest who in the sixteenth century said, 'O brave new world that hath such people in IT." After all, it is only an accident of history that Shakespeare did not have a computer. If he had what would he have done with this resource? It is an interesting conundrum that young learners today like to consider.

I wrote about my childhood experiences of computers at the bank some seven years ago in the preface to my dissertation about Computer Assisted Learning. My supervisor was a computer scientist. I admired his crisp, spare writing style: clearly expressed, simple ideas in a logical sequence. He rarely expanded on any subject. He scored through my Preface. "I really can not see what any of this personal stuff has to do with the design of Scoop. I suggest you ditch it. No-one will be interested."

I hope that he was wrong and that in this ethnographical study you have found some points to chew on in the adventure of Ms. Average as she travels on the quest for computer literacy. In looking back on these critical incidents I have myself learnt more about the barriers and challenges that many teachers' face when Information Technology (IT) becomes part of the teaching and learning arsenal.

Education and Software Engineering
Ten Years of Progress towards a
Recognised Professional Discipline

J. B. Thompson

Chair IFIP WG 3.4, School of Computing and and Technology, University of Sunderland, Sunderland, SR6 0DD, UK <barrie.thompson@sunderland.ac.uk>

Abstract: The discipline of Software Engineering has a history dating back to 1968. However, it is only during the last ten years that real efforts have been made to address it as a profession with appropriate educational support at university levels. The achievements and failures regarding movements in the US towards professionalism in the latter half of the 1990s are first considered. Then parallel and subsequent activities that have taken place on a broader front under the auspices of the International Federation for Information Processing (IFIP) are reported. The framework that the IFIP work has produced is then used in an evaluation of international progress over a ten-year period. Finally a summary of remaining challenges is given.

1.   Introduction

The formal history of the discipline of Software Engineering (SE) can be traced back to the 1968 NATO (North Atlantic Treaty Organisation) Conference on Software Engineering [15] where the first organised presentations and discussions took place. However, it was not until the late 1970's that the first academic programs in SE were offered. The programs, at masters level, were created at a number of universities in the USA and were based on the results of an effort initiated by the IEEE-Computer Society (IEEE-CS) [8]. Undergraduate courses began to appear in the UK and Australia during the 1980s but did not appear in the US until much later. The first two programs in the UK were at Imperial College in London in 1985 [7] and at the University of Sheffield in 1988 [5]. Also, during the 1980s the first text books aimed specifically at SE began to be published. For

Please use the following format when citing this chapter:

Thompson, J.B., 2006, in IFIP International Federation for Information Processing, Volume 215, History of Computing and Education 2 (HCE2), ed. J. Impagliazzo, (Boston: Springer), pp. 93–105.

example, the first edition of Sommerville's text "Software Engineering" [20] appeared in 1982 – by 2004 it was in its seventh edition and had grown immensely both in size and popularity. With regard to conferences addressing the educational and professional side of SE there are the long running Conferences on Software Engineering Education and Training (CSEET) that began in 1987. These were initially run and sponsored by the SEI (Software Engineering Institute) at Carnegie Mellon University but now operate under the auspices of the IEEE-CS. However, it was not until the 17th conference in 2004 that they started to be held outside the North American continent. During the 1990s, there were also a number of national and international SE specific events, outside the US, that have had streams that addressed education and professional issues. For example, the IFIP 1993 Working Conference in Hong Kong [4] and the UK 1996 conference on Professional Awareness in Software Engineering held in London [14].

It is very clear that it was only from the mid 1990s that real efforts were being made to address SE as a professional discipline with appropriate educational support at university levels. The remainder of this paper addresses the progress and otherwise that has occurred during the last decade. In section two I consider the achievements and failures regarding movements in the US towards establishing SE as a profession in the latter half of the 1990s. Then in section three I outline some parallel and subsequent activities that were taking place on a broader front under the auspices of the International Federation for Information Processing (IFIP). This work has provided a framework that can be used in evaluating the progress that has been made within SE. In section four, I highlight the successes that have been achieved and finally in section five I present what I believe are the remaining challenges.

2.   Achievements and Failures 1996-2000

In January 1996 Gary Ford and Norman Gibbs produced a SEI report entitled "A Mature Profession of Software Engineering" [9]. In this they proposed a model that they believed would characterise a mature profession. They also presented a general exploration and validation of their model using professions that existed at the time. Finally they used their model to describe what they believed could become a SE profession. The components of a profession and the interactions between them, as identified by Ford and Gibbs are reproduced in Figure 1. However, a major problem with this work is that it took a very US-centric view. Only in one of its appendices was a non-US situation considered and that was with regard to undergraduate SE programs. Also, there was perhaps an overemphasis on the mechanics of controlling a profession rather than what a profession should be about.

At the time of the Ford and Gibbs report the IEEE Computer Society (IEEE-CS) and the Association for Computer Machinery (ACM) were already working together towards establishing SE as a profession and there is no doubt that the report fed into this. In 1998, the IEEE-CS and ACM further formalised their co-operation with the creation of Software Engineering Coordinating Committee (SWECC), which was made responsible for coordinating, sponsoring and fostering all the various activities regarding SE. within the IEEE-CS and ACM's sphere of operation. These included areas such as standards of practice and ethics, body of knowledge, curriculum guidelines, and exam guidelines. Particular projects that SWECC promoted, and which I will return to later in this paper, were the project concerned with defining a Software Engineering Code of Ethics and Professional Practice [17], and the project concerned with defining a Software Engineering Body of Knowledge [22] – the SWEBOK project.

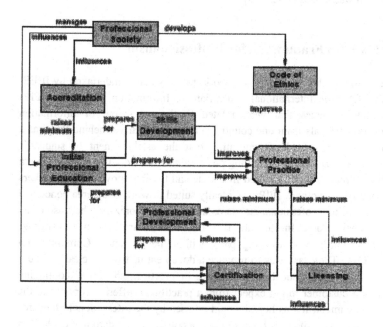

Fig. 1. Ford and Gibbs representation of the interactions among the components of a profession [9].

Then in June 1998 an event occurred that would cause a divergence of views on SE professionalism between the IEEE-CS and the ACM and which would eventually lead to the latter's withdrawal from SWEECC [2]. This event, which at fist appeared so positive, was the enactment by the Texas Board of Professional Engineers rules that recognised SE as a distinct engineering discipline [21]. These rules went into effect on 18th July 1998 and applications for licenses were accepted from 1st August 1998. This legislation enabled engineering licenses to be issued to

Software Engineers so that they could, within the State of Texas, legally represent themselves to the general public as an engineer, offer consulting engineering services to private and public entities, and perform engineering design or construction on public works. Unfortunately, a influential group within the ACM felt that that SE was not yet a mature discipline, that licensing was inappropriate at that time, and that the SWEBOK could be seen to be too closely related to the examinations that licensing would involve [2].

During 1999 and 2000, perhaps as a reflection of the growing rift between the ACM and IEEE-CS interest in SE professionalism appeared to wax and wane. Some papers relating to the topic appeared in major computing journals [e.g. 3, 10, 12, and 16]. However, at least in the US, a commonly held view was that professionalism was a "dead duck" [6].

3.   IFIP's 1998 Framework for Professionalism

During the 1990's, independently of the work that was being undertaken by IEEE-CS and the ACM, the International Federation for Information Processing (IFIP) started to address issues that were related to the movement of Information Technology professionals from one country to another. A driver behind this was a view from the World Trade Organisation that the establishment of standards regarding the qualifications of computing professionals was very important in an era of international treaties that promoted free trade and the free movement of workers from one country to another. IFIP was ideally suited to work in an area concerned with issues regarding professional standards and their harmonization because of its truly international nature. In 1997 the IFIP Executive Board handed the work on professional standards to a working party within the Technical Committee on Education (TC3). Their task was to produce a document that would clearly set out the standards of tertiary education, experience or practice, ethics, and continuing education that a customer might expect from a practitioner offering services to the public. This document, it was hoped, could be used by the International Standards Organisation and IFIP's member bodies to gain a consensus standard that could then be adopted by the standards bodies within each country. It was expected that the IFIP Member societies would administer the standard within their countries, giving the Member societies increased status and authority. During 1998 a small writing party met to produce a draft standard [13] - a copy of the text of which is appended to this paper. The main parts of the draft address the following areas:

- Ethics of professional practice,
- Established body of knowledge,
- Education and training,
- Professional experience,
- Best practice and proven methodologies and
- Maintenance of competence.

The draft was presented in August 1999 to the full TC3 committee meeting in Irvine, USA. At IFIP's World Computer Congress held in Beijing in August 2000 the harmonization project was re-considered within TC3 and it was decided to refer the draft document back to the Working Group concerned with Professional and Vocational Education (WG3.4) for further work to be undertaken.

It was felt that the most appropriate area within the field of Information Processing for consideration of professionalism was SE. This, starting in September 2000 a series of activities were undertaken to promote the IFIP Harmonization document and provide a forum for an analysis of its relevance to SE. These activities included conference presentations, panel sessions, participative workshops, and an International Summit that was co-located with the 2002 International Conference on Software Engineering (ICSE). It is estimated that these activities brought the IFIP Harmonization document to the direct attention of at least 350 individuals within the SE community and many more indirectly via conference proceedings and the workshop/summit reports. The overall reaction by the community was very encouraging. It has been recognised that the harmonization document essentially defines framework or meta model, which should truly assist advancing professional standards if it is used in a sensitive and appropriate manner. A summary of the work undertaken in promoting and evaluating the harmonization document and the most significant outcomes from the evaluations was included in paper [24] presented at the IFIP 2005 World Conference on Computers in Education.

4. Evaluations of Progress Against the IFIP Model

There are obviously similarities between what was proposed by Ford and Gibbs and the model in the IFIP Harmonization document. Perhaps the greatest differences are in the areas of controlling the profession and education. Regarding the former, the IFIP document says little since it would see this as the role of the member society or legislative body within the relevant country. However, it does place a greater emphasis on the underpinning of education both at university and during life long learning by an appropriate Body of Knowledge, recognised Best Practices and Proven Methodologies. To measure progress towards achieving a recognised professional discipline for SE evaluations can be performed against the six areas highlighted in the document. However, because of the close relationships between particular areas in some cases I will consider two or more together.

4.1 Ethics of professional practice

A major success that did result from the SWECC cooperation between the EEE-CS/ACM was the production of the Software Engineering Code of Ethics and

Professional Practice by a task force led by Don Gotterbarn of East Tennessee State University. The code is available [17] in two forms: a short version, which summarises aspirations at a high level of abstraction, and a full version which includes additional clauses. The latter provide examples and details of how the aspirations of the code should change the way persons act as SE professionals. Currently the eight areas that the code addresses are: Public, Client and Employer, Product, Judgment, Management, Profession, Colleagues, and Self.

The code in addition to being approved by both IEEE-CS and the ACM [11] has been widely adopted across the world [17]. In fact, it appears to be one particular project that has been outstanding in the lack of criticism associated with it. Perhaps this was partly due to the way it was developed and those involved [11].

4.2   Education and life-long learning

Three areas within the IFIP Harmonizsation document address education and what can be seen as life long learning activities. These are the sections on: Education and Training (which relates to undergraduate level activities), Professional Experience (which relates to supervised experience that normally follows graduation), and Maintenance of Competence (which relates to the learning and associated activities that practitioners should undertake throughout their professional lives so as to remain competent in the tasks that they undertake). The major success in the area of education has been the publication in August 2004 of the SE Volume of the IEEE-CS/ACM Computing Curricula [18]. Of particular note is the process that was adopted in the production of this volume. In addition to the direct work of four groups of volunteers (a Steering Committee, an Advisory Board, an Education Knowledge Area Group, and a Pedagogy Focus Group) there has been a particularly open development process which has attempted to involve as much of the community as possible via: public reviews by the SE community, invited reviews by recognised experts in the field, presentations at conferences to keep the community informed, articles in community publications, such ACM SIGSOFT Software Engineering Notes, open participative meetings and workshops at major conferences, including the 2002 and 2003 International Conferences on Software Engineering, which provided opportunities to provide information, carry out activities, and generate feedback. The work of the Education Knowledge Area Group was also supported by a major workshop that was partly funded by the National Science Foundation.

To close the loop on comments received, the project's web site contains a record of all the individual comments and the developers' responses to them [19]. This approach, the tools used to support the work, and the level of international participation in the effort have been formally recognised in the 2004 annual report of the ACM Education Board as setting standards for the development practices for all future generation ACM-sponsored curriculum guidelines. The production of

SE2004 Volume really is a major success as it can be seen to have given the SE discipline international academic credibility it so rightly deserves.

4.3 Knowledge

Two areas within the IFIP Harmonization document relate to the knowledge domain for Software Engineers. These are the area headed Established Body of Knowledge, and that headed Best Practice and Proven Methodologies. For a discipline which a few years ago had no agreed body of knowledge we could now view ourselves as being doubly lucky in that we now have two complementary expositions. First we have the SWEBOK [22, 23], of which mention has already been made in section 2 of this paper, and which provides a guide to the core knowledge that a practitioner with some four years of work experience should have access to. Secondly we have the Software Engineering Education Knowledge (SEEK) which forms an essential part of the Curriculum Document [18] and represents the knowledge appropriate to undergraduate study.

To a great extent those who have been involved with the SWEBOK project may be regarded as having been extremely unlucky in that it was viewed as a key element in the split between the ACM and IEEE-CS over licensing and the ACM's withdrawal from SWECC. The leaders of the project are to be congratulated for seeing the project to a stage where not only has the SWEBOK guide been published under the auspices of IEEE-CS [23] but it has also been adopted as a technical report by ISO (ISO/IEC TR 19759) [22]. The project has attempted to adopt a broad and international approach in the reviewing and of particular note is that the results of the process have been visible and are available on the project's web site. A milestone has clearly been reached with the production of the 2004 version of the guide. The developers are now embarking on the planned evolution phase of the Guide [22].

5. Outstanding Challenges

From the information presented in the previous section, one may infer that all is well and everything is a success. Unfortunately, this is not quite the case. The evaluations undertaken on the proposals in the IFIP Harmonization document [24] resulted in many positive outcomes the major of which was the acceptance of the framework itself. However, the area of Best Practices and Proven Methodologies was seen as particularly problematic. With questions being raised such as:
- How to test for "best practice"?
- How to enforce documentation of Best Practice and Proven Methodologies?
- Should it build upon existing standards?

The ongoing problems associated with poor quality software continues to be highlighted in published studies [1] and the indications are that if Best Practices do exist they are certainly not used as they should be, nor does it appear that they are being developed in the light of actual practical experiences.

Acknowledgements

This summary draws in parts from papers and reports which myself or myself and my colleague Prof. H. Edwards have produced relating to evaluations of the IFIP Harmonization document. Details of all these can be found in the reference list of the report presented to the 8th IFIP World Congress on Computers in Education [24].

References

[1]   BCS, The Challenges of Complex IT Projects, British Computer Society from: http://www.bcs.org/bcs/news/positionsandresponses/positions/complexity.htm, 2004.

[2]   Bagert D.J., ACM Withdraws from SWECC, in Forum for Advancing Software engineering Education (FASE), Volume 10, Number 07, July 2000.

[3]   Bourque, P. et al, The Guide to the Software Engineering Body of Knowledge, IEEE Software, Vol. 16, No. 6, pp35-44, November/December, 1999

[4]   Barta, B.Z., Hung, S.L. and Cox K.R. (Eds), IFIP Transactions A40, Software Engineering Education, Proceedings of the IFIP International Working Conference, Hong Kong, September 1993, North-Holland, Amsterdam, 1993.

[5]   Cowling, A., The First Decade of an Undergraduate Degree Programme in Software Engineering, Annals of Software Engineering, vol. 6, pp 61-90, 1998.

[6]   CSEE&T 2001 Comments at Workshop on Achieving a World-wide Software Engineering Profession, 14th Conference on Software Engineering Education and Training (CSEE&T 2001), February 19-21, 2001, Charlotte NC,

[7]   Finkelstein, A., European Computing Curricula: A Guide and Comparative Analysis, Computer Journal, vol. 36, no. 4, pp 299-319, 1993.

[8]   Freeman, P., Wasserman, A.I. and Fairley, R.E., Essential Elements of Software Engineering Education, Proc. of the 2nd International Conference on Software Engineering, IEEE Computer Society Press, 1976, pp. 116-122.

[9]   Ford, G. and Gibbs, N.E., A Mature Profession of Software Engineering, Software Engineering Institute, Carnegie Mellon University, Pittsburgh, Pennsylvania, Technical Report CMU/SEI-96-TR-004, 1996.

[10]   Gotterbarn, D, How the New Software Engineering Code of Ethics Affects You, IEEE Software, Vol. 16, No. 6, pp58-64, November/December, 1999

[11]   Gotterbarn, D Miller K, and Rogerson S. Computer Society and ACM Approve Software Engineering Code of Ethics, Computer October 1999 p 84-8

[12]   Lethbridge, T. C. What Knowledge Is Important to a Software Professional? IEEE Computer, Vol. 33, No. 5, pp 44-50, May 2000.

[13]   Mitchell I., Juliff P., and Turner J., Harmonization of Professional Standards, International Federation of Information Processing, 1998, at: http://www.ifip.or.at

[14] Myers, C., Hall, T. and Pitt D (Eds), Proceedings of the First Westminster Conference: Professional Awareness in Software Engineering (PASE'96), London, February 1996. (Published in edited form as: The Responsible Software Engineer, Springer-Verlag, London, 1997, ISBN 3-540-76041-5).

[15] Naur, P. and Randell, B. (editors), Software Engineering: Report on a Conference, Sponsored by the NATO Science Committee, (7 – 11 October 1968), Brussels, Scientific, Affairs Division, NATO, 1969.

[16] Pour, G., Griss M. L. and Lunz, M. The Push to Make Software Engineering Respectable, IEEE Computer, Vol. 33, No. 5, pp 35-43. May 2000.

[17] SEEPP Project details are availabe at the following Web Sites: http://computer.org/tab/seprof/code.htm, and http://computer.org/tab/sweec/SWCEPP

[18] Software Engineering 2004 (Curriculum Volume), available from: http://sites.computer.org/ccse/SE2004Volume.pdf

[19] Software Engineering 2004 (development details) at: http://sites.computer.org/ccse/

[20] Sommerville, I., Software Engineering, Addison-Wesley, Publishing Company, London, 1st Edition, 1982

[21] Speed J.R. Software Engineering: An Examination of the Actions Taken by the Texas Board of Professional Engineers, Octo-ber 12th 1998, Available from Texas Board of Professional Engineers Web site at: http://www.main.org/pebody/soft.htm

[22] SWEBOK Project Web Site, http://www.swebok.org

[23] SWEBOK Guide to the Software Engineering Body of Knowledge, Bourque P. and Dupuis R. (Eds), 2004 Version, IEEE Computer Society.

[24] Thompson, J. B. Evaluations of IFIP's Proposed Standards for Professionals. In Proceedings of the 8th IFIP World Conference on Computers in Education, (WCCE 2005), Session P10.3. University of Stellenbosch, Cape Town, South Africa, July 4-7, 2005.

Appendix
IFIP Harmonization Document

Harmonization of Professional Standards
Draft: October 1998
Summary

This document sets out an international standard for professional practice in information technology.
Practitioners who meet the standards will:
- publicly ascribe a code of ethics published within the standard.
- be aware of and have access to a well-documented current body of knowledge relevant to the domain of practice.
- have a mastery of the body of knowledge at the baccalaureate level.
- have a minimum of the equivalent of two years supervised experience before the practitioner operates unsupervised.
- be familiar with current best practice and relevant proven methodologies.
- be able to provide evidence of their maintenance of competence.

Purpose

The purpose of this work is to clearly set out an international standard for professional practice in information technology.

The components of the standards are:
- Ethics of professional practice,
- Established body of knowledge,
- Education and training,
- Professional experience,
- Best practice and proven methodologies and
- Maintenance of competence.

A customer has a right to expect that a practitioner offering information technology services to the public meets these standards.

This document will be offered as a draft standard to the International Standards Organization in anticipation that it will in turn conduct its process of obtaining consensus from its member bodies and hence the standard would be adopted by the standards bodies within each country.

It is expected that the IFIP member societies would prepare any local or regional adaptation of the standard. The administration process, which may include promotion, assessment and certification as well as the distribution of materials, may also be carried out by the IFIP member society.

The standard could also be incorporated in the requirements for a level of qualification of individual members in the member society.

Although the initial country or regional implementations may have differences, the intent is to move towards a common implementation.

Why Have Professional Standards?

The traditional professions such as accounting, medicine and engineering have long had standards which enable a qualification gained in one country to be recognised in another. The World Trade Organisation in conjunction with the International Standards Organisation has now taken an active role to create such standards under the General Agreement on Trade in Services (GATS).

The benefits of internationally recognised standards are that:

- the public is assured that safety or economically critical work is performed by competent individuals regardless of where in the world those persons gained their qualifications and experience.
- a client is assured that a person who meets such international standards is competent to carry out tasks in documented specific areas regardless of where the work is done or the output of the work is used (subject to recognition of issues of culture and locale).
- professionals are assured that their qualifications if recognised in one country will be accepted in other countries without re-examination (except possibly for being up-to-date).
- Under GATS, trade in products developed by practitioners who meet this standard cannot be restricted on the grounds that the developers were not competent or used inadequate professional practices.

Such standards will contribute to the attainment of a reputation for competence by the profession.

The standards will facilitate the obtaining of work by individual practitioners in the international arena.

To Whom does the Standard Apply?

This standard is primarily focused on practitioners involved in the development of software-based systems and related services. The standards are not necessarily intended to apply to other members of IFIP member societies such as:

- academics, who in general will be much more qualified but possibly in a narrow discipline and whose research may be at a more abstract level than practice.
- school teachers, who in general will be qualified to teach rather than to develop IT systems.
- users, who have input into the designs of computer systems but who do not construct them.
- electronic engineers, who design computers but who would normally be qualified as engineers.

It is recognized that these classifications may be blurred.

Harmonization of Professional Standards

The following clarifications are offered in this context.

Harmonization means that the standards of different countries would be brought together to be substantially the same. Any extremes from the commonality of these standards would gradually be pruned away until each country has the same standard by mutual consent.

Professional identifies the peculiar responsibility of a person with high levels of knowledge and related practical skills in a given discipline with respect to members of the public who do not have that knowledge or skill-set. It is particularly relevant to the information technology profession because it has significant impact on society at large. The power of the knowledge must be balanced by a sense of responsibility towards others. This definition is focused on practitioners, persons who actually develop, maintain and operate software systems for commercial or governmental purposes.

Standards are clear statements that reflect the minimum qualifications for mastery and knowledge of processes, skills and practice that a professional should have before undertaking work which may put an employer or client at risk, either physical or financial.

The field of Information Processing has many domains ranging from data management to embedded software systems. Any one individual cannot be expected to be expert in more than one or a few such domains. This needs to be recognized particularly in the body of knowledge required to be known by one person.

The changes within the many domains together with the dynamic development of new domains in information technology means that the standards themselves must be continuously developed and individuals must anticipate life-long learning.

The Standard for Professional Practice in Information Technology

Ethics of Professional Practice
A code of ethics acknowledges the professional responsibilities of practitioners to society at large, members of the public, employers, contracting parties and fellow practitioners.
Codes of ethics have been published by many member societies and IFIP itself.
Every implementation of the standard must include a code of ethics.
Such a Code of Ethics must be compatible with the culture of the society in which the practitioner normally works.
Practitioners must operate in a manner compatible with the culture of the locale in which they are currently working and in which the product may be used.
Practitioners must publicly ascribe to the code of ethics published within the standard.

Established Body of Knowledge
Several IFIP member societies have published bodies of knowledge, some of which have gained wide acceptance. Such recognised bodies of knowledge are divided into many domains determined by the various services carried out by practitioners. The body of knowledge on which any implementation is based should include at least the common components of these but also ensure that each domain is complete in itself for the domains adopted locally.
Mastery of such a body of knowledge forms the basis of preparation for practice. A practitioner must demonstrate mastery of at least one such domain as well as all core components identified in the body of knowledge.
Practitioners must be aware of and have access to a well-documented current body of knowledge relevant to the domain of practice.

Education and Training
Most practitioners will enter the workforce with prior education and training which will commonly be a baccalaureate degree assessing the mastery of the body of knowledge.
Institutions offering such education and training should be prepared to openly compare themselves to internationally well-known and recognised peer institutions offering similar programmes.
It is recognised that this level of mastery may be achieved by various combinations of education and experience. Nevertheless a practitioner must be able to provide evidence of such mastery to practitioners who have met this standard.
The minimum level of mastery of the body of knowledge must be at the baccalaureate level.

Professional Experience
Experience builds on knowledge in many essential ways. Such as:
*   It develops and improves practical skills and competencies.
*   It provides understanding of task definition in the users' terms.
*   It helps develop interpersonal skills that facilitate the communication and human interaction between all participants.
*   As many approaches to problem solution are not readily scaleable experience over a wide variety of problem types and sizes is desirable before working in an unsupervised environment. Experience is generally required in assessing task complexity.

- Task management, overall project management and quality management generally require experience.

Other professions have clear requirements for experience before allowing their members to practice without supervision.

In addition to a demonstrated mastery of the body of knowledge a minimum of the equivalent of two years supervised experience is recommended before the practitioner operates unsupervised.

Best Practice and Proven Methodologies

Experienced practitioners have identified and documented many practices and methodologies the use of which generally leads to successful project outcomes. Where such best practice and proven methodologies are available the practitioner should use them unless a particular task has exceptional attributes.

Member societies drawing on all available international sources should encourage the documentation and promulgation of best practice and proven methodologies.

Practitioners should be familiar with current best practice and relevant proven methodologies.

Maintenance of Competence

To maintain demonstrated competence practitioners must be familiar with new developments in their domains of practice.

Such developments may be reflected in the body of knowledge, best practice and proven methodologies as well as in specific skills.

Familiarity with new developments may be obtained through formal education or peer interaction.

There may be assessment of current competence by formal examination, peer assessment or employer or client acknowledgement of successful work.

A practitioner should participate for at least the equivalent of 10 days per year in activities that contribute to maintaining competence. It is recognised that in different locations the opportunities for such ongoing development may vary.

The standard in each country or region must state how this requirement will be met and the role of the IFIP member society in monitoring this function.

Practitioners must be able to provide evidence of their maintenance of competence.

Drafted by Ian Mitchell, FNZCS, Peter Juliff, FACS and Joe Turner, FACM.

Early Computer Awareness Courses in Australian Secondary Schools
- Curricula from the Late 1970s and Early 1980s

Arthur Tatnall and Bill Davey

[1] Centre for International Corporate Governance Research,
Victoria University, Melbourne, Australia., <Arthur.Tatnall@vu.edu.au>
[2] School of Business Information Technology, RMIT University,
Melbourne, Australia <Bill.Davey@rmit.edu.au>

Abstract. Today there is no need to introduce secondary school students to computer technology, but in the early 1980s, the situation was quite different. In Australia in the late 1970s and early 1980s considerable importance was put on the introduction of Computer Awareness courses in secondary schools. The justification for such courses was the perceived need for children to be prepared for living in a society which was fast becoming dependant on the widespread application of computer technology, and that few people then understood the use and implications of this technology. Unlike in parts of the United States, no distinction was made in Australia between Computer Awareness and Computer Literacy, with the Australian curricula involving elements of each. This paper outlines the reasons for the development of Computer Awareness courses in Australia and describes their content. It discusses the consequences of these courses and why they were prominent in the 1980s.

1.   Introduction

In most developed countries around the world today, secondary school students are very aware of information technology and of the many use of computers. In Australia, most secondary school students now know a good deal about the Internet and broadband, play computer games, make extensive use of computer software and take photos using their mobile phones. This was, however, certainly not the case in the late 1970s and early 1980s when the first PCs began to make their appearance in Australian schools. Also quite significantly though, few Australian teachers were then aware of how to use a computer, what computers could be used for, or what the

Please use the following format when citing this chapter:

Tatnall, A., Davey, B., 2006, in IFIP International Federation for Information Processing, Volume 215, History of Computing and Education 2 (HCE2), ed. J. Impagliazzo, (Boston: Springer), pp. 107–116.

implications of their use might be. It was into this climate that the first secondary school courses in Computer Awareness (or Computer Literacy as it was sometimes known) were formulated and delivered. This paper discusses the content of these early courses, what driving factors led to their development, what resulted from their delivery, whether they were successful, and why they were essentially a phenomenon of the 1980s that then ceased to exist in this form.

2.   Computer Awareness and Computer Literacy

Moursund (1983) suggests that the idea that there was a need for the general student population to become computer literate began in the U.S. in the late 1960s, leading to the development of a number of courses and individual units in the early 1970s. He describes these early courses as being in Computer Awareness rather than Computer Literacy, in that they aimed only to give students a level of understanding that would enable them to talk sensibly about computers, and involved little or no experience of actually working *with* computers. Moursund argues that courses like this had little personal relevance to most students and that just being *aware* of computers had little impact on their lives. He suggests rather, that students using computers in applications like Computer Assisted Learning and other curriculum areas had more impact.

Computer Awareness courses in Australia, however, began to appear in the late 1970s and early 1980s when the first microcomputers started to be seen in schools. Unlike the situation described by Moursund, distinctions between Computer Awareness and Computer Literacy were not made in Australia, and Australian Computer Awareness courses were always much more practical and involved a good deal of computer use rather than being almost wholly theoretical.

In the Australian state of Victoria in 1980 a report to the Education Department Computer Policy Committee noted that: "The case for computer education in schools is based largely on the need for children to be prepared for living in a society which is fast becoming dependant on the widespread application of computer technology." (McDougall 1980 :3). It went on to suggest that: "Computers have been called electronic 'brains' and there is no doubt that in the popular view, they are surrounded by an aura of mystery and are credited with powers they do not possess. The result is that most people outside the computing profession have attitudes of awe and fear towards computers and feel helpless and powerless in a highly computerised society." (McDougall 1980 :3) It saw a need for computer education to begin by imparting an "informed understanding of the power and capabilities of computers and also of their limitations ... to every school pupil as part of a general education for modern living." (McDougall 1980 :3). The McDougall (1980) report came up with several important recommendations:

- Schools should be encouraged to offer computer awareness education for all students.

- Where it is desired to teach programming this should be in Computer Studies units rather than normal mathematics classes.
- A major commitment should be made to in-service education of teachers for Computer Awareness and Computer Studies.
- Each school should own a microcomputer or interactive terminal facility with at least the BASIC language, a standard typewriter keyboard and disk storage.
- A large pool of courseware programs for use in a wide variety of subject areas must be developed.

Also in 1980 the Secondary Computer Education Curriculum Committee was formed with a membership made up from members of the Secondary Mathematics committee, the Board of Inspectors of Secondary Schools and a number of practicing teachers (Tatnall 1992). The brief of this committee was the production of Computer Awareness course guidelines, the investigation of Computer Science as a discipline, the publication of computer education articles, the collection and propagation of public domain software and the provision of in-service education.

3. Computer Awareness at Watsonia High School in 1979

In the late 1970s computers were just starting to appear in Australian high schools, the most common being the Apple II. In 1977 Watsonia High School, in the northern suburbs of Melbourne, obtained an Apple II microcomputer with 16Kb RAM, a television monitor and a cassette tape drive as the result of a curriculum innovations grant submission to the Federal Government. (The authors of this paper were at that time teachers at this school.) In 1979, Watsonia High introduced what was to be one of the first Computer Awareness subjects in Victoria into the Year 10 curriculum. This was to be a core subject taken by all 150 Year 10 students. The new subject came mainly from the initiative of one science teacher at the school who was then also a member of the Education Department's Secondary Computer Education Committee. The idea was for the subject to run for the whole year and consist of three parts, each of one term's duration and delivered by a teacher who understood and could relate to this area (Tatnall and Davey 2004). The teaching team consisted of this science teacher, a commerce teacher and a teacher of social science. Together they then set out to determine the requirements for the new subject that consisted of the following units:

> How a computer works, computer programming, history of computer technology.
> Business and commercial uses of information technology.
> The social implications of increased use of computers.

As secondary school curriculum in Victoria was school-based and a matter to be determined by the whole teaching staff of the school, the next step was to convince the remainder of the teaching staff to vote for this change to the Year 10 curriculum. Given the interest in computers at the time, convincing other teachers did not prove to be too difficult.

In its first year, with only one microcomputer and some access to a mark-sense card system at a nearby university, the new subject involved a good deal more theory than practical use of computers. With additional hardware however, the subject became much more practical in subsequent years. The subject was immediately popular with the students most of whom were intrigued by the new computer. It was also seen as worthwhile by their parents, many of whom saw the possibility of better jobs for their children if they learned how to use these new machines. The subject remained in place at the school until the late 1980s.

4.   Secondary School Computer Awareness Courses in Victoria

In Victoria, the Secondary Computer Education Committee put an early priority on the introduction of Computer Awareness in the middle secondary school years, and was also involved with the development of a new Computer Science subject at senior secondary school level. In a 1980 curriculum document (Secondary Computer Education Committee 1980) the Committee noted that although computers had become indispensable in the operations of science, business and government, they did not currently play a significant role in Victorian secondary education. The justification made by the Committee for introducing computers into the curriculum went along the lines that as computers and related technology were beginning to exercise such an important and growing influence on society, that part of the school curriculum concerned with preparation for living in society should contain at least some elements of computer education (Secondary Computer Education Committee 1980). The Committee's Year 10 curriculum guidelines noted that: "… we define Computer Education in terms of computer 'awareness' – the possession of skills and knowledge to enable informed judgments to be made on the basis of what is seen or heard about computers." (Secondary Computer Education Committee 1980 :1). It added that "… the future citizen, ignorant of computers, will be functionally disadvantaged in a computer oriented society. In terms of 'social obligation' therefore, a strong case can be made for Computer Education. Since computers have significant social, political and economic consequences, an awareness of these consequences is essential to informed decision-making and to the democratic process." (Secondary Computer Education Committee 1980 :1).

Of course there were those who argued that there was no need to introduce a new curriculum area to teach about computers as if computers were to become common in society then students would find out what they needed to know about them informally without the need to study them at school. They would do this in the same way that they found out about telephones, television or aeroplanes. In reply,

McDougall (1980 :4) notes that "… this argument does not allow for the fact that computing technology is developing at a rate much faster than the other three technologies mentioned, and there are very few adults who can tell students what they might want to know about computers."

As determination of the details of junior and middle secondary school curriculum in Victoria was seen as a matter for each individual school to decide, the Committee was not able to be prescriptive but only to offer guidelines and advice. The guidelines for the proposed new Year 10 Computer Awareness subject (Secondary Computer Education Committee 1980 :4-14) specified the following content:

Section 1 (15% of available time):

> Historical development of the computer: from the abacus, Pascal's adding machine, Babbage's difference engine and early electronic computers through to the microcomputer.
>
> Structure of the computer: Analogue and digital computers. Input and output, processing, backing store.

Section 2 (25% of available time):

> Hands-on experience in operating a microcomputer (booting the system, loading programs, running programs, creation and use of files, word processing, general computer usage).
>
> Algorithms – the concept of an algorithm, simple flowcharting.
>
> Elementary programming in BASIC.

Section 3 (60% of available time):

> Use of computers in Government, industry/commerce, science/research, the arts, at home.
>
> Implications of computer use for society. Political, economic and social implications.

The document strongly stressed the interdisciplinary nature of this subject matter and that Computer Awareness should not be equated with Computer Programming.

5.   The Commonwealth Computer Education Program

In April 1983, the Federal Minister for Education and Youth Affairs announced that the Government would set up a National Advisory Committee on Computers in Schools. In its report *Teaching Learning and Computers in Schools* (Commonwealth Schools Commission 1983) the Committee then made comprehensive recommendations covering curriculum development, professional development, support services, software/courseware, hardware, and organisation. The report indicated that priorities for curriculum development should be:

1. The provision of Computer Awareness activities for all students in the earlier years of secondary schooling.

2. The integration of computing into the school curriculum: 'computers across the curriculum'.

3. Optional, in-depth Computer Studies courses at the secondary level.
4. Curricula which meet the special needs of relevant disadvantaged groups.

As the first priority in curriculum development, Computer Awareness courses around the country were given a considerable boost. In the period 1984-1986, the Commonwealth Government provided Aus$19m to support the program.

6.   Computer Awareness in Victorian Technical Schools

Up until the mid-1980s, the Victorian Education Department had three very separate (and often non-cooperating) divisions: Primary schools (year P-6), Secondary Schools (year 7-12) and Technical Schools (year 7-11), each of which pursued its own policies and directions. This was in evidence in the Computer Education area, particularly in the often apparent friction between the Secondary and the Technical Divisions (Tatnall 1992). These divisions had radically different ideas on policy; that of the Technical Schools Division being towards *industry standard equipment* and training for employment, while the main concern of the Secondary Schools Division was (after the recommendations of the McDougall report) for Computer Awareness. This important distinction in policy was partly due to the historical differences between the two divisions, the Secondary Division having (traditionally) considered its role as in both provision of a general education to all students, and in preparation of some students for tertiary studies; while the Technical Division had always been primarily concerned with preparation of students for apprenticeships, and training students for employment. It is thus not surprising that the Technical Division should have stressed *computer industry compatibility* as important in education. The problem remained until 1983 when the divisions were finally abolished.

In 1983 the Technical Schools Division brought out its own guidelines for a Computer Awareness course (Computer Studies Curriculum Committee 1983). These guidelines indicated that such a course should contain the following components: familiarity with computing equipment and processes, knowledge of the variety of computing technology and the way it is used, and an insight into the implications of the implementation of computing technology both for society as a whole and for the individuals in that society. The course was structured around the following main sections:

- Computer applications and implications   40%
- Using a computer   30%
- Components of a computer   20%
- History of computers   10%

7. Computer Awareness Courses in Other States

Victoria was not alone in placing emphasis on Computer Awareness courses and most other Australian states also produced Computer Awareness curriculum guidelines. One example is the state of Queensland's Guidelines for Secondary School Computer Awareness (Curriculum Services Branch 1983). In much the same way as the Victorian course guidelines this suggested the following elements of such a course:

- Computer history: pre-computer age, computer development, establishment of computers in society.
- Computer applications: information and data processing, simulation and modelling, artificial intelligence, computer control.
- Computer effects: positive and negative effects of computer usage.
- Computer technics: operation, peripheral devices, software and programming.

8. Drivers for Computer Awareness Courses in Australia

A number of factors in the 1980s acted to drive the concept of Computer Awareness courses into a significant place in the school curriculum. Some of these drivers acted right across the country, while others acted primarily only at the local school level. Firstly there was the sincere belief by many proponents of Computer Education that it was vitally important for all future citizens to have some understanding of computers, what then could do, and perhaps even more importantly, what they could not do. This driving force came from a small number of pioneering educators rather than from students, parents or the general public. This force acted right across Australia.

Another important driving force, acting mainly at a local level, was a need to involve more teachers in the use of computers. If you were teaching in a school where you were the only teacher with any knowledge of computers what you needed most was some other colleagues of like mind. Few teachers had studied computing anywhere in their own university courses and there was no time to wait for teachers to be given in-service professional development training, even if you could find enough people to deliver this training. There is an old saying that the best way to learn something is to try to teach it, and teaching Computer Awareness offered a fairly gentle introduction to computing for a number of teachers who were then later able to go on to other better things. To make good use of computers in the classroom however, what do teachers really need to know? At the very least they need to be computer aware and delivering, or even observing and discussing school Computer Awareness courses made teachers also computer aware. At a later stage, after the commencement of the Commonwealth Computer Education Program, in-service education for teachers was given a very high priority in Victoria and stress was placed on professional development activities that were aimed at a 'non expert' clientele. The results of this stress on beginners were mixed with some of those who received this training soon finding that they were unable to get any assistance to make any use of computers when they returned to their schools.

The third driver, also acting mainly at a local level, was a need to justify putting more computer equipment into the school (Tatnall 1990). If your school had only a single Apple II computer, how could you convince those with the funds to purchase more? One answer was to offer courses, such as Computer Awareness, that were seen as worthwhile and attractive to students, that could be run initially with a small amount of computer hardware, but which would clearly run much better with more. This offered a powerful argument to the proponents of the technology.

We are not suggesting that these forces were enacted in the 1980s with a full understanding of their consequences. It is only with hindsight that they are apparent.

9.   The International Perspective

Authors such as Moursund (1983) trace the beginnings of computer awareness courses in the USA to the late 1960s, leading to the development of a number of courses and individual units in the early 1970s. Writers at the end of this period (Kurland and Kurland 1987, Brooking 1983) suggest that early use of computers was for administrative use in schools that blossomed into computer clubs and programming instruction. The emergence of US Federal initiatives, such as the NSF sponsored PLATO system, produced CAI applications spread fairly widely through that country. Writers of this time trace real penetration of broad computer awareness programs to the introduction of the microcomputer. Several authors (including Kurland, Spresseer and Dyck) suggest that the publication of Seymour Papert's "Mindstorms" in 1980 and the associated discussion were the real beginnings of computer literacy courses in the USA and the UK. During this period David Morsund, Alan Kay and Seymour Papert were all invited to Victoria (at separate times) by the Computer Education Group of Victoria. Through these contacts between thinkers in the USA and Australia, much of the history of development in Australia was synchronised with that in the USA, but in a much smaller breeding ground, with much more local autonomy. It seems to have been the case in both countries that the education system was being dragged into computer literacy courses by local groundswell. Kurland reports (1987) that "In the 1981-1982 school year, for example, an estimated 27% of the money used to purchase computers came from sources outside of the normal school channels". In the parallel world of the UK, Brooking (1983) laments "... there is a remarkable lack of computer expertise as more and more schools require micros." It can be argued that the picture of computer awareness courses presented here from the Australian perspective is a reflection of those changes taking place in the USA, and the UK. A parametric demonstration of this is that each country produced its own manufactured computer in response to the educational needs of schools at the time. In the USA the Tandy TRS 80 and Apple II, in Australia the Microbee, and in the UK the BBC computer.

10. Conclusion

In 2006 in Australia, like most developed countries, secondary school students are generally very *computer aware* and also quite *computer literate* so that there is no need now for any form of formal Computer Awareness course in schools. Many subjects in the school curriculum now make good use of computers in various ways and so all students get considerable exposure to this technology. The only people who need additional computer literacy training now are mainly those who have not, for any reason, worked their way through the normal school system.

Given that it is not still offered by schools, one way that they can easily obtain access to such training is to undertake course such as those leading to an International Computer Drivers Licence (Australian Computer Society 2005). These courses have modules such as: basic concepts of IT, using the computer and managing files, word processing, databases, presentations, and information and communication. The Danish Ministry of Education also have a Junior Computer Drivers Licence (Danish Ministry of Education 2004). Many public libraries also offer introductory computer courses.

While school students and the public at large knew and understood little of computers in the early 1980s, ready access to a wide range of technologies has now made such knowledge and understanding widespread. While there was a significant need in the 1980s to offer formal courses in what computers were, what they could do, and the implications of their use, the need for such courses died with the 1980s. There is still a need to ensure that students are computer literate, but this can now generally be done through computer use in normal school subjects.

References

[1] Australian Computer Society (2005). Are you Licensed to Drive a Computer? Web, Date accessed: December 2005, www.acs.org.au/icdl
[2] Brooking A C (1983). The Problem of Producing Teachers with Computing Expertise Within the School System, *Proceedings 14th ACM SIGCSE Technical Symposium 1983*

[3]   Commonwealth Schools Commission (1983). Teaching, Learning and Computers. Report of the National Advisory Committee on Computers in Schools. Canberra, Commonwealth Schools Commission.

[4]   Computer Studies Curriculum Committee (1983). Computer Awareness - Year 9, Year 10. Melbourne, Education Department of Victoria.

[5]   Curriculum Services Branch (1983). Computer Awareness: Guidelines for Secondary Schools Years 8-10. Brisbane, Department of Education Queensland.

[6]   Danish Ministry of Education (2004). Junior Computer Drivers Licence. Web, Date accessed: December 2005, http://eng.uvm.dk/news/junior.htm?menuid=05

[7]   Kurland, D. M. and Kurland L.C. (1987) Computer Applications in Education: A Historical Overview, *Annual Review Computer Science* , Vol 2: 317-358

[8]   McDougall, A. (1980). Computers and Post-Primary Education in Victoria: a Study of Needs. Melbourne, Education Department of Victoria, Computer Policy Committee.

[9]   Moursund, D. (1983). *Precollege Computer Literacy: a Personal Computing Approach.* Eugene, Oregon, International Council for Computers in Education.

[10] Secondary Computer Education Committee (1980). Year 10 Computer Education: Guidelines for Secondary Schools. Melbourne, Education Department of Victoria.

[11] Tatnall, A. (1990). "Designing the Australian Educational Computer." *Education* **110**(4): 453-456.

[12] Tatnall, A. (1992). The Growth of Educational Computing in Australia. *History, Context, and Qualitative Methods in the Study of Education.* Goodson, I., F. and Mangan M. J. London, Ontario, University of Western Ontario, Canada. **Vol 3:** 207-248.

[13] Tatnall, A. and Davey, B. (2004). "Improving the Chances of Getting your IT Curriculum Innovation Successfully Adopted by the Application of an Ecological Approach to Innovation." *Informing Science* 7: 87-103.

From Learning to Use Towards Using to Learn
About Lessons to be Learned from
ICT-Education in the Netherlands

Jan Lepeltak

Institute for Education and Communication, Noordelijke Hogeschool Leeuwarden (NHL-University) 8917 DD Leeuwarden Rengerslaan 10, The Netherlands
www.nhl.nl/ictendidcatiek, www.frieslandleernetwerk.nl <j.c.lepeltak@iec.nhl.nl>

Abstract. Implementing ICT in secondary education and teacher training is not a complete success story in the Netherlands. One of the reasons is that for a long time the focus was on the system and learning to use the machine. By introducing the European Computer Driving License (ECDL) and it's educational variant in the 1990's the focus remained on the machine and the use of general applications we know from MS-office. Although a lot of effort is put in the training of teachers still less than 50% of the secondary school teachers in the Netherlands use ICT in there lessons. On the basis of the experience of more then 20 years of ICT implementation and research in cognitive learning theory, it is possible to give an account of this. Using to learn seems more and more a condition for learning to use.

1. Introduction

A survey in the Netherlands in 2005 shows that in secondary education (from 12-18 years) in 2005[1], 47% of the Dutch teachers use ICT in there lessons. What we see is a very slow growth in the use of computers in the learning process within the schools. In 2002 66% of the interviewed teachers expected that they would use ICT within three years. From this same 2002 survey we learned that in fact 41% of the teacher used ICT in there lessons. It seems almost as if the use of ICT is slowing down in secondary education in the Netherlands. The situation in primary education seems better. In 2002, 72% of the primary school teachers were using ICT and they

---

[1] TNS NIPO onderzoek ["research"] januari 2006 in opdracht van St.Ict op school

---

Please use the following format when citing this chapter:

Lepeltak, J., 2006, in IFIP International Federation for Information Processing, Volume 215, History of Computing and Education 2 (HCE2), ed. J. Impagliazzo, (Boston: Springer), pp. 117–127.

expected that in 2005 93% would use ICT. Reality is that in 2004 84% used ICT which is a nice figure compared with secondary education.

What could be the reason of this difference in use between primary and secondary education? The large majority of teachers in primary as well as in secondary education have positive attitude towards the use of ICT in teaching.[2]

As I will point out it is not availability of hardware or the access to the internet. Is it the software? Alternatively, has it to do with training and the professional development of teachers? That seems more likely if you consider that more than 60% of the teachers have no skills or skills on a very beginners level in the use of ICT in education as a added value.[3]

In this paper, it will be tried to show that there are reasons to believe that it is the combination of lack of innovative software and the way the professional development of teachers was setup in the Netherlands that can explain the slow implementation of ICT in secondary schools. ICT was far from every day practice: teaching in a regular subject area.

2.   Training and the Curriculum During the "Learning to Use" Approach

The formal introduction of information technology in Dutch schools goes back too 1984. Dutch government presented in that year a plan to parliament called the INSP (INformatics Stimulation Plan)[4]. It was an overall plan with a special education paragraph. In the years 1984-1987, the focus was on secondary education. The approach toward the school was integral: every school should be facilitated with hardware in a computer classroom, teachers should be trained and educational software developed. The idea was that in every school three teachers should attend training. Afterwards they would disseminate there knowledge and skills to their colleagues in their schools. This did not happened enough though.

Training was not perceived as adequate by many teachers. In their rapport, the school inspectors[5] mentioned several problems: some teachers who already taught information science for several years and were pioneers within their schools experienced that they knew more then there trainers. On the other hand there were teachers send to the training by there school management who hardly ever used a PC. So a generic approach was not satisfying. Schools received start package in the

[2] ICT Education Monitor 2003-2004. Neut, Irma van etc. *ICT in the Netherlands. Learning for the future.* Nijmegen/Tilburg 2004. Facts and Figures 2003/2004. p. 39 also on see
   http://www.ict-onderwijsmonitor.nl/
[3] See publication referred to in note 2 p.37
[4] *Informatica-Stimuleringsplan. Onderwijsbijlage. Versnelde invoering van informatietechnologie in het onderwijs.* Ministerie van Onderwijs en Wetenschappen. Zoetermeer, januari 1984.
[5] *Het Nivo-project in de scholen.* Inspectierapport 25. Zoetermeer 1988.

1980's with a special spreadsheet program (PC-calc), a word processor (PC-Type) and a D-base program (PC-file). Teachers were learned to use these tools.

Almost 70% of the content in the "basiscursus" handbook[6] was technology orientated with special attention for IT-applications, programming and system development. But it was not all technology. A special chapter about the information society should also be mentioned. For many teachers there was not much of a relation with there subject teaching. A lot of theory not much attention for the pedagogical and organizational aspects teachers complained.[7]

Because of the top-down approach there was clearly not a situation as mentioned by Fulhan in his advisory report for the Canadian government about introducing new educational technologies (NET). In the second part of the report, he states:

> "The best models of use will grow out of local implementation. The strategic ideas in this report are centrally built around the idea of "backward mapping. Good implementation must rest on what people in schools are really up against. Thus, the Ministry needs to engage local school personnel in an active collaborative search for the best ways of using NET. Cumulative, shared learning about NET is the key of the process."[8]

Although the proposed curriculum was certainly more than just "Learning to use", as you will later see, fact is that what happened in the school was often just "Learning to use". One of the most popular schoolbooks Babbage, was (but there are still new editions) a "non-nonsense" course (as the publisher calls it) that students could use individually in combination with there computer, almost without a teacher. It learns them to use a PC and some of its tools.

3. Informatics as a New Subject Area in Secondary Schools

Schools for secondary education started in 1984 with a new experimental subject area called "civil information science" (burgerinformatica) a project for students form 12 – 16 years. The national institute for curriculum development SLO coordinated the project. The curriculum was a combination of computer awareness and computer literacy. Its main general purpose was "The development of knowledge and skills that makes it possible for students to react adequate in

---

[6] Casimir, Gerda and Cor Nagtegaal. *Nivo-basiscursus Informatiekunde*. Zeist, 1987

[7] See note iii

[8] See Fullan, M., and M.B.Miles ands S.Anderson. *Strategies for implementing microcomputers in schools: the Ontario Case. Ministry of education, Ontario, April 1987.* quoted by Jan Timmer in his study about the use of educational software in secondary education in the Netherlands. Opstapreeks nr. 32. Zoetermeer 1991.

situations where the use of data-processing systems where possible ore necessary. And students should be able to make critical evaluation of the social meaning and impact of the use of such systems."[9]

This general goal has been specified in five sub goals that dominated the information science curriculum for the next twenty years.

1. Learning to work with, in general (collect, select ,evaluate, process and distribute data without computers)
2. Learning to work with data processing systems, the computer as:
    i. a tutor, and learning machine i.e. in some role as a teacher
    ii. a tool (word processor, calculator etc.)
    iii. constructor i.e. using the programming language Logo
    iv. an object in terms of it's hardware features: open it up and show it's components and where they for.
3. Gaining insight in some important applications of information technology i.e. systems for seat reservation, human-machine interaction.
4. Gaining insight in some of the implications of IT for society: e.g. privacy, lose of certain jobs etc.
5. Developing insight in the basic principles of data processing systems.

Because of these goals, four areas for learning were identified.

1. Use of applications
2. The social implications
3. Problem analysis and programming
4. Building principles ('architecture") of hard- and software

After the school reform in the Netherlands of 1993, Informatiekunde (the new name) became a school subject with a curriculum of 80 hours. However, it was practiced between 20 and 40 hours on the school timetable. The school inspectors also claim in a report[10] that this is not enough to make this a serious subject within the curriculum. The national institute for curriculum development developed the core objectives for this subject area with as long-term objective of integrating this learning to use skills in the regular subject areas (math, language, and sciences).

4. New Hardware and the Introducing of MS-DOS

The first hardware used in a national school project in 1983 was made in the Netherlands: the Philips P2000 computer and the Aster a company that went bankrupt soon afterwards. All were 8-bit computers.

---

[9] Raamwerk ["framework"] *Burgerinformatica. Stichting voor leerplanontwikkeling.* Enschede 1983
[10] See also note iii

It was in the year 1985, when MS-DOS personal computers where introduced in secondary education in the Netherlands. With its commando-driven interface not a tool easy to handle but a PC that could partly be manufactured in the Netherlands by IBM, Philips and Tulip Computers. No WYSIWYG, and it has also not very much in- and external memory (640Kb was the limit of directly addressable memory).That made learning to use also a more legitimate issue.

Apple introduced in 1984 the first PC with a graphical interface for the consumer and small business market. It formed the basis of a modern personal computing. "The Mac's elegant system software was its great accomplishment. It displayed a combination of aesthetic beauty and practical engineering that is extremely rare" [11] wrote Paul Ceruzzi in it's history of modern computing.

Before the MS-DOS introduction schools in secondary education where already experimenting with for example CP/M machines. British Acorn-BBC network were installed in Dutch computer classrooms. The importance of having an emerging educational standard should not underestimated. In the UK, it was the start of an emerging educational software industry,

There was strong a lobby for the Apple approach, but without success. In 1990 Bill Gates signed a Windows contract with the Dutch government who started to supply elementary schools with a special MS-DOS computers called the Comeniuscomputer, after the famous 17th century Tsjechian philosopher and pedagogue Jan Amos Comenius. It was installed with the new Windows interface.

The choice was made on the basis of a rapport from the Centre for Education and Information Technology (COI) published in 1987. There were also efforts to promote the MSX2-computers who were popular as game computers at that time for gaming. Main argument (although the cost aspect played a role as well) for not choosing the Apple Macintosh line was the fact that they were manufactured by only one company and the MS-DOS machines by a lot of companies. [12]

5.   Software and the Curriculum

The Netherlands, like most other northern European countries where reasonable equipped during the 1990's. Important is in this respect the research of T. Plomp, and W. Pelgum in there Comped-studies in which the international development of the use of computers in education was measured and compared. [13]

Still there is in the present days not a lively and strong educational software market in the Netherlands. An important European conference took place in 1986 called Eurit 86. On this first European conference on education and information

[11] Ceruzzi, Paul E. *A history of modern computing.* P.273-276 MIT press Cambridge, 1998.

[12] Schoenmaker, J. *Apparatuur en besturingssystemen voor het basisonderwijs.* COI.Enschede 1987.

[13] Pelgrum, W.J., and Tj.Plomp, Tj. *The IEA study of computers in education: Implementation of an innovation in 21 education systems.* Oxford, (1993). UK: Pergamon Press.

technology, the main theme was Developments in educational software and courseware. In addition, IFIP acted as a sponsor. Important other issues were methodology of courseware development, implementation and national plans, teaching programming and instructional design, intelligent tutoring and expert systems.[14]

A new initiative to stimulate educational software development called the Poco project was launched in 1987. In the Poco-project educational software was developed by various organizations and later published by publishing company's .

Although millions of Euros (then guilders) were invested in the stimulation of software development during 1987-1991 a commercial independent market did not develop. Of course, one of the reasons has to do with the use of the Dutch language. The Dutch market is a relative small market, and the peculiar way in which the delivery of educational content is organized in the Netherlands - where the commercial publishers have a de facto monopoly- makes commercial educational software development not easy. It is all together unclear if there is a return on investments developing educational software considering the illegal copying practices in those days. Even large government funded developing programs did not led to the start of a successful software market in secondary education.

In the second half of the 1990s, the emphasis on information science was not an issue anymore. This could be an excellent moment to shift from learning to use toward using to learn. Unfortunately, this did not happen. A strong lobby for the educational variant of the so-called European Computer Driving License (ECDL) seemed partly successful. With a small educational adjustment, it became an educational driving license. School managers send there teachers to ECDL-courses. However, the government never made it obligatory. The ECDL approach for teachers is controversial. Teachers want to learn more about how they could use ICT in there lessons and not just follow a course word, PowerPoint, or Excel.

In the Netherlands, there is not a national curriculum as for example in England. Only at the end of secondary education, there is a national examination. Learning objectives though are formulated. For primary education and the first years of general secondary education, certain objectives that should be reached are formulated. The situation in vocational education is more complex. Although there is not a national curriculum it does not mean that school develop there one curricula. Most of the curricula are developed by the authors of schoolbooks on the basis of curriculum examples. The majority of the schoolbooks are more les tradition in there pedagogy. That implies that they are course driven and have an instructional character. ICT comes with it as an extra. Educational publishers say that they are willing to develop more innovative material other then so called book plus

---

[14] See Moonen, Jef and T.Plomp (ed.) *Eurit 86. proceedings of the first European conference on education and information technology.* Pergamon press. Oxford 1987.

production (traditional course with some software) but the majority (70%) of the market asks for "traditional" material they claim. Recent surveys support this.[15]

6.   The Shift from Learning to Use to Using to Learning

The key problem seems that in the last 15 years there was not enough attention for using ICT in the learning process and its pedagogical implications in the Netherlands. This focus on the use and knowledge of systems seems the be international phenomena in the midst of the 90's of last century as we can see in a UNESCO document in which a Informatics curriculum for secondary education is formulated.[16] Developing some kind of computer literacy was considered to be an important aspect of school learning.

One of the main reasons is the lack of knowledge and experience in using ICT in the classroom. A disturbing fact in the Netherlands is that also in higher education i.e. the teacher training centers more than 60% of the teacher trainers claim that they should like to have more knowledge about educational use of ICT.[17] In a recent policy document of the ministry of education, quality assurance of the teacher education is an important issue. During a parliamentary discussion in June 2005 the necessity of a quality impulse was supported by must of the members of parliamentary education committee.[18]

So what we see is that despite of the fact that every school in the Netherlands has a free broadband connection with internet, the existence of a national educational network (kennisnet) and an average pupil-computer ratio of 9:1 in elementary and secondary education[19] educational use in secondary education is below expectation.

Are the other successful examples? More successful seems the Swedish approach where in the Itis-project[20] professional development, and school development were integrated. The button line is a school tailored approach, with an focus on education, improvement of learning and proven or expected added value for the use ICT.

As stated four guiding principles have underpinned the planning of the action program of Itis and shall be applied to its implementation in the municipalities:

1. Equal standards between schools and quality for pupils

---

[15] See ICT in the Netherlands. Fact and figures 2003-2004. IVA/ITS Nijmegen/Tilburg 2004. and http://www.ict-onderwijsmonitor.nl/

[16] See p. 5 *Informatics for secondary education. A curriculum for schools*. Produced by a working party of IFIP. Unesco document , Paris 1994.

[17] See http://www.ict-onderwijsmonitor.nl/ section Hoger onderwijs

[18] See http://www.eerstekamer.nl/9324000/1/j9vvgh5ihkk7kof/vh1jf30xeuxg/f=x.doc

[19] See note v

[20] See http://www.logos-net.net/ilo/150_base/en/init/swe_7.htm

   2. School development[21]
   3. Supplementing and reinforcing programs planned and already
      completed by the municipalities.
   4. Increasing the school's accessibility to the Internet and e-mail

In the development of "learning to use" curriculum material the concept
mental model played an important role. Users develop a mental model of a system
and on the basis of this model they can also use other similar systems. Nevertheless,
it should be an adequate model. Our mental model of a typewriter should not be
similar on that of a word processor. If it is, the user can easily be identified by the
hard return after ever line. A mental model is a cognitive construction. It deals with
the way people think about what's happening within a system.[22]

We consider learning to be more effective as it perceived as meaningful,
embedded in authentic situations.[23]   It is in what we now call the social
constructivist approach of Lev Vygotsky where we find a great emphasis on the
importance of interaction between people (children, teachers, parents) in cognitive
development. Anchoring instruction in real life problems that have to be solved and
creating rich environments that stimulate to interact about real life problems and
situated learning is becoming more and more mainstream in the use if ICT for
learning.[24]   By situated learning we mean the physical and social context within
which learning takes place this remains an integral part of which is learned.[25] That is
hardly the case in the traditional technology driven courses where one is supposed to
learn to work with software applications in isolated way. Children learn to use word
processors by learning to express themselves by writing, learning to use
spreadsheets by e.g. during statistic research in there environment. Learning to use
creative tools, mind maps by exploring there creativity. It is this more constructivist
approach - opposite of the mechanistic, behaviorist – that is now in our full
attention.   This approach differs fundamentally from the more mechanistic,
behaviorist approaches in which trough training and instruction one learns to use
ICT.

What we learn from the Dutch situation is that it is difficult to change patterns
that are followed for years. In countries where ICT is recently introduced, we could
learn from new approaches by action research methods and the exchange of free

---

[21] Note: The Itisproject is now integrated in the national Swedish schooldevelopment plan. See:
   http://www.skolutveckling.se/in_english/
[22] A mental model is an explanation in someone's thought process for how something works in the real
   world. It is a kind of internal symbol or representation of external reality, hypothesised to play a
   major part in cognition. The idea goes back to Kenneth Craik (1943) and Philip Johnson-Laird (1983)
[23] See Bereiter, C. *Education and mind in the knowledge age.* Mahwah, New Jersey LEA Publishers.
   (2002).
[24] See Maddux, Cleborne D. , D.Lamont Johnson and Jerry W.Willis. *Educational Computing. Learning
   with Tomorrow's Technologies.* Second ed. Boston. 1997.
[25] See Wood, David. *How children think and learn. The social contexts of cognitive development. 2e
   edition.* London 2005.

open source material. Education should primary be a matter of student/pupils/ teachers and parents. The involvement of large soft- and hardware companies is not automatically a benefit for developing school systems with ICT. Different then in elementary school, teachers in secondary schools are subject orientated i.e. they are teaching math, language, physics, history etc. Only by developing concrete plans and projects for the use of ICT, that is integrated in there subject areas and every teaching works. That is why in physics teaching in the Netherlands, where there is longstanding tradition in the use of science labs, ICT is well integrated in the curriculum. From the start in the 1980's tools like IP-Coach and coach lab, developed by Prof. Dr. Ton Ellermeijer of the University of Amsterdam, were introduced to support modern teaching of physics.[26]

7. Conclusions: Toward Development of Community of Practices CoP

The first hardware used in school had a commando-driven user interface (MS-DOS) and word processors like WordStar dictated the focus learning to use the machine. Unfortunately, this led to a practice that is still very manifested in the Netherlands. In a 2004 national report we read "In 1999, the training of teachers was based on acquiring basic skills and learning to use standard ICT-applications. In 2002, this does not seem to have changed a lot. Teachers are still "learning to use" instead of "Using to learn".[27]

During the WCCE conference in July 2005 in Stellenbosch, South Africa the so called Stellenbosch declaration[28] was formulated. It states that good teaching skills are more important than good ICT skills. It put the teachers where he belongs: together with the pupil/student in the center of the learning and teaching process. ICT should empower the teachers and should not be seen as a barrier that has to be taken. The integration of ICT in the curriculum will lead to new pedagogies and new roles for teachers and active learning.

On the basis of our past experiences we can discriminate a top down instructional ("learning to use") approach focused on ICT use and a more bottom up constructivist approach focused on learning ("Using to learn"). In this scheme, I will try to sum up some of the differences. The were in a preliminary form also mentioned in[29]

---

[26] See also http://www.cma.science.uva.nl/english/index.html

[27] Lam Ineke etc. *Ilab. Dutch National Report IVLOS. Centre for ICT and education. Utrecht University. Utrecht 2004.* see www.theknownet.com/ilab/uploads/sector_national_reports

[28] See http://www.unesco-iicba.org/index.php?option=com_content&task=view&id=76&Itemid=1

[29] See Lepeltak, Jan en Verlinde, Claire, *Education for the twenty-first century: issues and prospects, Contributions to the work of the International Commision on Education for the Twenty-first Century,* chaired by Jacques Delors, 1998, Pagina 281-298.

	LEARNING TO USE Traditional dessimation model	USING TO LEARN CoP-model
Training	Generic: one curriculum for all (top down). A curriculum set up by specialist	Tailored: on the spot. On the basis of school/teachers needs
Content	Learning isolated skills. Knowledge as a function for these skills	Integrated e.g. Word-processing in learning to write stories or reports
Pedagogy	Instruction based. Decontextualised learning. Individual	Social constructivist: Collaborative learning in situated in authentic context
Assessment	Individual testing with certificate	Products, port folio
Role Teacher	Directs process	In mentoring role
Knowledge	Is distributed by teachers to learners	Is shared and build up together
Organized	In school setting	In learning network or Community of practice
Research	Quantitative statistic. Methods from Neopositivist social studies.	Qualitative, Practice based action research: Cyclic. The participants as reflective professionals
Dissemination	Through research reports and scientific publications and periodicals. On academic conferences	Through publishing on Internet. Direct communication to peers and presentations on seminar

The emerging Community of Practice/Learning network[30] will play the role of a starting expert center where all the participators (students, teachers, teacher trainers, soft- and hardware specialist) share knowledge and experience, A model we are trying to implement in Indonesia you se below

However, the question remains, How can we effectively implement ICT in our schools? For countries that are in a developing phase, the next scenario seems promising as a starting point[31] within small communities. Plans are now developed to experiment on a larger scale in Indonesia with Nahdlatul Ulama (NU), the largest Moslem organization in Indonesia. NU is exploring the possibilities to stimulate the use of ICT in Indonesian primary, secondary schools, and teacher education.

---

[30] See for a definition of Wenger's notion of Community of Practice
   http://fdhis.inknoise.com/CommofPractice/2004/12/30/0001
[31] See the world e-citizensproject in http://www.mirandanet.ac.uk/

8.   Seven steps for integration

Step 1   Organize: A small starting seminar in which participants can articulate the possibilities and challenges.

Step 2   Form a CoP in which teachers, students, teacher trainers, ICT-specialist and advisers participate.   Investigate issues of infrastructure, content, and expertise among participators

Step 3   Choose a platform - Virtual learning environment that can be used for your emerging learning community to exchange experience, content and communication.

Step 4   Choose one or two priories for development e.g. writing and physics. And collect resources.

Step 5   Make general plans for a education project in which you do practical e.g. you environment.

Step 6   Make an overview for the necessary ICT-skills and integrate the training in the project. E.g. the use of internet (starting with email) but also the use of tools as PowerPoint, etc.

Step 7   Use ICT for learning and define a cyclic action research project for students and teachers that's can be linked with curriculum goals. (See step 5.) For example an environmental project about the quality of the water of a river nearby or a (rain) forest. Elements from writing, science (chemistry and geography) can be integrated

Developing country's could build up their capacity in developing e-community's in which teachers, teacher trainers, subject specialist, experts and students work together, share knowledge and experience and develop a learning network.

Human Resources Education in Computing at Simón Bolívar University, Venezuela
1972 to 1985

Julián Aráoz and Cristina Zoltan

1 Aráoz - Department of Statistics and Operation Research, Technical University of Catalonia, Edifici C5, 2 Planta, Campus Nord, Jordi Girona, 1-3, 08034 Barcelona,, Spain. <julian.araoz@upc.edu>
2 Zoltan - Departament of Llenguatges i Sistemes Informàtics, Technical University of Catalonia, Barcelona, Spain. <zoltan@lsi.upc.edu>
3 Aráoz and Zoltan - Also Universidad Simón Bolívar, Caracas, Venezuela.

Abstract. In this work we describe the efforts of the Computing Coordination at Simón Bolívar University, Venezuela, for forming Human Recourses in Computing at graduate and postgraduate levels in the years from 1972 to 1985. We also consider the background given by the Scientific Computer Program at the Calculus Institute, Buenos Aires University, that begun in 1962 and by the Computation Licentiate Program at Science Faculty, Venezuelan Central University, that begun in 1967. We close considering the impact that programs and professors from Simón Bolívar University have at national and regional levels.

1. Introduction

In this work, we want to emphasize the importance that the studies of Computing, designed and implemented in the Simón Bolívar University (USB), Venezuela, had for the development of the profession in Venezuela and the impact and influence that it had in those years in South American countries of Hispanic speech.

We will discuss the efforts at graduate and postgraduate levels in the years from 1972 to 1985. We select these years because the programs begun in 1972 at USB and stabilized with very good results in the middle 1980s, hence 1985.

Please use the following format when citing this chapter:

Aráoz, J., Zoltan, C., 2006, in IFIP International Federation for Information Processing, Volume 215, History of Computing and Education 2 (HCE2), ed. J. Impagliazzo, (Boston: Springer), pp. 129–137.

We begin considering the background given by the Scientific Computer[1] Program at the Calculus Institute[2] (IC-UBA), Buenos Aires University, that started in 1962, but was official in 1964, and by the Computation Licentiate[3] Program at Science Faculty, Venezuelan Central University (UCV), that begun in 1967. We also consider the impact that the programs and professors from USB had at national and at regional levels such as at UCV, Guyana University, Venezuela, Latin-American Center for Informatics Studies[4] (CLEI), and Latin-American Informatics School[5] (ESLAI). We wish to emphasize that, unlike historians, the authors of this paper were active actors of this history.

2.   Background

In this section, we give the facts that were at the origin of the studies in informatics at the USB.

2.1   Informatics at the Venezuelan Central University, 1960–1965

In 1960, almost all the computing facilities available in Venezuela belong to the oil industry. However, at the Faculty of Science in the Venezuelan Central University (UCV) (Caracas, Venezuela) there was some computing related activity, because there was a IBM 1620 installed since 1960 in the newly formed Department of "Numerical Calculus and Data Processing" (CNDP–UCV). It was dedicated to give support to some engineering activities and science research. The Department offered short programming courses but had no university educational project until 1966. At that moment, the Science Faculty received more than two hundred professors from Argentina.

2.2   The long sticks night

The IC–UBA, where the University of Buenos Aires computing facility was installed, was a center giving support to the degree of "Computador Científico" offered by the University since 1962[6]. The Argentinean University crisis occurred in 1966 when the Argentinean tyrannical government decided on the intervention of the universities. In particular, the Science Faculty was violently invaded by the army. This act was called *The Long Sticks Night* and it produced the resignation of most of the professors and technicians.

---

1 Computador Científico
2 Instituto de Cálculo
3 Licenciado en Computación
4 Centro Latinoamericano de Estudios en Informática
5 Escuela Superior Latino Americana de Informática
6 Was officially approved in 1964 and in the same year three students obtained their degrees.

The IC–UBA practically disappeared. Nicolás Babini refers to the fact that the process of building a corps of teachers and researchers was badly suspended by the massive group of people resigning to the University (see Babini (2003)).

In the same work Babini also signals that the winners were the universities that received the resigning people. Some of them where Asunción del Paraguay (Universidad Católica), Montevideo (Universidad de la República) y Caracas (Universidad Central de Venezuela) among others. Several of these professors were captured by the CNDP–UCV, allowing the expansion of human resources and promoting the offering of a degree in computer science.

2.3   Informatics at the Central University, Caracas, Venezuela, 1966–1975

With the reinforced faculty, the CNDP–UCV began to offer in 1967 a scientific oriented degree named the "Licenciatura en Computación"[7]. Even if the pensum was programmed in 1966, using the experience of the IC–UBA, it was very similar to the recommendations of *Curriculum 68* (Atchison, Conte, Hamblen, Hull, Keenan, Kehl, McCluskey, Navarro, Rheinboldt, Schweppe, Viavant, and David M. Young (1968)).

The degree was offered by the Mathematics and Physics School, based on the Department of CNDP–UCV, but soon, as the degree became more demanded by students, the department became the "Computing Department" under the direction of Manuel Bemporad (see Bemporad (1989)). Afterward a School of Computing was created in the Faculty of Science.

The program was highly demanded, reaching in 1975 to a peak of more than 2000 students (Venezuelan population at the time was over 12 million inhabitants (see Faces-ULA)). But the students were more interested in obtaining a professional degree, rather than a science degree. In general, they start working after a couple of semesters of studying because of the rapidly expanding of computer personal demand.

Meanwhile the CNDP–UCV, tried to convince the Engineering Faculty at the Central University to start a program in Computing, closer to an engineering discipline, but the Engineering Faculty was afraid of the volume of students in the discipline. The CNDP–UCV also promoted in the Economics Faculty programs related to computing. Nevertheless, both efforts failed. From 1958, the Faculty of Sciences of the UCV, saw the population of registered students grow about 10.5 times, passing from the position 8th to 3rd in number of enrolled students among the faculties in the University (see Méndez (2001)), mainly by students enrolling in computer science.

---

7 Was officially approved in 1968

However, unfortunately there were very few graduates. The main reason was that Caldera's government closed the UCV for a year and the students went to the labor market and were lost for the university. Another problem was the amount of time taken by the students in writing their thesis and most of them never finished the degree.

3.   Informatics at the Simón Bolívar University Caracas, Venezuela (USB)

The computing studies at the USB had three differentiable periods. In the first period, the undergraduate degree was very close to the one offered by the CNDP–UCV and there was a recycling master program. The second period corresponded to the establishment of an innovative Computer Engineering program and a Computer Science master program. The last one corresponded to the Faculty consolidation and program diversification.

3.1   Informatics at the USB 1972–1975

The Simón Bolívar University (USB) was created in 1967 as a Technological Institute and started its activities in January 1970 (USB) and in 1972 there where offered degrees in informatics (graduate and undergraduate degrees). The degrees in computing started in 1972 with the names of "Master in Computer Science" and "License Diploma in Computing", respectively. This university received an important group of engineering professors from the Central University that was undergoing a "renovation movement", movement that ended in 1969 with an intervention of the university by the government (see Méndez (2001)).

At that time, the only graduate degrees specialized in computers where degrees offered to graduates in other disciplines like physics, mathematics and engineering. These degrees were a kind of way to change professional orientation. The initial graduate program at the USB was of this kind.

In 1974, the undergraduate degree changed its name to "Computer Engineer", changing also the program orientation viewing the profession as a new engineering branch. This change was easily implemented due to the fact that the Simón Bolívar University has the matrix organizational structure (see USB).

3.2 Informatics at the USB 76–79

3.2.1 Engineering undergraduate program

In 1976, a group of 44 students obtained their degree in computing engineering. At that year, the curricula suffered a mayor restructuring. One of the main reasons for these was that the changes in the area had such a speed that it was mandatory to give students a solid basic preparation that allows to rapid learning of new techniques diminishing the emphasis in teaching techniques.

The USB Computing Coordination felt that there was a need for having a very solid basic formation, allowing the professional to be able to quickly adapt to technological changes, for that the new version emphasized on finite structures as a requirement programming courses. These believe was sustained against the opinion of the people on the mayor computing centers that hired our graduates (see Aráoz (1989)).

With this in mind, during 1976, an important adjustment of pensa was made and it had great impact in the success of the later generations. This program is still valid with small modifications.

The important changes were:

1. Algebra and logic moved to the second year courses (first year was common to all students). This changes where looking to set these courses as the basic ones for any other computer course. Especially logic and algebraic structures were required for the first course that teach how to program.
2. More emphasis was set on algorithm analysis and data structures, replacing the data processing courses and graph theory (in a math oriented style).
3. A group of elective courses became mandatory: operating systems, comparative study of programming languages, and computer architecture.
4. In this program the students select a trio of specialized subjects from programming languages, operating systems, computer architecture, information system and teleprocessing, and they ought to take three courses (3 terms = 1 year) in each branch. This allows specializations at the undergraduate level.
5. Every computer course has a 4-hour theory and 3-hour laboratory per week, these laboratory give appropriate practice to students.
6. Replace the thesis by a half time, three-term project controlled on time and scope. This change reduced the graduation span.

The main idea behind the program changes was to give a solid basic formation in order to help them to be prepared to cope with the rapid changes in the discipline. The pensa changes set in 1976 where mainly driven by the changes suffered by the discipline since 1966. A very similar style is seen in the *Curriculum 78* of the ACM (see Austing, Barnes, Bonnette, Engel, and Stokes (1979); Aráoz (1989)).

3.2.2 Postgraduate studies

At the graduate level the changes where the following:
1. Turn the degree into a real postgraduate one in computing with a research orientation, asking the students entering the program to have a degree in computing (or take remedial courses). The recycling task was left to other degrees (Like the one in system Engineering).
2. The course level changed drastically. All the students were required to take a group of basic courses:
   - Computability Theory
   - Computational Mathematics
   - Theory of Algorithms

   Afterward a group of specialized courses, preparing the student for writing the thesis.

   The areas where selected among the most demanded ones and those having a research group backing it. The areas where at the time:
   - Computer graphics
   - Optimization
   - Numerical Analysis
   - Algebraic Calculus
   - Language Theory
   - Computer Networks
   - Operating systems
3. At the same time, the work started to reinforce the research groups to back up the Master program. Best students where sent to pursue doctoral studies in universities having agreements with the USB, mostly in USA and France.

While part of the faculty studied abroad, a "Project of Doctoral Studies" was developed, but was not implemented until the rest of the disciplines offered by the university developed doctoral studies.

3.3   Informatics at the USB 80–85

At this period the USB Computing Faculty has consolidated, being the large computer science Ph.D. group in Spanish–America, almost surely. The reason for this was that the USB Computing Coordination hoped to open a doctoral program in 1980 and had prepared for this for four years. However, the USB had no doctoral programs at that time, and therefore did not approve it. Nevertheless, most of the Ph.D. people in computer sciences that returned to the country worked in the USB and in addition, the Faculty came from ten different countries.

The USB Computing Coordination had strong ties with Computing Schools in USA, Europe and South America. This marked that in 1979 when the CLEI[8] was founded in Chile the only group (outside Chile) that was prepared for organizing a Latin–American Conference, with pre–published proceedings, in one year was the USB Computing Coordination. Other countries demanded two years.

In this period, the USB Computing Coordination started developing the concept of "Software Workshop", as a way to have an activity longer than term laboratories. This was inspired in the "Architecture Design Workshops". This concept was used in other centers.

4. Outside Impact

4.1 Impact on other universities in Venezuela

Most of the Computing Programs, either Engineering or Licentiate, created in Venezuela have a strong influence from the USB graduates and faculty. The CNDP–UCV formed its instructors[9] sending them to the USB Computer Science Master Program.

The University of Guyana, Venezuela, asked the USB Computing Coordination to design its computing engineering program. Here and in ESLAI (Babini (2003); Atchison, Conte, Hamblen, Hull, Keenan, Kehl, McCluskey, Navarro, Rheinboldt, Schweppe, Viavant, and David M. Young (1968)) we implemented the idea of the "software workshop". Ours graduates and faculty worked in the careers at The Andean University (Mérida), Metropolitan University (Caracas), Orient University (Cumaná-Margarita), among others.

4.2 Impact to other Latin American countries

During these years, the developing of Computer Science and Engineering Curricula and human resources formation at the USB was a very successful experience that has an important impact in the developing of the area in Latin America. The USB Computing Coordination actively participate in helping the computing programs in Latin-America, main contributions were:

- Founders of CLEI and organization of Panel 80.
- Design, teaching, direction and advising of ESLAI[10]. This was a very successful school organized by the Argentinean Government in 1984.

8 Centro Latinoamericano de Estudios en Informática
9 First level of teachers

10 Escuela Superior Latino Americana de Informática

- Design of the engineering, master and doctoral pensa for the University of the Republic (Uruguay) and evaluation of the Uruguayan computing research system at Uruguay.
- Evaluation and advising of the UNESCO proposal for Computing Curricula in Latin America in 1976.
- Congress presidency and advising in computing to several Latin American countries.

5.   Final Remarks

In this paper, we have describes the three stages that underwent the developing of the informatics curricula at the USB until its stabilization. After 1985 doctoral studies were added to the graduate level, as the master program continuation. However, there are still missing postgraduate programs with a professional orientation and also recycling and update programs.

At the undergraduate level the curricula is almost the same, having minor changes due to new technologies. Given that for many years the student admission to the engineering program had a quota of one hundred students per year, the computer engineering undergraduate population accounts for about the 10% of the six or seven thousand undergraduate students at the USB.

The population that obtained the computer engineering degree until 2001, according to USB was about 2600, out 16500 obtaining a university degree at the USB. Graduates were easily absorbed by the industry (in Venezuela and abroad) due to their rapid adaptation to technological changes and the short period needed to become productive. We believe that solid basic formation is still a valid paradigm for the informatics' curricula design.

References

[1] Julián Aráoz. Desarrollo de la computación en la USB. In Gonzalo Viana, Carlos Di Prisco, Jesús Zambrano and Roger Soler, editors. Informática en el Desarrollo Nacional, pages 27–36. Fondo Editorial Acta Científica Venezolana, 1989.

[2] William F. Atchison, Samuel D. Conte, John W. Hamblen, Thomas E. Hull, Thomas A. Keenan, William B. Kehl, Edward J. McCluskey, Silvio O. Navarro, Werner C. Rheinboldt, Earl J. Schweppe, William Viavant, and Jr. David M. Young. Curriculum 68: Recommendations for academic programs in computer science: a report of the ACM curriculum committee on computer science. Commun. ACM, 11(3):151–197, 1968. ISSN 0001-0782. http://doi.acm.org/10.1145/362929.362976.

[3] Richard H. Austing, Bruce H. Barnes, Della T. Bonnette, Gerald L. Engel, and Gordon Stokes. Curriculum 78: recommendations for the undergraduate program in computer science— a report of the ACM curriculum committee on computer science. Commun. ACM, 22(3):147–166, 1979. ISSN 0001-0782. http://doi.acm.org /10.1145/359080.359083.

[4] Nicolás Babini. La Argentina y la computadora. Editorial Dunken, New York, NY, USA, 2003.

[5] Manuel Bemporad. Evolución de la computación en la U.C.V. Gonzalo Viana, Carlos Di Prisco, Jesús Zambrano and Roger Soler, editors, Informática en el Desarrollo Nacional, pages 21–26. Fondo Editorial Acta Científica Venezolana, 1989.

[6] Faces-ULA. 2005. URL http//iies.faces.ula.ve/censo/pobla\s\do5(v)ene.htm/.

[7] Nelson Méndez 2001. http://www.analitica.com/bitblioteca/nelson\s\do5(m)endez /renovacion.asp.

[8] USB. 2005. http://www.usb.ve/conocer/pdf/boletin_estadistico_1997_2001.pdf.

[9] USB. 2005. http://www.usb.ve/universidad/institucional/estructura.html.

Language History – A Tale of Two Countries

Bill Davey and Kevin R. Parker

[1] *School of Business Information Technology, RMIT University,
Melbourne, Australia <billd@rmit.edu.au>*
[2] *Idaho State University, Pocatello, Idaho USA < parkerkr@isu.edu>*

Abstract. This paper looks at the relationships between industry computer languages and those taught in universities. By considering the differences between two of the first countries to embrace programmable computers (USA and Australia) we find patterns that seem culturally independent. History shows a set of recurring problems for academics in choosing languages. This study shows that academics should be informed by history when making those decisions.

1. Introduction

The dawn of the history of programmable computers can be traced back to Eckert and Mauchly's departure from the ENIAC project to start the Eckert-Mauchly Computer Corporation. The fourth programmable computer in the world (SCIRAC) was developed in Australia. This computer, manufactured by the government science organization (CSIRO), still exists as a complete unit at the Museum Victoria in Melbourne. The computer was used into the 1960's as a working machine at the University of Melbourne. Australia's early entry into computing makes the comparison with the United States interesting.

These early computers needed programmers, that is, people with the expertise to convert a problem into a mathematical representation directly executable by the computer. The first programmers were mostly mathematicians or engineers who programmed in machine code of some form. Many of them used hardwiring to achieve their ends. Few if any of these early programmers had any formal education in machine language programming.

Please use the following format when citing this chapter:

Davey, B., Parker, K.R., 2006, in IFIP International Federation for Information Processing, Volume 215, History of Computing and Education 2 (HCE2), ed. J. Impagliazzo, (Boston: Springer), pp. 139–151.

vInitial computer-related offerings by universities were courses in engineering or physics. Academia's landscape changed with remarkable speed as the twin paths of computer science and information systems degrees were quickly established in most developed countries. In Australia the University of Sydney introduced a course called "The Theory of Computation, Computing Practices and Theory of Programming" in 1947 (Tatnall and Davey, 2004). The speed of the introduction of specialized degrees paralleled the introduction of hardware and software in industry. The speed of change meant that both industry and university sectors were required to make very difficult choices between hardware and software alternatives.

At that time the connection between the computing industry and academia was tight. Industry progressed due to innovation from university academics, and many industry leaders moved to teaching and research positions. In Australia the 1960's saw Gerry Maynard move from the Post Office to set up a degree at the Caulfield Technical College, Donald Overheu move from the Weapons Research Establishment to the University of Queensland, and Westy Williams leave the public service to start a program at Bendigo Technical College (Tatnall and Davey, 2004). Much of improvement of software and the emergence of languages occurred in university research departments, performed by passionate academics focused on discipline-based research rather than on industry needs.

2.   The History of Language Selection

The first languages were the individual machine languages developed to control specific central processing units. UNIVAC's C-10 language was one of the first to use mnemonic instructions, like "a" for add and "b" for bring, and by the late 1950's universities had discovered (and in most cases created) higher-level languages.

> I remember a lecture given by a colleague, Peter Sefton, in the late
> 1950s on a new language called Fortran, which he said he thought
> might relieve some of the tedium of programming in machine
> language (Smillie, 2004).

The development of FORTRAN began in 1954 and culminated in the first release in 1957. ALGOL, released in 1958 with a major update in 1960, introduced recursion, indirect addressing, and character manipulation, among other features. Many universities adopted it as the language for use in their computer programming courses because it was a precise and useful way for capturing algorithms (Keet, 2004). COBOL was developed in 1959 and was widely used for a number of decades in business applications.

As early as 1960 there were 73 languages in existence (Sammet, 1972). By 1967 there were 117, and by 1971 there were 164 (Sammet, 1972). Of these only ten, ALGOL, APT, COBOL, Comit, FORTRAN, IPL, LISP, MAD, MADCAP, and NELIAC, appeared on all the lists. Sammet identifies the period from 1960 to 1970 as the decade in which the programming language field maturated. During this time, the battle over the use of higher-level languages was clearly won in the sense that machine coding had become the exception rather than the rule.

By 1972, most universities in Australia and the USA had established computer science or information systems (the latter often called "data processing") degree programs. Almost all computer science degree programs offered ALGOL, FORTRAN or LISP, while most data processing programs offered COBOL. In Britain BASIC was also important. During the late 60s, schools experimented with various languages like PL/I.

This situation changed most markedly with the introduction of Pascal. The first version of Pascal was released in 1970. Wirth began teaching Pascal to engineering and physics students in 1971 (Wirth, 1993), but the real impact of Pascal had to await the release of the P-machine in 1973 (Wirth, 1993).

The mid-1970s brought about another important change – the introduction of the microcomputer. These machines came with BASIC and revolutionised the teaching of computer courses in high schools. Most secondary schools immediately started using BASIC, but this trend did not impact university programs. With the introduction of Pascal in the 1970s, most universities adopted Pascal for their introductory programming course. Some authors attribute this to two pragmatic factors: the invention of the personal computer, and the availability of Pascal compilers (Levy, 1995).

Pascal compilers were always far slower than the languages used in industry, but the speed was well within the limits needed in a teaching environment. At this time academics used arguments to justify the divergence from using industrially common languages. For example, Merritt (1980) wrote

Since Pascal is a widely available and well-designed language, it was suggested that Pascal provided a unique language environment in which these features that support high quality program construction can be learned. However, it is reasonable to expect that reliable software will be a priority, that the connections between good programs and language features will continue to be made, and that language features will develop along the lines presented here. Information Systems graduates will be in systems development and management roles.

Of course Wirth himself admits that logic is not really the most important underlying cause of human decisions, "But it was probably my stubborn persistence rather than any reasoned argument that kept Pascal in use"(Wirth, 1993).

The use of Pascal in academia was eventually superseded by languages used in industry, beginning with C and C++, and eventually shifting to Java and C#. As recently as 1996 a survey of CSAB accredited programs showed the most popular first language was still Pascal at 36% of the responding institutions, followed by C++ at 32% and C at 17% (McCauley and Manaris, 1998).

The selection of programming languages in university curricula in the US and Australia is almost identical, with some interesting differences. The current distribution in Australia is shown in Table 1.

Table 1: Languages taught (de Raadt et al. 2003b)

Language	Number of courses	Weighted by students
Java	23	43.9%
VB	14	18.9%
C++	8	15.2%
Haskell	3	8.8%
C	4	5.5%
Eiffel	2	3.3%
Delphi	1	2.0%
Ada	1	1.7%
jBase	1	0.8%

This is a close approximation to the statistics in US universities. One historical difference between the countries involved Ada. When the US Department of Defense mandated Ada for their applications the language experienced a surge in US colleges, which declined after 1997 when the mandate was removed.

3.   How Universities Choose Languages

The problems that must be faced in designing an introductory course are many and varied. These range from those of interdepartmental politics in the case of service courses to logistical challenges if substantial numbers of students must be accommodated (Solntseff, 1978). A cursory glance through back issues of computer-related journals such as the ACM Special Interest Group on Computer Science Education (SIGCSE) Bulletin makes it apparent that discussions about the introductory programming language course and the language appropriate for that course have been numerous and on-going (Smolarski, 2003). The selection of a programming language for instructional purposes is often a tedious chore because there is no well-established approach for performing the evaluation. The informal process may involve faculty discussion, with champions touting the advantages of their preferred language, and an eventual consensus, or at least surrender. As the number of faculty, students, and language options grows, this process becomes increasingly unwieldy. As it stands, the process currently lacks structure and replicability.

A list of the factors that affected the choice of a programming language for an introductory course at one US university is ably discussed in Smith and Rickman (1976). According to Solntseff (1978), there "appears to be no other discussion in the literature of comparable thoroughness".

A current study carefully examines a first programming language for IT students (Gee et al., 2005). A more recent study examines over 60 papers relevant to language selection in academia (Parker et al., 2006). Over the years languages have been invented to solve problems. Other languages have been invented to make teaching algorithms easier. This has lead to two sometimes conflicting lines of arguments by academics about which languages they should use in university courses: choose a language that is commonly used or is expected to be commonly used in industry, or choose a language that best supports concept development in students. Thus, there have been two distinct arguments for language selection that have been extant throughout the history of languages: pragmatic versus pedagogical.

The pragmatic approach recommends choosing a language that will help students get a job after graduating. The pragmatic approach is impacted by a language's industry acceptance as well as the marketability of individuals proficient in its use.

3.1 Industry acceptance

Industry acceptance refers to the market penetration (Riehle, 2003) of a particular language in industry, i.e., the use of a language in business and industry. Often referred to as industrial relevance, this can be assessed based on current and projected usage, as well as the number of current and projected positions. Stephenson (2000) claims that this factor has the greatest influence in language selection, as indicated by 23.5% of schools that participated in his study. Lee and Stroud (1996) point out that real-world acceptability is a factor that once had little weight, as indicated by the earlier use of ALGOL and Pascal, but that attitude does seem to be changing. They note that for their students being able to have an industrially accepted language on their résumé is a significant consideration for them. A 2001 census of all Australian universities revealed that perceived industry demand was the major factor in the choice of an introductory language (de Raadt et al., 2003a). King (1992) agrees that many language decisions are made on the basis of current popularity or the likelihood of future popularity; he notes that choosing popular languages has a number of practical benefits, including increased student motivation to study a language that they have heard of and know is in demand, as well as a good selection of books and language implementations that will be available for a popular language.

3.2 Marketability

Marketability refers to the employability of graduates. This may include regional or national/international marketability, based on the placement of a program's graduates. Language selection is often driven by demand in the workplace, i.e., what employers want. Not only are marketable skills important in future employability, but students are more enthusiastic when studying a language they feel will increase their employability. (de Raadt et al., 2003a).

Language marketability is stressed in several studies. The census of introductory programming courses conducted by de Raadt et al. (2003a) emphasizes the importance of employability. In fact, the most commonly listed factor in language selection (by 56% of the participants) was the desire to teach a language that provides graduates with marketable skills. Watt (2000) discusses the need for transferable skills that will be useful in whatever career the student chooses to pursue. Emigh (2001) agrees that the primary concern in language evaluation must be the demand in the workplace and argues that when deciding on a new language one must take into account employers' expectations of graduates. Further, graduates' marketability can be improved by exposing them to several languages (de Raadt et al., 2003a). They cite, for example, that a progression from C to C++ to Java will qualify a graduate for more advertised positions than exposure to any single language in isolation. An example of this argument is:

> There is perhaps an implication here for the choice of platform and language. Extrinsically motivated students aspiring to a lucrative career will demand to be taught those tools that are currently in vogue in the industry. Universities may have to accept that pedagogical issues in the choice of platform and language must be secondary to marketing concerns. (Jenkins, 2001)

3.3   Pedagogy

Smolarski (2003), McIver and Conway (1996), and Howland (1997) question whether changes in the curriculum and programming courses should be as driven by industry as they often seem to be. They argue that decisions about the language used in an introductory course are made based on what language would be most useful for a student in finding a job, rather than on how well it underscores fundamental skills that prepare the student for subsequent courses and help to make any software being developed by the student well-written and error-free (Smolarski, 2003).

3.3.1 Avoiding the complexities of industrial environments

These arguments also call attention to the possibility that the purposes of teaching problem solving and introducing a professional grade language into the first course conflict because students end up focusing on difficulties associated with that language and its environment (Johnson, 1995; Jenkins, 2002; Gee et al., 2005; Allison et al, 2002; Kelleher and Pausch, 2005). "A language that requires significant notational overhead to solve even trivial problems forces the language rather than the techniques of problem-solving to become the object of study" (Zelle, 1999).

3.3.2 Clear problem-solving principles

A teaching language should have attributes that help teach fundamentals of all programming tasks. This is the argument used by Wirth (1993), Kölling et al. (1995), and all the other inventors of languages designed for classroom use, and is exemplified by proponents of the various "pure" teaching languages. The argument quickly becomes one that urges use of a language not common in industry. An example of such an argument is:

> A new teaching language is required to meet the needs for teaching .... This language does not have to be a real world production language and thus can avoid the compromises in conceptual cleanness for efficiency that cause many of the problems with existing languages. (Kölling et al., 1995)

3.4 The winner?

The relevant importance ascribed to both the pragmatic and practical approaches is illustrated by a recent survey of academics, shown in Table 2. The primary reason for language selection reported by the survey is marketability, cited by 56.1% of the respondents, followed by pedagogical benefits, cited by 33.3% of the academics.

Table 2: Reasons for choosing language (de Raadt et al. 2003b)

Used in industry / Marketable 56.1%
Pedagogical benefits of language 33.3%
Structure of degree/dept politics 26.3%
OO language 26.3%
GUI interface 10.5%
Availability/Cost to students 8.8%
Easy to find appropriate texts 3.5%
OS/Machine limitations of dept 1.8%

The task of anticipating industry needs is complex. Emigh (2001) points out that four to five years pass between when a student begins a program of study and when he or she attains a position requiring programming skills. Even if a curriculum teaches a newer programming language, there is no guarantee that employers will still be looking for that language when the student enters the work force. Further, some trends are difficult to understand. Currently in Australia there seems to be a demand for multi-skilled programmers (de Raadt et al. 2003a). The average advertisement required 1.84 languages. 48% of jobs required more than one language. C++ appeared as a requirement in around 30% of advertisements, as did Java. Visual Basic was next with 21%, followed by C with 17%.(de Raadt et al. 2003b). The Gottleibsen reports (Gottliebsen 1999; Gottliebsen 2001) on job advertisements in Australia for a sample of years shows 128 languages advertised in 1999, 3822 positions for C++, 2555 for Visual Basic, 1052 for Java, and 4678 for COBOL. By 2001 there were 206 languages in demand by industry, with 4359 positions for C++, 2680 for Java, 3369 for Visual Basic, and 1087 for COBOL.

An interesting omission from most programming language selection approaches is the ability to produce output using the language. Experiments such as that conducted by Zeigler (1995) could be used to help decide the issue. The same 60 programmers developed code in both Ada and C, the same work environment was used, as were the same debugging tools, same editors, same testing tools, and the same design methodology. Most of these programmers had masters degrees in computer science, and the more experienced programmers tended to work more in C. When first hired, 75% of the programmers knew C, while only 25% knew Ada. Despite the bias in C's favor, the experiment showed that the cost of coding in Ada is about half the cost of coding in C, because code written in Ada contained 70% less bugs discovered before product delivery and 90% less bugs discovered after product delivery (Zeigler, 1995). Note that this approach is limited by the shear quantity of programming languages available, well into the thousands today. A one-to-one comparison of all possible candidates cannot possibly be preformed.

Student perceptions also play a part in this debate. There exist several languages designed for teaching (Pascal, LOGO), but any department using one of these today would be an object of ridicule (Jenkins, 2002). It is true that programming languages designed for teaching purposes are not used to any extent by industry. Therefore student perception is that these languages are of little practical worth and further assume that, in general, they lack the advanced facilities of other languages (Gee et al., 2005). If that argument were to be carried to absurdity then the overwhelming choice would be COBOL, which now has an installed base of "more than 200 billion lines of code, and 5 billion lines of COBOL are written every year" (Langley, 2004).

Parker et al. (2006) propose a set of criteria for the selection of a programming language in an academic setting. Their work is based on papers by researchers in both Australia and the United States. Each of the criteria has been used in one or more previous studies that evaluate programming languages. This extended set of selection criteria points to a more formal and mature approach to language selection. As our current period moves into history, we may be able to see the early years of the twenty first century as a time of fundamental change in language choice.

4. Trends in Language Selection

The debate over programming language selection has been ongoing since the introduction of programming classes in university curriculums. A sampling of papers published over time provides some insights into the trends observed during given time periods.

Dijkstra (1972, p. 864) stated that

"...the tools we are trying to use and the language or notation we are using to express or record our thoughts are the major factors determining what we can think or express at all! The analysis of the influence that programming languages have on the thinking habits of their users ... give[s] us a new collection of yardsticks for comparing the relative merits of various programming languages."

Sime (1973) noted a need for an empirical approach to evaluate programming languages for unskilled users rather than experienced users, a trend that he observed in language evaluation papers prior to his work. Yohe (1974) pointed out that the development of problem-oriented languages began in the late 1950s, and they now offered an alternative to assembly language, although that was still the most basic tool available to most programmers. The availability of so many languages, however, presented a new problem in the selection of a language best suited for a particular task. Friedman and Koffman (1976) stressed the need for structured programming as a replacement to the older versions of FORTRAN, noting that "teaching disciplined programming at an elementary level is a nearly impossible task in the absence of a suitable implementation language" (p.1). Smith and Rickman (1976) were also seeking a replacement for FORTRAN, developing a well-designed set of criteria, including pedagogical factors, resource constraints, and political issues through which they "graded" ALGOL W, APL, Assembler, Basic, COBOL, EULER, Structured FORTRAN, LISP, Pascal, PL/I, and SNOBOL. In 1977, Furugori and Jalics reported that the results of their survey indicated that over half of the respondents still used FORTRAN in their introductory courses, while PL/I was used in a quarter of the schools. Finally, in 1978, Schneider indicated a trend toward the use of Pascal in classes. He pointed out that Pascal was the language that best met two critical and apparently opposing criteria – richness and simplicity. Pascal was rich in those constructs needed for introducing fundamental concepts in computer programming, but simple enough to be presented and grasped in a one-semester course.

The 1980s were marked by an increase in the number of available languages, which led to increased uncertainty about which to choose for the introductory programming course. Various paradigms were also introduced during this period. Boom and Jong (1980) performed a critical comparison of multiple programming language implementations available on the CDC Cyber 73, including Algol 60, FORTRAN, Pascal, and Algol 68. Tharp (1982) also pointed out the variety of languages available, including FORTRAN, COBOL, Jovial, Ada, Algol, Pascal, Pl/I, and Spitbol. He discussed several recent comparisons of programming languages on the basis of their support of good software engineering practices, availability of control structures, the programmer time required for developing a representative non-numeric algorithm, and the machine resources expended in compiling and executing it. Soloway, Bonar, and Erlich (1983) discussed recent research into finding a better match between a language and an individual's natural skills and abilities. Their study explored the relationship between the preferred cognitive strategies of individuals and programming language constructs. Luker (1989) discussed the alternatives to Pascal, noting that many instructors at that time were choosing between Ada and MODULA-2. He then examined the paradigms available, including functional programming, procedural programming, object-oriented programming, and concurrent programming.

King (1992) looked at the evolution of the programming course from the *Computing Curricula 1978* to the *Computing Curricula 1991* recommendations. He noted that the 1980s saw the creation of several important languages while at the same time several languages of the 1970s became popular. He also discussed the increasing popularity of various programming paradigms during the 1980s, including the imperative or procedural paradigm, the concurrent or distributed paradigm, the database paradigm, the functional or applicative paradigm, the logic-programming paradigm, and the object-oriented paradigm. He continued by proposing a set of criteria for the selection of programming languages. Howatt (1995) also proposed an evaluation method for programming languages. His criteria included the broad categories of language design and implementation, human factors, software engineering, and application domain. He went on to provide an evaluation approach. Howland (1997) also presented an extensive list of criteria that the author felt were important in choosing a language for introductory computer science instruction, but concluded that the selection of a programming language should be made primarily on the basis of how well key programming concepts may be expressed in the language.

By the turn of the century, the object-oriented paradigm was becoming more prominent, as was the importance of security. The Ad Hoc AP CS Committee (2000) noted that in their study of language selection for CS1 and CS2 classes three main principles emerged: emphasis on object-orientation, need for safety in the language and environment, and a desire for simplicity. Wile (2002) stated that programming language choice is subject to many pressures, both technical and social. He organized the pressures into three competing needs: (1) those of the problem domain for which languages are used for problem solving; (2) the conceptual and computing models that underlie the designs of the languages themselves, independent of their particular problem domains; and (3) the social and physical context of use of the languages. He also observed a trend:

> It is clear that the role of general-purpose languages had shifted by
> the end of the millennium. The days of writing an entire application

"from scratch" in a single language to build a stand-alone system that accomplishes a task are over. Modern software engineering process uses general-purpose languages as the integrating medium for extensive functionality offered by database packages, web-based services, GUIs, and myriad other COTS and customized products that interface via an application program interface (API). At the same time, "contextual concerns" for security, privacy, robustness, safety, etc., universally dominate applications across the board (p. 1027).

Roberts (2004a) observed another trend, that the growth in the popularity of the object-oriented paradigm and the decision by the College Board to move the Advanced Placement Computer Science program to Java led an increasing number of universities to adopt Java as the programming language for their introductory course. He further pointed out in (2004b) that there were two additional challenges in which dramatic increases had a negative impact on pedagogy: (1) the number of programming details that students must master has grown, and (2) the languages, libraries, and tools on which introductory courses depend are changing more rapidly than they have in the past. Finally, Gee Wills, and Cooke (2005) pointed out another trend that is becoming increasingly evident (and controversial). They mentioned several studies that the recommended the use of scripting languages to teach programming concepts because they provide "not only a proper programming environment but also an instant link into the formation of active web pages".

5. Conclusion

While there have been various differences throughout the years between Australia and the United States in the teaching of programming languages, there is a pattern that seems culturally independent. Across the two countries there has been, and still exists, a fundamental disagreement between taking a pragmatic or pedagogical approach. The pragmatic approach recommends choosing a language that will help students get a job after graduating. The pedagogical approach insists that the language used in introductory programming classes should be designed for teaching programming concepts and problem solving and should minimize complexities so that more time can be spent on developing design skills. There has been no consensus on which approach is optimal, but the ultimate lesson is that neither approach is sufficient by itself. There are additional critical factors that must be considered when selecting a programming language. Recent studies have examined a variety of factors that must be taken into account, and while pragmatic and pedagogical concerns are still near the forefront, they must be tempered by an awareness that other factors impact the selection process. The bottom line is that academics must carefully assess the best interests of the students, weigh all variables in the language selection process such as those listed by Parker et al., (2006), and choose a language accordingly. As Johnson (1995) points out, "the greatest danger to our university system is the lemming-like rush to do the same thing, to be one with the crowd, to be part of the current fashion industry of computing."

References

[1] Allison, I., Ortin, P., and Powell, H. (2002). "A virtual learning environment for introductory programming." Proceedings of the 3rd Annual conference of the Learning and Teaching Support Network Centre for Information and Computer Sciences, Loughborough, UK.

[2] de Raadt, M., Watson, R., and Toleman, M. (2003a). "Introductory programming languages at Australian universities at the beginning of the twenty first century." Journal of Research and Practice in Information Technology 35(3): 163-167.

[3] de Raadt, M. d., R. Watson, et al. (2003b). "Language tug-Of-war: Industry demand and academic choice." Australasian Computing Education Conference (ACE2003), Adelaide, Australia., Australian Computer Society, Inc.

[4] Emigh, K L. (2001). "The impact of new programming languages on university curriculum." Proceedings of ISECON 2001, Cincinnati, Ohio, 18, 1146-1151. Retrieved July 10, 2005 from http://isedj.org/isecon/2001/16c/ ISECON.2001.Emigh.pdf

[5] Gee, Q. H., Wills, G. and Cooke, E. (2005). "A first programming language for IT students." Proceedings of the 6th Annual Conference of the Learning and Teaching Support Network Centre for Information and Computer Sciences, York, UK.

[6] Gottliebsen, C. (1999). Computer market results 1999. C. Gottliebsen. Bayswater, GIMA

[7] Gottliebsen, C. (2001). Icon index trend report 2001. Icon index Trend Report. B. Youston. Bayswater.

[8] Howland, J.E. (1997). "It's all in the language: yet another look at the choice of programming language for teaching computer science." Journal of Computing in Small Colleges, 12(4): 58-74, http://www.cs.trinity.edu/~jhowland/ ccsc97/ccsc97/

[9] Jenkins, T. (2001). "The motivation of students of programming." ACM SIGCSE Bulletin , Proceedings of the 6th annual conference on Innovation and technology in computer science education ITiCSE '01 33(3).

[10] Jenkins, T. (2002). "On the difficulty of learning to program." Proceedings of the 3rd annual conference of the Learning and Teaching Support Network Centre for Information and Computing Science, Loughborough, UK.

[11] Johnson, L.F. (1995). "C in the first course considered harmful." Communications of the ACM 38 (5): 99-101.

[12] Keet, E. E. (2004). "A personal recollection of software's early days (1960–1979): Part 1." IEEE Annals of the History of Computing (October–December).

[13] Kelleher, C. and Pausch, R. (2005). "Lowering the barriers to programming: A taxonomy of programming environments and languages for novice programmers." ACM Computing Surveys 37(2): 83–137.

[14] King, K.N. (1992). "The evolution of the programming languages course." Proceedings of the Twenty-Third SIGCSE Technical Symposium on Computer Science Education, Kansas City, Missouri, pp. 213-219.

[15] Kölling, M., B. Koch, et al. (1995). "Requirements for a first year object-oriented teaching language." ACM SIGCSE Bulletin , Proceedings of the twenty-sixth SIGCSE technical symposium on Computer science education 27(1).

[16] Langley, N. (2004). "COBOL integrates with Java and .NET." Computer Weekly. http://www.computerweekly.com/articles/article.asp?liArticleID=133085

[17] Lee, P.A., and Stroud, R.J. (1996). "C++ as an introductory programming language." in M. Woodman (Ed.), Programming Language Choice: Practice and Experience, London: International Thomson Computer Press, pp. 63-82.   http://www.cs.ncl.ac.uk/old/ publications/books/apprentice/InstructorsManual /C++_Choice.html

[18] Levy, S. P. (1995). "Computer Language Usage In CS 1: Survey Results." SIGCSE 27(3): 21-26.

[19] McCauley, R. and Manaris, B., (1998). "Computer science programs: what do they look like?" Proceedings of the 29th SIGCSE Technical Symposium on Computer Science Education, February, pp. 15-19.

[20] McIver, L. and Conway, D.M. (1996). "Seven deadly sins of introductory programming language design." Proceedings of Software Engineering: Education and Practice (SE:E&P'96), Dunedin, NZ, pp.309-316.

[21] Merritt, S. M. (1980). "On the importance of teaching Pascal in the IS curriculum." ACM SIGCSE Bulletin , Proceedings of the eleventh IGCSE technical symposium on Computer science education SIGCSE '80 12(1).

[22] Parker, K. R., T. O. Ottaway, et al. (2006). "Criteria for the selection of a programming language for introductory courses." International Journal of Knowledge and Learning 2 (1/2) 119-139.

[23] Riehle, R. (2003). "SEPR and programming language selection." CrossTalk - The Journal   of   Defense   Software   Engineering   16(2):   13-17, http://www.stsc.hill.af.mil/crosstalk/ 2003/02/Riehle.html

[24] Sammet, J. E. (1972). "Programming languages: History and future." Communications of the ACM 15(7): 601.

[25] Smillie, K. (2004). "People, languages, and computers:A short memoir." IEEE Annals of the History of Computing (April–June): 60-73.

[26] Smith, C. and Rickman, J. (1976). "Selecting languages for pedagogical tools in the computer science curriculum," ACM SIGSE Bulletin 8(3): 39-47.

[27] Smolarski, D.C. (2003). "A first course in computer science: Languages and goals." Teaching Mathematics and Computer Science 1(1):137-152. Retrieved November 10, 2005 from http://math.scu.edu/~dsmolars/smolar-e.pdf

[28] Solntseff, N. (1978). "Programming languages for introductory computing courses: a position paper." ACM SIGCSE Bulletin 10(1): 119-124.

[29] Stephenson, C. (2000). "A report on high school computer science education in five US states." http://www.holtsoft.com/chris/HSSurveyArt.pdf.

[30] Tatnall, A. and B. Davey (2004). "Stream in the history of computer education in Australia." History of Computing in Education. J. Impagliazzo and J. A. N. Lee, Kluwer Academic Publishers.

[31] Watt, D.A. (2000). "Programming languages–Trends in education." Proceedings of Simposio   Brasileiro   de   Linguagens   de   Programacao,   Recife,   Brazil, http://www.dcs.gla.ac.uk/~daw/ publications/PLTE.ps

[32] Wirth, N. (1993). "Recollections about the development of Pascal." ACM SIGPLAN Notices, The second ACM SIGPLAN conference on History of programming languages HOPL-II 28(3).

[33] Zeigler, S.F. (1995). "Comparing development costs of C and Ada." Rational Software Corporation, Santa Clara, Calif., March 30.

[34] Zelle, J. M. (1999). "Python as a first language." Proceedings 13th Annual Midwest Computer Conference (MCC 99), March 18-19, Lisle, IL.

Computing Behind the Iron Curtain and Beyond Hungarian National Perspective

Maria Raffai

Chair for Information Science, Szechenyi Istvan University,
Egyetem ter 1., 9026 Győr, Hungary, http://www.sze.hu
<raffai@sze.hu>, http://rs1.sze.hu/~raffai

Abstract: At the beginning of the computing era it was a great challenge to write a running program in order to solve different mathematical, statistical tasks, and to get the appropriate results by using a computer. At the university where I had began my studies we started to get acquainted with computers using a Russian made machine, named URAL 2. Looking back to the roots and thinking of the Hungarian born pioneer of computer science: the polymath John von Neumann, I had intended to deal with the history of computing at the very beginning of the eighties. Although there is a wide range of computing history literature worldwide (most of them in English), there are not any publications dealing with the Hungarian results. As I was one of the first graduates on computing taught by the Pioneers, I am forced to perform research on all materials dealing with the Hungarian achievements in computing, to protect the values of the past as long as it is not too late and also to make the results known!

1. Historical Background

In order to understand the evolution process, to see the efforts and difficulties this country has undergone during the realization of her purposes the main streamline had always been to comprehend the political background. The end of the Second World War resulted with a situation, which had great influence on both the social and the technical evolution. The world was divided into two parts; the government of the Soviet Union directed the Socialist Block. Because of this status the countries belonging to this authority were blocked from the achievement of the other parts of the world, and could produce development and go forward only with difficulties. Hungary belonged also to this block. Though Hungary has had several relations to

Please use the following format when citing this chapter:

Raffai, M., 2006, in IFIP International Federation for Information Processing, Volume 215, History of Computing and Education 2 (HCE2), ed. J. Impagliazzo, (Boston: Springer), pp. 153–165.

western enterprises and professionals, the main line of the research and the innovation was directed by the Soviets up to the end of eighties. But telling the truth at the beginning of the eighties the situation started to turn more liberal, the relations could open wider even towards the western countries and the United States. The experts and some university students could take study tours to foreign countries outside the socialist block, and there was also possibility to purchase computers from all over the world.

2.   Computing Eras

Although the computing evolution process is reckoned from the end of the Second World War, the roots of building automatic working machines in Hungary lead us back to the 18th Century when Farkas KEMPELEN had developed and built a *speaking machine* (1773) and a *chess automat* (1796). Later then Ányos JEDLIK discovered the *theory of self-induction* and the *dynamo principle* (1861). He was also the first who constructed *electromagnetic rotating machine*. But to our great regret Hungary could never become known of their scientific issues; therefore the discovery of dynamo is assigned to Werner Siemens (1867). The next considerable innovative results worth to mention were the *automatic airdefence fire controller* and the *targeting unit* designed by István JUHÁSZ (1925-1939). After a successful show in Sweden (1932) the GAMMA Inc. produced more then 1 000 targeting units and sold in several foreign countries 0, 0.

2.1   The five-era view of computing in Hungary

Looking back to the evolution of Hungarian computing we can distinguish five eras as it is shown on Figure 1. But for the reason that a conference paper is only a frame to prescribe scientific research results, it is impossible to give full details on the discussed theme, so I have to focus only on some very important milestones not losing sight of the inherences. Let us see the main characteristics and the most important events/achievements!

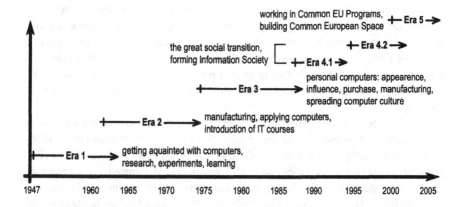

Figure 1. The Five-Era View of Computing Evolution in Hungary

2.2   The beginnings up to 1964

The first epoch can be dated back to 1947-1964. At that time some electrical engineers, mathematicians and economists had started to get acquainted with the principles of electronic calculators and with the new technique. They tried to gather information about the first built computers and they performed uncountable research work and conducted experiments in different laboratories. The research and experimentation work was strongly influenced by John von Neumann's activity; by the first computers having built in the USA[1], by the documentations about the computers having developed in Europe and also in other parts of the world but mainly in the Soviet Union.

The first László KOZMA's calculators were created in 1936. Their improvements such as the quick calculating machine of the telephone exchange elements, the remote controlled solution via telex line or the magnetically wired transfer memory were designed and manufactured at the Antwerpen Bell Telephone Company. Returning back to Hungary in 1943 he continued his research on telephone networks at the Technical University of Budapest where he constructed the first Hungarian Computer named as MESz-I using a digital binary signal-receiving system (1976).

László KALMÁR first started to be interested in the central problems of mathematical logic and set theory, and by 1956, he developed the idea of building a *logical machine.* This machine used logical operations such as conjunction, disjunction and negation for evaluating the true value of formulae containing logical variables. As performing tools, he used an electric circuit made solely switching

---

[1] The first translation about the architecture of ENIAC was published in the Hungarian Scientific Journal in 1947. The article was prepared by Tihamér NEMES, who also developed a mechanical logical machine in 1954.

elements. By the end of the 1950s, an idea came up for constructing a computer, which directly performs a program written in a high level programming language. Kalmár started to work on the principles of such a computer and designed it in great details. Later a research team in Szeged University directed by Dániel MUSZKA improved these designs as a *formula directed computer* (1960). Beside developing logical machine Kalmár and Muszka created *a sensor controlled memory model of conditional reflex* in the form of a ladybug. This artificial animal model is still working.

The efforts to build a Hungarian computer with similar characteristics as the ones constructed in the US - as for instance the ENIAC - were launched in 1956 with the KKCS (Cybernetic Research Group) established as an institute of the MTA (Hungarian Academy of Sciences). The group was designated for building a computer produced by fully Hungarian design, named by B-1 as the smaller version of the ENIAC. However, as the team had lacked the practical experience they asked for the help of the Soviet engineers. Finally, by the common ascent the KKCS had the task to build a middle-sized computer, the *M-3* on the basis of Soviet plans. The head of the development was Bálint DÖMÖLKI (now he is the member of the IFIP General Assembly). The computer that was built in two Years from 1957 could perform 50 operations per minute, its magnetic drum capacity was 1024 words and data input worked with punched tape. This machine used to work first in a newly established Computer Center, and later it had been moved to Szeged University where it had been working until 1968.

Being proud of the achievements of my motherland, it is sorrowful that because of political reasons and/or the lack of any chance to make success and gain acknowledgement some of Hungary's very valuable scientists had felt to be forced to leave Hungary to follow their own scientific aims, which had the result of being known worldwide. Nevertheless, those who remained at home had no possibility to acquire the same world/regional-fame.

2.3   Computers in Work and Manufacturing: Epochs between 1964-1989

After having built the first computers in Hungary, there was a very progressive developing and manufacturing process under way. As the first step in this process it is worth to reference *a computer for supporting data processing and administration* constructed in the Hungarian Telephone Factory by László EDELÉNYI and László LADÓ in 1959. After having built the prototype of EDLA-I the engineers constructed the next generation that used already transistors. The most remarkable element of this computer was the *foil memory* developed by Tibor SZENTIVÁNYI and Ottó BÁNHEGYI, which can be regarded as *the ancestor of the floppy disc*.

In the process of scientific and physical H/S development several Hungarian enterprises played very important role. Not aspiring to entirety we have to mention the VILATI, KFKI, MOM, Videoton, BRG and the SZKI. In these factories computers and peripheral units had been designed and produced. Let us list some mass-produced devices:

1964   Hunor Calculator and EMG-830 computer (EMG Co.)

1969-   Production of TPA-series as the clone of Deck's PDPs: TPA-1100, TPA-1140 (PDP-11 and VAX-11), the IC-based TPA models (following the architecture of the PDP-8 family; all developed and produced by KFKI)

1970-   Production of the R 10 minicomputer (Videoton Co.), disk units and floppy disk drives (MOM)

1982-   Exporting software to the western countries and manufacturing of the first Hungarian developed personal computers (SZKI/Sci-L), and produce of personal computer for schools: the HT school computer (Híradátechnika Co-operative) and the PRIMO home computer (MTA SZTAKI)

Beside using Hungarian made computers and despite of COCOM limit, this small socialist governed country had always found the possibility to procure computers of excellent qualification from different foreign countries. At the end of the sixties some ICL, IBM, Siemens, CDC, BULL, Elliott computers had been purchased and used for the industrial, research and state administration works. As at that time there were not enough well trained technicians and software experts for maintaining and repairing computer failures the computer centers required professional help. In order to satisfy this demand and giving quick aid a nationwide enterprise with county affiliations had been founded (SZÜV).

Clearly understanding the history on computing in Hungary, looking back to the computer manufacturing, it is essential to mention the political and economic changes in 1968 (New Economic Mechanism of Hungary) as the most remarkable program of the East European socialist block. In the same Year on the conference managed by the Soviets the social countries what at that time had belonged to the KGST decided to produce her independently designed computers in country-level cooperation, sharing the manufacturing work of the products. In the frame of the *ESZR named program* the Soviet Union produced the central processing unit of the R-20, R-22 and R-40 computers (semi-compatible with the IBM S 360/40 and 370 Series), Bulgaria was signed to produce the disk units, East Germany to Robotron series, and Hungary to the displays and the R-1x series of mini computers (R-10, R-12 and later R-15).

With putting more and more produced and also purchased computers into use the demand for people who taught and learned computing, who developed applications and even for those who used them on effective way was progressively increasing. During the second half of the 1970s, the number of such professionals was quickly growing. Characterizing the results and the consequences of the second and third epochs in the Hungarian computing it can be stated, that by the end of the eighties the employees and the pupils had got accustomed to the computers, learned how to use them, and they also could already take advantage of their capability.

2.4   The home computer craze

The early 1980s brought significant changes in the attitude and also in usage of computers. The appearance of the personal computers such as ZXs, Commodores, and later the Hungarian made HTs and PRIMOs became more and more popular, and instead of being afraid of the computer centers with closed doors the leaders started to familiarize themselves directly with the PCs. At that time, they thought that the personal computers will solve their business problems, and that they do not need the mainframes anymore. However, this conception was condemned to death because of the lack of solutions for storing and managing the necessary amount of data.

But anyway, the use of home and personal computers no matter if they were purchased or produced, played very important role in computerization in Hungary! As the State Administration introduced an effective supporting system in the school year of 1982-1983 by what the secondary/high schools could get at least one, but in average more school computers, not only the university students could get acquainted with computers and their usage but the computers became friends of every schoolboys and -girls. It is unambiguous that this school computer program was the first step to a paved way for spreading general computer literacy in Hungary!

Beside the school computer program there have been proved results also in hardware and software R+D activity as the scientists and engineers achieved internationally recognized results. The home graphical color display designed by SZTAKI, the ArchiCAD program, the optical character recognition system (Recognita software), the image processing systems, the MPROLOG used for expert systems are the most well known competitive achievements had been sold on the world market.

2.5   The great socio-political transition

The last decade of the 19th Century brought significant changes in Hungary. The most remarkable and important to mention was the secession from the Soviet Union's socialist system and transform into a capitalistic system. It was a great shock not only for the individuals but also for the companies, administration and the different institutes. That means that the decade of the nineties brought significant changes not only in the social economic system but also in computing in Hungary.

The transition concerning to the electronization has began with the MTA's Information Infrastructure Development Program (IIF or I^{2}F program). This program was declared after approving the Hungarian Information Strategy, and served as the basis for modernizing the information infrastructure in the research and development processes and in the academic and university communities. In the scope of this program fighting with realization problems the infrastructure and support services achieved the acceptable technical and organizational level with those of the most European countries. After having deployed the majority of the available network resources between the Years of 1990-1994 the services of eMail and message handling, the file transfer, remote job entry and interactive processing, the bulletins and the distribution lists have been already accessible. In early 1996 already about 80,000 users[2] had access to the internet, we had altogether 17,000 hosts connecting to it, and we had altogether 10 000 email addresses. The IIF program is continuously updated –let the target community be young or elder– it has also newer and newer plan elements in order to give the Hungarian population the possibility to join accessible to the international electronic circulation.

3.   Computer Science in Education

3.1   The pioneer universities

The scientific and engineering background gave a stable base for special courses in the frame of the high education institutes. The first attempts took place in Szeged, from that time revoked as "the cradle of education of computing", where a cybernetic seminar was announced in 1956 followed by a course for program designer mathematicians already in 1959. The mathematicians could get computer skills on the deployed M3 (from 1963), on a Minszk-22 computer (from 1968), and later they became acquainted with the R-40 (from 1975), which was the social semi-clone of the IBM System 370. The "Szeged School" created and directed by professor Kalmár played a definitive role in the Hungarian computerization process. Having excellent conditions (professors and computers) the JATE named University at Szeged was the first one in Hungary, which got afloat courses in the field of Computer science in the Academic Year 1960-1961. Parallel to Szeged the Budapest Technical University (BME) having also a good technical basis with MESZ-1 computer (1958) could also start very early with programmer training.

At the beginning of the sixties a very intensive innovation started in the application of computers not only in business and administration but in the academic sphere as well. Most of the universities received the opportunity to purchase computers in order to apply them in scientific research and education. For the initiatives of Béla KREKÓ the University of Economics (MKKE) deployed the

---

[2] The population of Hungary was at that time around ten million.

Russian made URAL 2 computer in 1960 and started with the course for mathematician planners. Nowadays we call this kind of education as a course on business information science. In some years, the most significant universities joined the education programs in computing. The Eötvös Lóránd University of Sciences (ELTE; 1961), the University of Debrecen (a Poland made Odra 1013 in 1963) also belonged to the pioneer institutes.

From national budgetary reasons it was impossible to support all the universities with expensive computers, the Ministry of Education established a University Computer Center in 1964 in order to serve the administrative and research work of every institutes. Beside the effective settled tasks the Center, named ESZK played a very important role in making the computing culture general.

3.2   The first special courses

During the eighties already many Hungarian enterprises had been deployed and used computers to support data processing, to solve operation research problems and the administrative and management tasks, so there was an urgent need to find highly trained, erudite professionals in the field of computer science. In order to satisfy this demand and to give professional help in installing and serving computers an institute was established in 1972. The SZÁMOK international education center of informatics (later it has changed to SZAMALK) was dedicated to train the professionals on the different field of IT such as system analysts and designers, programmers, operators, technicians etc. In this period more than 6 500 students was graduated and received diploma yearly, and nowadays this institute fulfills the requirements with 20 000 students even from 50 foreign countries.

3.3   Educational process fulfillment

The early courses focused mainly to teach computer programming first in machine code, in Assembly, and later in ALGOL, Fortran and/or Cobol. As these courses specialized mainly for training electrical engineering, mathematics, programming and economic with specialty of applied mathematics they organized trainings to develop practice mainly in writing and testing programs not taking care of the platform-independent logical design of the problem. Despite of having at the first time only elementary knowledge on computing the professors and the assistants obtained skills in teaching. As a result, during the years, excellent experts had been growing up and by the end of the 1980s, the situation was mature enough to introduce special computer courses at every universities and colleges. In the curriculums, we can recover all subjects relating to the different special fields of ICT such as information system design, system and software development methodologies and tools, operation system concepts, computer and network architecture, data modeling and database design, CASE tools, programming languages etc.

By the end of the nineties about 4,000 students graduated yearly in Hungary in the different fields of computing. Most of them got their degree at technical universities and colleges, 45.5% of them had advanced degrees. As it can be seen from the Table 3, most of the graduates are specialized in technological knowledge (almost 75%), 20% in program designer, and only 5.8% in business related areas.

Table 3. The Number of Students Graduated in Computing

Course/Degree	Univ. Degree	College Degree	Sum	Ratio
Technical informatics	970	1990	2960	74.74%
Program designer mathematician	600	170	770	19.44%
Business information systems	130	0	130	3.28%
Programmer w. spec. in economics	100	0	100	2.52%
	1800	2160	**3960**	
	45.50%	54.50%		100%

In the existing higher education structure, the leading universities justify their degrees based on market demands, and add permanently new courses to the existing set. Although these courses show only small differences instead of harmonizing the knowledge structures of the curriculums the different programs competed for the students what caused great divergences in skills, qualification and degrees, and made almost impossible for the students to switch their study field and path, and try to make their institutions more attractive. Some additional factors underlined the urgent need for a wide coordination not only inside the country but even wider in whole Europe:

- The budget is almost 100% government funded, so the degree of financial support strongly depends on the lobbying of the university leaders.
- The existing IT infrastructure of the universities is very heterogeneous.
- The students' skills and experiences in using computers are in most cases limited to personal computers and to access to the internet.
- The level and currency of professors' knowledge is different: there are even institutes without adequately qualified teachers.
- There is great lack of high quality instructors because of low salary.
- The teaching materials (books, supplements, lab manuals, exercises, case studies etc.) are missing or they are outdated.
- The existing dual system makes impossible to move between programs or from one university to another.
- The quality assurance process is exhausted and stops with the accreditation.

3.4   The common European Space on Higher Education

The great breakthrough in higher education system started in 1999 when the education ministers of 29 European countries signed the Bologna Declaration in order to harmonize the European education systems and unify the degrees. The ultimate goal was to create a common European Higher Education Space by 2010 with performing competitiveness in six objectives: (1) Easily readable and comparable degrees, (2) Unified degree structure based on a three-cycle model: Bachelor degree, Master's and Doctoral degrees, both as postgraduate degrees, (3) Establishment of a system of credits - such as in the ECTS system, (4) Increased mobility of students and teachers, (5) promotion of European co-operation in quality assurance with a view to develop comparable criteria and methodologies, and finally (6) promotion of the European dimension in higher education: closer international cooperation and networks; language and cultural education. Although the Bologna Declaration strives to unify the education systems in Europe it clearly stated that in the new system the diversity of cultures, languages and educational traditions remains a priority. The universities keep their independence and autonomy, but also underlined that this new system requires constant support, supervision and adaptation to the continuously changing needs.

Replacing the wide variety of IT courses, the Hungarian Committee recommended three courses as the first level of the two-stage education system (BSc): (1) a course for technical computing, (2) a course for program design, and (3) a course for business information systems. Only these programs and degrees will be introduced in the Hungarian higher education system, of course with some considerations to the regional needs and the traditional specialties of the universities. The new courses have been implemented already in the 2004/2005 academic Year.

4.   The Role of the John von Neumann Computer Society

As the number of computer professionals had been growing by the end of seventies there was and urgent need to establish a forum where the specialists can meet, discuss their problems and results, make the newest issues known, namely change their mind and ideas. After the initiatives in 1968, the *John von Neumann Computer Society* was founded. The main effort was to bring people dealing with and interested in computers together, to give them chance to publish their experimental and scientific results, to organize presentations, and last but not least, to make computing culture generally possessed. As it is defined in its Constitution the main goals of the society are

- to study computer and information technology,
- to inform the specialists about the new scientific theories and results, the hardware/software solutions and the user's experiences, and bring the parties together,

- to promote the development of computer science and diversification of the applications,
- to disseminate applications and help to solve current problems,
- to publish the newest results and to organize exhibitions, programs, conferences, lectures and workshops as well as
- to spread the culture of computing, provide education for computer professionals.

The John von Neumann Computer Society is committed in supporting the activity of scientists and also the company professionals by organizing conferences and running workshops as well as by managing regular events through its technical committees. The Society is responsible for supporting the realization of new ideas in computing and for providing the necessary institutional framework for the IT-innovation. The NJSZT is charged to set up and update the law on data base security, to create the Code of Ethics binding on all members, to play a leading role in the nation-wide dissemination of computer literacy and to form the strategy and to give solutions for forming Information Society in Hungary. As a special importance the Society pays particular attention to the young people's education and to spread the information culture among the civil (non IT-professional) population.

The Society not only represents Hungary in a number of international organizations of high prestige, but takes active part in the work of these establishments. Through these relations, the members of the Society can also benefit from participating in international projects. The NJSZT is a member of the IFIP International Federation for Information Processing, the CEPIS (Council of European Professional Informatics Societies), the EFMI (European Federation for Medical Informatics), the IAPR (International Association for Pattern Recognition), the ECCAI (European Coordinating Committee for Artificial Intelligence), the IEEE (Institute of Electrical and Electronics Engineers) and the ECDL Foundation European Computer Driving License. In the past three decades the Society as an active member of IFIP and IEEE played and is still playing through their active members very important role in forming the IT-based modern society in Hungary.

5. Conclusions

Summarizing the most remarkable occurrences and the achievements of the Hungarian history on computing we can conclude that in spite of the underprivileged political and economic circumstances the computing evolution can be proud of its results even in international acknowledgment.

Mentioning only the most important milestones I have to highlight the achievement of László KOZMA and László KALMÁR, who both later gained the acknowledgement of IEEE Computer Society in the form of *Computer Pioneer Award* in the honour of their academic and technical results (1996).

But being proud of the achievements of my motherland it is sorrowful –that because of political reasons and/or the lack of any chance to make success and gain acknowledgement– some of Hungary's valuable an successful scientists had felt to be forced to leave Hungary to follow their own scientific aims resulted of being known worldwide. But for those who remained at home there was no possibility to acquire the same world/regional-fame.

After having been changed to a competitive and open country of the world in 1989 the computing firms recognized that they could gain profit mainly on assembling hardware from kits (mainly PCs) and from developing software involving added value. The European Union membership (Hungary joined to European Union on the 1st of May 2004) and the activity to form the Information Society forces the Hungarian people to come closer and closer to the developed countries (e.g. USA, JAPAN and EU countries).

Drawing a definitive conclusion from the Hungarian evolution of computing:

> I am convinced that the education system and the spreading countrywide computing culture in Hungary are the most important and most significant strength in the survival process.

References

[1] Kovács, Gy.: Forty Years of the Hungarian Computing and the Volan Elektronika Rt., 1999.
[2] Kovács, Gy.: Old Timers of Computer Technology, International Computer Olympiad, Veszprem, 1996.
[3] Lukács, J.: From the Punched Tape to the Informatics – The TPA History – KFKI Group-MTI, 2003.
[4] Raffai, M.: The Almanac of Computing in Hungary – InForum Publisher, 2000.
[5] Raffai, M.: The Half Century of Computing – Springer Hungarica, 1997. The original title: Az informatika fél évszázada
[6] Szentgyörgyi, Zs.: A Short History of Computing in Hungary – IEEE Hungary Section, Budapest, 1996.; IEEE Annals History of Computing. Vol. 21. No. 3 1999.
[7] Neumann, J.: First Draft of a Report on the EDVAC – Contract between the United States Ordnance Dept. and the University of Pensylvania (No.: W-670 ORD 4926) 1945.

Abbreviations used in the paper

CEPIS:	Council of European Professional Informatics Societies
CoCom:	Coordinating Committee for Multilateral Export Controls of the non-Communist Countries during the Cold War
ECCAI:	European Coordinating Committee for Artificial Intelligence
ECDL:	Foundation European Computer Driving
EFMI:	European Federation for Medical Informatics
ESZR:	Unified System of Computers (USC)
IAPR:	International Association for Pattern Recognition
IEEE:	Institute of Electrical and Electronics Engineers
IEEE:	International
IFIP:	International Federation for Information Processing
JATE:	József Attila University of Sciences
KFKI:	Research Center to investigate problems of Physics
KGST:	Council for Mutual Economic Assistance, the so called COMECON
KKCS:	Research Group for Cybernetics belonging to the Academy of Sciences
MOM:	Hungarian Optical Factory Inc.
MTA:	Hungarian Academy of Sciences
R+D:	Research and Development
SZÁMALK:	Computer Applications and Service Company
SZKB:	Intergovernmental Committee on Computing
SZKI:	Computer Research and Innovation Center
SZTAKI:	Computing and Automation Research Institute as a Cybernetic Research Group, an institute of MTA
SZÜV:	Computational and Data Processing Services Inc.

Revolutionary Development of Computer Education – A Success Story

Nandasara S.T. , Samaranayake V. K. and Yoshiki Mikami

[Nandasara, Samaranayake] University of Colombo School of Computing (UCSC) No. 35, Reid Avenue, Colombo 3, Sri Lanka <{stn, vks}@ucsc.cmb.ac.lk>, http://www.ucsc.cmb.ac.lk [Yoshiki] Nagaoka University of Technology, Nagaoka, Niigata, Japan, <mikami@kjs.nagaokaut.ac.jp>, http://www.nagaokaut.ac.jp

Abstract. The University of Colombo, Sri Lanka has been in the forefront of the "Computer Revolution" in Sri Lanka. It has introduced the teaching of computer programming and applications as early as in 1967, more than a decade before other educational institutions, thereby producing, over the years, a large number of pioneer computer scientists and IT graduates out of students entering the university from a variety of disciplines. They are presently employed as researchers, educators, data processing managers, analyst programmers, software engineers and in many others in the professional field of information technology, not only in Sri Lanka but also in other countries. Established in 1870 as the Ceylon Medical College by the government of that day under the leadership of Governor Sir Hercules Robinson, the University of Colombo could claim to have been associated with higher education for over 130 years. The University has become a center of excellence of international repute that contributes significantly towards national development and human resource development in the field on computer science and information communication technology, particularly in the South and South East Asian Region. This paper presents the milestones of the success story, which did not occur without a policy, plan, leadership, group work, collaboration, and donor support.

1. Introduction

The Democratic Socialist Republic of Sri Lanka, known in short as Sri Lanka is a free, sovereign, and independent democratic socialist republic. It is an island in the Indian Ocean located closer and to the north of the equator. With a total land area of 65,610 sq. km., it spans a length of 445 km. and a breadth of 225 km., encompassing

Please use the following format when citing this chapter:

Nandasara, S.T., Samaranayake, V.K., Mikami, Y., 2006, in IFIP International Federation for Information Processing, Volume 215, History of Computing and Education 2 (HCE2), ed. J. Impagliazzo, (Boston: Springer), pp. 167–180.

beaches, green vegetation, a mountainous mass somewhat south of centre with heights reaching about 2,500 meters, surrounded by broad plains.

Sri Lanka has a population of 19 million of whom the majority is Sinhalese (74%). Other ethnic groups are made up of Sri Lankan Tamils, Indian Tamils, Moors, Malays and Burghers. Although it is a multi-religious country, Buddhists constitute the majority (69%) and other religious groups are Hindus, Muslims and Christians. Sri Lanka has 46% of its population below 20 years. The literacy rate is 91%, one of the highest in Asia. Considering the infant mortality rate and the Life Expectancy etc., Sri Lanka continued to rank high in the world by indicators of Physical Quality of Life.

In terms of various e-readiness criteria, Sri Lanka is also ranked higher than neighboring Asian countries in spite of her relatively low penetration of computers, internet and other telecommunication media. According to the United Nations Report on e-Government Benchmarking [1], Sri Lanka is ranked at the eleventh among twenty-three countries in East/Southeast/South Asia region. Especially she marked a high ranking in Human capital index and E-Participation index.

Table 1. UNPAN's E-Government and E-Participation Index 2003

Country	E-Government Readiness				E-Participation	
	Index 2003	Web measure	Telecom	Human capital	Country	Index 2003
Singapore	0.746	0.703	0.666	0.87	Philippines	0.672
Korea	0.744	0.607	0.675	0.95	Korea	0.483
Japan	0.693	0.524	0.626	0.93	Singapore	0.466
Philippines	0.574	0.747	0.064	0.91	Japan	0.431
Brunei	0.549	0.266	0.250	0.86	Mongolia	0.379
Malaysia	0.524	0.480	0.292	0.80	**Sri Lanka**	**0.293**
Thailand	0.446	0.380	0.117	0.84	Indonesia	0.259
Indonesia	0.422	0.432	0.045	0.79	India	0.259
China	0.416	0.332	0.116	0.80	Pakistan	0.155
Maldives	0.410	0.262	0.069	0.90	Nepal	0.138
Sri Lanka	**0.385**	**0.279**	**0.036**	**0.84**	Cambodia	0.138
India	0.373	0.522	0.027	0.57	Malaysia	0.121
Vietnam	0.357	0.183	0.048	0.84	Thailand	0.103
Mongolia	0.343	0.140	0.040	0.85	China	0.069
Myanmar	0.280	0.087	0.003	0.75	Maldives	0.034
Nepal	0.268	0.319	0.006	0.48	Vietnam	0.017
Cambodia	0.264	0.127	0.004	0.66	Brunei	0.017
PNG	0.250	0.170	0.031	0.55	Bhutan	0.017
Pakistan	0.247	0.297	0.026	0.42	Bangladesh	0.017
Lao	0.192	0.048	0.007	0.52	PNG	0
Bangladesh	0.165	0.092	0.004	0.40	Myanmar	0
Bhutan	0.157	0.035	0.015	0.42	Lao	0
DPRK	0	0	0.011	0	DPRK	0

Source: UNPAN, e-Government Benchmarking Report 2003.

Another survey [2] conducted by regional association of information processing societies in the region, SEARCC (Southeast Asia Regional Computer Confederation), shows that age cohort of IT professionals over 40 occupies 15% in Sri Lanka (see Fig. 1 & 2). This percentage is the second largest next only to Japan among eight countries surveyed. It means that IT manpower training started since as early as the 1980s at substantial degree in Sri Lanka. Later in this paper, we reveal that this cohort corresponds to those who were trained under certificate courses offered by the University of Colombo during 80's. Actually, most of the senior managers in the IT Industry today had gone through training programs introduced during 1980s. Moreover, graduate level professionals trained later through 1990s were added to the pool of IT professionals.

In this article, authors try to describe historical process of IT education in this country. They also try to show how higher education sector has been instrumental in this process.

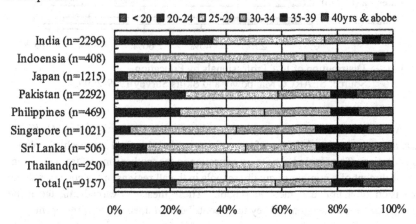

Fig. 1. Distribution of ICT Professionals by Age Group

2. Computing and Computer Education at the University of Colombo

2.1 Background: Sri Lanka - The land of free education

Before going to the recent development of computer education in Sri Lanka, the paper goes back to the traditions of education in the country. The world's first museum and library were built in Sri Lanka 2200 years ago. The museum housed the parts of the ship that brought the *Bodhi* sapling to Sri Lanka from India in 3rd century B.C. In 1805, after the British invasion, education system was developed based on the British System and University of Colombo established in the year 1870, as the Ceylon Medical College.

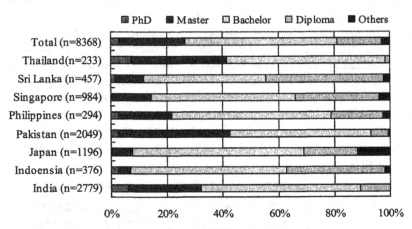

Fig. 2. Distribution of ICT Professionals by Education
Source: SEARCC Manpower and Skills Survey 1999-2000

A few years before receiving independence from the British, Hon. *C. W. W. Kannangara*, the then Minister of Education introduced several far-reaching policies in education. They included primary education in the mother tongue, free education, establishment of a number of quality schools in the all regions of the country and the provision of a mid day meal in school. These measures earned him the name "Father of Free Education". They have contributed immensely towards opening up higher education to the masses as opposed to the elite that benefited until then.

2.2   Teaching FORTRAN without computers

Teaching of computer programming and the use of computer applications for research at the University of Colombo commenced in 1967.   The ICL 1901 computer at the State Engineering Corporation was used free of charge thanks to the encouragement given by their management towards the introduction of computing at the Universities in Sri Lanka. A few years later in 1971, the Department of Census and Statistics allowed the University free computer time on their IBM 360/25. The fact that these installations were close to the University of Colombo, the interest of both organizations in statistical and scientific applications helped the university researchers to make very good use of this invaluable gesture.

According to the development plan of the Faculty of Science [3] introduced in 1967, first teaching was restricted to FORTRAN programming to staff and students as an extra curricular activity. However, within a few years a combined course in Computer Programming and Numerical Methods was introduced as a paper in Applied Mathematics for the general degree. A single course unit in Computer Programming was introduced in the late seventies. The number of courses offered increased in late 1970's and the course unit system operating at the University of Colombo made it possible to offer a range of third year degree options. After the study on the introduction of Computer Studies submitted to the Ministry of Higher Education by Prof. Reeves (*Reeves, C. M.* [6]), Computer programming and Applications became a part of most postgraduate and undergraduate courses in the country.

During the initial stage of this activity, the practical sessions were not available for the students due to the non-availability of computer(s) at the University of Colombo. However, the students who were keen to take the course unit in FORTRAN programming had to imagine the machine's internal functionality and code accordingly to solve problems only on the paper and then transferred to punched cards and sent to the computer elsewhere. One of the significant achievements in computing history in Sri Lanka noted here; the introduction of the Glossary of Technical Terms for Mathematics and Computing [7] for Sinhala & Tamil languages in 1956 is unforgettable.

The above programmes were initiated by the Mathematics Department of the University of Colombo, which was at that time developing the field of Applied Statistics. A Statistical Unit that was established in 1968 at the request of the Department of Mathematics, the Department of Geography, and the Faculty of Medicine did not survive long, due manly to the loss of several key staff members to overseas universities. However, thanks to the support received from the staff of the Department of Applied Statistics of the University of Reading, UK with British funding, the Statistical Unit was revived. Reading was involved in a link arrangement since 1974 and helped the Statistical Unit to progress steadily to become a National Center for Statistical Research, Teaching and Consultancy.

2.3   Computer Programming Course Units for non-science students

Under the Higher Education Reforms that took place in 1972 (*Prof. Jayarthne* Report), the Department of Mathematics and the Statistical Unit of the University of Colombo made the remarkable attempt to initiate new course units in Mathematics, Statistics and FORTRAN Programming for Faculty of Art degree students following the newly introduced Special Degree in Development Studies. 30 students were selected among 210 reading for the above degree and given the opportunity to follow a special degree stream that was specially designed and managed by the

Department of Mathematics of the University of Colombo. This combination of art and computing education is a unique and visionary attempt ever seen.

2.4   First computer of the University of Colombo

The requirement of the Statistical Unit of the University of Colombo in the form of computing support for research, consultancy and teaching resulted in a substantial increase on the computing field. Soon thereafter, it was felt that the Statistical Unit should have its own computer for teaching and consultancy in addition to using the free computer time available for research at the Department of Census and Statistics as indicated earlier. An HP9825 desktop microcomputer (HP claimed that this is a Calculator) was obtained under the link arrangement with British Government Assistance in 1977. This introduced in-house computing at the University of Colombo and a small computer center was established in the same year. Unfortunately, difficulties arising out of the non-availability of local servicing facilities made this excellent machine (at that time) rather unpredictable. In 1978, the HP9825 microcomputer was send back to UK for repairs, and it was lost in the process and was never seen again. In 1980, a serious attempt [4] was made to fulfill the need for computing power with a modern computer, capable of statistical work and therefore having a configuration allowing the implementation of some of the well-known statistical packages. The result was the purchase of a Data General Eclipse S/140 mini computer with time sharing, multi user interactive capabilities together with adequate disc storage (20 MB), RAM (128 KB) and a magnetic tape drive with three terminals. The purchase was made possible by the pooling of funds from Netherlands Universities Foundation for International Cooperation (NUFFIC), University Grants Commission (UGC) and the Equipment Vote of the Faculty of Science of the University of Colombo. Authors wish to record our appreciation of this timely assistance to introduce a multi-user, multitasking computer to the University of Colombo. One major objective in selecting the particular computer configuration was the implementation of third party software packages used worldwide such as GLIM, MINITAB and SPSS which have been implemented on these machines.

Up to the early seventies, teaching was confined to one member of staff. In the late seventies, more were available and the support staff recruited for the Statistical Unit were able to double up as teachers of computing. Some of the academic staff who had obtained their postgraduate degree in statistics in overseas also devoted a considerable amount of their efforts towards matters relating to computer applications [5].

2.5   Computers go public

One of the main demarcation points of history of computing in Sri Lanka was the introduction of computers for assisting the Commissioner of Elections for processing and telecasting results for the National Presidential Election held in November 1982. In late 1981, thanks to the Reading-Colombo Link programme, Colombo made a request to Overseas Development Assistance (ODA), UK for assistance to purchase a few BBC microcomputers, due to be released to the market in 1982. When they did arrive, in October 1982, this remarkable microcomputer was an immediate success and the Compute Center received much publicity among the public by their computer display that enabled the telecast of the 1982 Presidential Elections. This saw the use of computers to process election results and the release of results as graphics displays for telecasting. For this, floppy disk drives for the BBC microcomputer were used even before they were introduced to the UK market. This process of release of results of every national election has continued without a single break thereafter, with technological improvement at every stage. In addition, this was the one of the early attempt to introduce local language processing in the country.

The BBC microcomputer has been exploited for use as a tool for teaching statistics, programming and for research in addition to its value as an aid for promoting computer literacy. In 1983, ODA, UK granted GBP 10,000/- in addition to the GBP 3,000/- given in 1982 and the UGC grant for microcomputers was used together with this grant to establish a networked laboratory of 13 BBC microcomputers and also purchase several stand alone BBC microcomputers with disc drives, second processors and other peripherals and software.

2.6   First ever computer courses for public and government employee

With high publicity received by the University of Colombo due to the release of the Presidential Election results, the Computer Center was able to inaugurate a Certificate Course in Computer Applications for the general public, to be held during week ends, not interfering with the undergraduate courses. These courses were primarily meant for the employed to gain knowledge of computer applications rather than to those wanting to learn computer programming for employment. Furthermore, preference was given to those in the scientific and educational sectors. Literacy courses were conducted for students of the Institute of Workers' Education of the University of Colombo and proved to be a success. This success is reflected in Fig.2 where the large number of high ranking IT professional in the industry are holding diplomas and it is the highest among region.

As highlighted by the National Computer Policy for Sri Lanka [8], University of Colombo realized an important aspect of the its Computer Center's extension work through a Computer Literacy programme in Schools. In early 1983, the Ministry of Education introduced Computer Assisted Education to three schools as a pilot project and the University of Colombo helped the Ministry in launching its Computer Education Programme through teacher training. Managing the selection and training of the Sri Lankan team to the International Olympiad in Informatics (IOI) where during the period of participation since 1992, 3 gold, 5 silver and 14 bronze medals have been won. The IOI of 2004 in Greece saw an excellent performance from the Sri Lankan team which won one gold and three bronze medals coming fifth among Asian countries.

While developing its computing facilities and skills of its staff in computing, the University of Colombo also took steps to encourage actively the use of computers in scientific research. A computer exhibition on "Computers for Scientific Research" was held by the Computer Center during Annual sessions of the Sri Lanka Association for the Advancement of Science (SLAAS) in December 1982 and several seminars, training sessions etc. have been held since then. The large number of computers and applications exhibited at the Natural Resources, Energy and Science Authority of Sri Lanka (NARESA) sponsored "National Exhibition on Science and Technology" held in 1985 clearly indicated the advances made by then.

Due to the demand increased, the Data General Mini Computer was upgraded to have 15 terminal and later facilities at the Computer Center was upgraded with an additional Data General MV2000 with 1MB RAM and AOS/VS operating system. There were by then three microcomputer laboratories of BBC microcomputers and accessories at Colombo University. The IBM-PC and WANG-PC computers were in heavy demand. A Kaypro 2 received as a gift, and the RadioShack TRS80-16 were used for student projects as well as consultancy work.

The staff of the Computer Center have succeeded in making the BBC a terminal for the Data General Mini Computer thus making available a versatile and low cost terminal as well as a device for data transfer between two computer systems. "INSTAT", a Statistical Package for the BBC microcomputer, developed with the collaboration of the University of Reading in the UK, was released to the overseas market [9].

2.7   Early regional training activities

The University of Colombo was involved with the organisation of the Asian Regional College on Microprocessor in June 1984 supported by the International Centre for Theoretical Physics, Trieste, Italy and co-sponsored by the UGC and The Council for Information Technology (CINTEC). This benefited 40 foreign and 32 Sri Lankan participants. A sum of US$ 120,000/- was raised for the Collage. Of this US$10,000/- was funds earmarked for the University of Colombo by UNESCO. This resulted in a valuable set of books being made available for the Library. Another international course was supported by the University of Reading and cosponsored by the Computer Center and the Statistical Unit in December 1984, on "Statistics in Agriculture", with a heavy bias towards computer use in agriculture. Fourteen foreign and ten local participants took part and they were supported by several international and national organizations including the Agrarian Research and Training Centre, Sri Lanka. This was repeated in 1985 for 30 local participants. In 1984, the Computer Center helped the British Council and the Ministry of Education to conduct two-week courses on "Computer Education" for school teachers and curriculum developers. All these activities have provided valuable experience to the staff and have also contributed significantly towards promoting the development of computer applications in the country.

2.8 Staff exchange programmes and postgraduate training

British Assistance for Statistics provided for staff training in Computing too through the link with the University of Reading, UK. The UGC initiative following the Reeves Report [6] also provided training in Computing at the University of Wales, UK. Subsequent support from the UNDP helped continue this trend. Many staff members returned with a Diploma, M.Sc., M.Phil., and PhD. in Computer Science during 80's and 90's as a result of these initiatives. Many received training in Japan too. Although there was some staff loss to the private sector or overseas, new blood was pumped into the Center. Incentives in the form of job satisfaction, additional remuneration received from extension courses and consultancy work, and an ever improving range of available hardware and software and good work environment, together with challenging projects made many stay, in spite of much better job prospects elsewhere.

2.9 Collaborative research activities

A collaborative research project on crop and climate data between the University of Colombo and the University Reading resulted in a data base being developed at Colombo University and many local and overseas groups and Research Institutes were able to obtain data for their research. This Crop and Climate Database project computerised the range of daily climate data, including temperature, rain, wind etc. collected from 100 metrological stations established around the island for the past 100 years.   This, together with the consultancy work done in the areas of Agriculture, Health and Education made the Computer Center a very useful resource in Sri Lanka. It developed expertise in the packages INFORMIX, SAS and SPSS and became the only expert group for such packages in the county at that time [13][14].

The Collaborative work with Research Institutes such as the Rubber Research Institute (RRI), Tea Research Institute (TRI), Coconut Research Institute (CRI) and

Meteorology Department grew during early 1980's with advice given on computing including evaluation of needs and assistance in purchasing of computer equipment and also training.

2.10 Establishment of a fully pledged academic department for computing

In January 1985, the existing Department of Mathematics split into two departments [10]; one remained as the Mathematics Department and a new Department of Statistics and Computer Science (DSCS) was established. It was only in 1986 that the formal separation took place as the separation of activities was not a simple exercise.

The Department of Computer Science (DCS) of the University of Colombo was established in year 2001 by splitting the Department of Statistics and Computer Science (DSCS), which functioned since 1985 as part of the Faculty of Science of the University of Colombo. While the DCS was responsible for undergraduate and postgraduate training in Computer Science, the Department of Statistics (DS) was responsible for statistical education in both undergraduate and postgraduate education. Although the University of Colombo, its first batch of students specializing in Computer Science and obtaining the B.Sc special degree graduated in 1992, the first such group in Sri Lanka.

2.11 Establishment of Institute of Computer Technology (ICT)

In early 1984, the University of Colombo Computer Center, while consolidating its position as leading computer installation and consultancy service, worked on plans for the establishment of an Institute of Computer Technology (ICT) with the assistance of the Japanese Government [11][12].

An initiative of CINTEC, the University of Colombo, and the UGC resulted in the establishment of the Institute of Computer Technology (ICT) at the University of Colombo in 1987 as an Institute established under the Universities Act [15]. The ICT was provided with the largest mainframe computer system in the country then with other peripherals and staff training under Project Type Technical Co-operation of the Japan International Cooperation Agency (JICA), Government of Japan. The ICT was to conduct Postgraduate Training programs to produce Analyst Programmers for the country. This was a result of the Japanese Mission's visits to the Computer Center of the University of Colombo in April 1984 and in February 1986 in relation to the proposed Institute and very hard negotiations to win from among several proposals from other countries. Finally, the University of Colombo was able to convince the Japanese Mission as well as the Government of Japan, the need of such institution. This was a milestone of success of computer education in Sri Lanka.

2.12 Third country training programmes

The Japanese assistance provided to the ICT resulted in building sufficient capacity both in human resources and in facilities. The donor having seeing the satisfactory completion of this phase moved on to the next where the ICT was expected to use these resources to provide training for those from other (Third) countries through the Third Country Training Programme (TCTP). Accordingly, from 1993 to 1998 a TCTP in Structured Systems Analysis and Design was held annually for 20 participants from 15 Asian countries. On successful completion of this program, a second TCTP in Information Systems Engineering was conducted from 1998 to 2002 for 20 participants each from 18 Asian, Far East and African countries. This programme continues up to today and has trained more than three hundred participants. In 1998, the ICT received the JICA President's Award for the Best Regional Training Center among its 60 JICA assisted countries. This excellent concept of south - south cooperation was later introduced to Sida, the Swedish international development agency who sponsored a TCTP in the Design, Installation, Management and Maintenance of Network Systems for twenty participants from Asian, African and even Latin American Countries for the last few years.

2.13 Year 2000 and beyond

The developments in Computing indicated above resulted in the University of Colombo becoming a Centre of Excellence by the dawn of the new millennium. Several landmark events took place thereafter enabling the consolidation of the status it had built up in the last three decades of the 20th Century.

The ever increasing demand for IT graduates both globally and locally combined with the inadequacy of the state sponsored free education system prompted the staff of the ICT to launch a very innovative external degree program for the Bachelor of Information Technology Degree (www.bit.lk) This was an instant success with over 5000 students registering for year one in 2000. The ICT developed the curriculum and was to hold the examinations while the University of Colombo was to award the degree. The private sector was to provide the training as the students were registered as external and not internal students. This was supplemented by web based course details, quizzes, model papers and answers and also by a weekly TV programme. This was an excellent example of Public Private Partnership with over 50 private institutions preparing students.

In 2002, the ICT and the DCS merged to form the University of Colombo School of Computing, UCSC, as a centre of higher learning affiliated to the University of Colombo with a fair amount of financial and administrative autonomy [16]. This merger helped to bring together over 50 academic staff with around 15

Ph.d's and a large number of postgraduate qualified IT specialists and also all the resources of the two institutions under a single entity (www.ucsc.cmb.ac.lk). The UCSC has three academic departments and five centres. It is now enjoying the status of being the best IT centre for higher education in the country with intake of 240 students annually for its B.Sc (Computer Science) and B.ICT degree programs, over 2000 annually for its external degree BIT and 200 annually for its three M.Sc programs in Advanced Computing, Computer Science and IT and many extension courses as well as consultancy, research and development activities. In addition, the UCSC conducts third country training programs with funding from Japan and Sweden and has research collaboration with several international research groups. Examples are the IDRC funded PAN localisation project and the Pandora Distance Learning project, both involving regional cooperation. UCSC has recently established an Advanced Digital Media Technology Centre (ADMTC) with JICA assistance, National e-Learning Centre with Swedish government support and the BIT program will be converted into an e-Learning based e-BIT with EU support and collaboration with Swedish and Dutch universities. UCSC has a reputation for producing excellent graduates for the fast developing IT industry in the country which includes international software leaders who have outsourcing facilities locally.

3.   Conclusion

Sri Lanka has throughout its recorded history given priority to human development and in particular towards education. This has resulted in a high quality of life even though pure economic indicators make the country one that is still developing. In the field of computing, which was recognized as important even in the late sixties, a strategy of sharing whatever knowledge one had without awaiting expensive resources has shown results [17, 18, & 19]. Another aspect was the policy of computers for all ages, professions and for the society at large. The development of Computer education has been well planned taking into account not only the currently available technology but also future trends as envisaged by the policy makers. This included the provision of resources both human and material and the strategic and optimum utilization of limited donor assistance. These initial steps have quite rightly led to international recognition and regional collaboration.

Today, the UCSC continues to grow from strength to strength, proving beyond doubt, the benefits of the initial planning and positive approach of the successive development phases of its predecessor institutions and their members. Its stature as a centre of international repute and success is also a strength to the many donors who have assisted in the early development efforts who can now see positive results from their investments in development.

Acknowledgements

The authors have relied on their vast experience in this area and on the many activities they have engaged in with a multitude of others who took part at various stages in the events recorded in this paper. Authors wish to thank all those who collaborated and participated in the many events over the past few decades. The contribution made by the authorities of the University of Colombo, and its predecessors; the ICT, DSCS, DCS, the Computing Services Centre, Department of Statistics and the Department of Mathematics is also gratefully acknowledged.

References

[1] UNPAN, Report on e-Government Benchmarking, (2003)
[2] Report on the Regional ICT Manpower and Skills Survey 1999-2000, Southeast Asia Regional Computer Confederation (SEARCC).
[3] Development Plan of the Faculty of Science, University of Colombo, (1975).
[4] Proposal for the purchase of a mini computer for the University of Colombo, (1980).
[5] Samaranayake, V. K., A Brief Note on the Activities and Future Plans of the University of Colombo on the Development of Computer Applications in Science, Proceeding of the Third National Computer Seminar, Computer Society of Sri Lanka, (1982).
[6] Reeves, C. M., On the Introduction of Computer Science in to Degree Studies in Sri Lanka – A report to the Ministry of Higher Education, (1983).
[7] Glossary of Technical Terms, Dept. of Educational Publication, Government Press, Sri Lanka, (1956).
[8] A National Computer Policy for Sri Lanka – Report of the special working committee of the Natural Resources, Energy and Science Authority of Sri Lanka, (1983).
[9] Stern, R. D., Statistical Software on Microcomputers, Proceeding of the Annual Sessions of the Computer Society of Sri Lanka, (1984)
[10] Proposal for the Establishment of a Computer Centre, A Department of Computer Science and Statistics and the commencement of a Postgraduate Diploma Courses in Computer Science submitted to the University Grants Commission, University of Colombo, Sri Lanka, (1984).
[11] A Proposal for the Establishment of an Institute of Computer Technology with the assistance from the Japanese Government, (1982), Revised Versions (1983 & 1985).
[12] Samaranayake, V. K., Report of the visit to Singapore and Japan in connection with the Institute of Computer Technology Project, (1984).
[13] Stern, R. D., Burn, R., Abeysekera, S., Nandasara, S. T., Samaranayake, V. K., Kodikara, N. D., "The Need for Good Statistical Software on Microcomputers for Agricultural Research in Sri Lanka", Microcomputers for Development: Issues and Policy. (1985).
[14] Nandasara, S. T., Kusuma A. Gunawardena, Liyanage, W. M., "Data Analysis: Then and Now", Proceedings of the Annual Sessions of the Sri Lanka Association for the Advancement of Science. (1987).
[15] Ordinance establishing the Institute of Computer Technology, under the Universities Act (1987).

[16] Ordinance establishing the University of Colombo School of Computing, under the Universities Act (2000).

[17] Samaranayake V. K., "An Overview of Human Resources - needs, availability and plans for the future". Proceedings of the 21st National IT Conference, Colombo, Sri Lanka, (2002).

[18] Samaranayake V. K., "Fifty Years of Information Technology" A chapter in "Fifty Years of Sri Lanka's Independence - A Socio - Economic Review." Ed. A.V. de S. Indraratne Colombo, (1998).

[19] Samaranayake, V. K., "Five Decades of Education at Reid Avenue: Some Personal Reflections, University of Colombo Review (to be published in the University of Colombo Review) (2006).

The First Decade of Computer Science in Argentina

Pablo Miguel Jacovkis

*Departamento de Computación and Instituto de Cálculo, Facultad de Ciencias Exactas y
Naturales, Universidad de Buenos Aires, Ciudad Universitaria, 1428 Buenos Aires
<jacovkis@dc.uba.ar>, http://www.dc.uba.ar/people/profesores/jacovkis/homepage.html*

Abstract. Computer science has a curious history in Argentina: it began late (more than ten
years later than in USA), had a ten-year span of flowering, was completely destroyed by the
military dictatorship in 1966 and, disregarding some advances in small universities in the
1970s, began to weakly revive in 1983. In this article we shall analyze the ten-years long
(1956-1966) "golden age" of computer science in Argentina, that is imbedded into a "golden
age" of Argentinean universities.

1. Introduction

For reasons that Babini [2] clearly explains, Argentina entered the computer age
with a considerable delay. In fact, Argentina entered the computer age after Perón's
fall, in 1955, that is, one decade after the electronic "protocomputer" ENIAC began
to function [7]. This decade of delay had, unfortunately, political causes. The
policy of maximum possible autarchy during almost all the years of the first Perón
administration (1946-1955), plus his mistrust vis-à-vis the universities, which he
considered essentially unfriendly to his government (and from where he fired as
many opponents as he could), caused a considerable delay in many areas, and
therefore a tremendous damage. With regard to informatics no benefit can be
ascribed to Perón's policies; on the contrary, the cost due to the theoretical and
commercial delay was extremely high. During Perón administration, as Babini
indicates in his book, the most advanced equipment consisted of tabulators based on
punched cards. There was no research in informatics, and very few people realized
what was happening abroad.

Please use the following format when citing this chapter:

Jacovkis, P.M., 2006, in IFIP International Federation for Information Processing, Volume 215, History of Computing and
Education 2 (HCE2), ed. J. Impagliazzo, (Boston: Springer), pp. 181–191.

2.   The Historic Context 1955-1966

Only after Perón's fall, in September 1955, due to a military coup d'état, can we speak about development of informatics in Argentina. On the one hand, it was easier to import foreign equipment, so that the eventual arrival of computers to Argentina was facilitated. On the other hand, autonomy was guaranteed to the national universities, and in some of them a group of intellectuals that considered science and technology extremely important for any project of development in Argentina acquired a strong influence; in particular, this group was particularly significant at the University of Buenos Aires, the most important one. The political climate during almost all the period 1955-1966 was very curious: a grave and not solved political crisis originated in the proscription of the Peronist Party. Consequently, a lack of legitimacy of the constitutional authorities (Presidents Arturo Frondizi, 1958-1962, and Arturo Illia, 1963-1966; President José María Guido administration, 1962-1963, was in fact a military government, that did not changed anything, in which Guido was a puppet). Such was the framework under which this group of intellectuals exerted their strong influence, above all in the University of Buenos Aires, and partially replaced the old guard of conservative professors.   These intellectuals considered that universities had a social responsibility and had to be instrumental to the national development and to the transformation from a developing to a developed country; in a sense, their ideas were based on an almost naïve belief in the power of science and technology, "soft" as well as "hard", as a tool for development. They created university degrees in political economy, sociology and psychology (areas that the military and the conservatives suspected of "communism"); they created an university publishing house that during many years was the most important in Latin America. In addition, they supported all kind of science and technology and, of course, they were interested in computer science and the fascinating perspectives that this science seemed to offer.

Therefore, during the almost eleven years that the university was governed autonomously, a peculiar situation happened in which a large group of people in different universities, and specially in the School of Science of the University of Buenos Aires, with an unusual enthusiasm, contributed to transform the university structures. They became modern and democratic centers for teaching and research, under the constant menace of a governmental intervention, given that this project was considered communist by many powerful political actors, among them of course the Army.

The menace materialized one month after the coup d'état that, on June 28, 1966, overthrew President Illia and replaced him by a military dictator, General Juan Carlos Onganía: on July 29, 1966, the government revoked the autonomy of the universities. Some hours later, the Police entered violently into the School of Science of the University of Buenos Aires, and savagely struck students, graduates and faculty, in a brutal incident that from then on was called "the night of the long sticks" [10]. And this was the end of the "golden decade" of the Argentinean universities (anyway, let us not forget that the transformation of the Universities was partial, at most: the Dean of the School of Law of the University of Buenos Aires was appointed Justice of the Supreme Court by General Onganía).

3. Computer Science During the Period 1955-1966

The "golden decade" 1956-1966 was witness of an impressive development in the School of Sciences of the University of Buenos Aires. The development began in 1955 with the new Dean José Babini, during whose administration the departmental organization of the School was implemented, full-time professors were appointed and scientific research was stimulated, and continued under the administration of Rolando Víctor García, Dean between 1957 and 1966. The outstanding personality and leadership of García was extremely important in overcoming the permanent budgetary and bureaucratic difficulties of state institutions (see for instance [6]). García strongly supported the decision of the University, in 1957, of constructing a new building on the new University Campus. They would move there the School of Sciences, as part of an ambitious plan to bring the Schools - or, at least, several of them - to that campus (incidentally, the plan was only partially completed: besides the School of Sciences only the School of Architecture and a Department of the School of Engineering eventually moved to the Campus). In addition, here we must mention García's Deputy Dean, Manuel Sadosky.

Among all the figures that contributed to the creation and development of computer science in Argentina Manuel Sadosky clearly stands out. When the University of Buenos Aires began its reorganization after Perón's fall in 1955, Sadosky joined the School of Sciences as a Professor at the Department of Mathematics (he was very soon elected Deputy Dean of the School), and began to think in the development of applied mathematics. In those times, most scientists considered the computer only as a device with which calculations with many numbers could be done very fast (what, of course, is true) and so as a powerful tool for helping other sciences, and particularly applied mathematics. Sadosky could easily intercommunicate with the scientists: he was an applied mathematician himself (a *rara avis* in Argentina, then and perhaps now) who had realized the eventual power of computers. He had fellowships in France and Italy at the end of the 1940s and he had written a book on numerical analysis [13] (a very successful book that only became obsolete when Argentinean scientists began to use massively computers in the 1960s: Sadosky wrote his book before the introduction of computers in Argentina). Sadosky decided then to carry out three fundamental projects: to obtain a computer for the School, to create an institute of applied mathematics, as an institutional "base" for using the computer, and to create a computer science degree.

The institute, named "Instituto de Cálculo", began to work in 1960, and was definitively approved by the High Council of the University of Buenos Aires in 1962, as the first institute in agreement with the new regulations of the University. Sadosky was its Director since the beginnings until the 1966 coup, and he was helped by his main collaborator, the mathematician Rebeca Guber. A detailed description of the first years of the Instituto del Cálculo may be consulted in the interview to Sadosky [14]; a semblance of his personality may be seen in [3]. The Institute, although associated with the Department of Mathematics, was a "de facto" Department of Computer Sciences, because all research and development in computer science in Buenos Aires was carried out there; besides the senior researchers, many graduate and undergraduate students worked day and night at the Instituto, with an amazing enthusiasm, in many different projects, all original and challenging.

With regard to the computer, it is interesting to see the process that finished with its acquisition. Firstly, it was necessary to decide whether the computer should be bought (abroad) or should be constructed in our country. In fact, both ideas were implemented, with different results: at the School of Engineering of the University of Buenos Aires, there was a project, directed by Humberto Ciancaglini, to build a computer, named CEFIBA (Electronic Computer of the School of Engineering). The computer was built between 1958 and 1962 and, in spite of the tremendously unfavorable circumstances, (see [2]), the project was useful to train the participants. CEFIBA was above all an ambitious exercise, discontinued after the 1966 coup d'état.

On the other hand, the School of Sciences decided to buy a computer. A committee was formed, whose members were Sadosky, Alberto González Domínguez and Simón Altman (Altman, who had worked at Oxford University, was the only one that had experience with computers), that prepared the international tender. There were bids from four firms, namely IBM, Remington and Philco from USA and Ferranti from UK. Once it was decided that the computer to be bought was the Mercury II from Ferranti (for which a group of scientists of the University of Manchester had created a programming language, Autocode, easy to learn and friendly for scientific applications), a grant was requested to the University of Buenos Aires and to the recently created National Council for Science, to pay for the £152,099 purchase. The fact that Rolando García was the Deputy President of the National Council of Science helped to convince its Board of Directors to approve a grant at the end of 1958. Specifically, as García tells [6], the President of the Council, Bernardo Houssay, was opposed to the purchase (he said that he, Houssay, had won the Nobel Prize in spite of not having tools so expensive) and it was necessary that, according to García's strategy, other member of the Board, Eduardo Braun Menéndez, convinced Houssay not to assist to the meeting of the Board in which the grant was assigned. After that, all was made with incredible precision:

the building where the computer would be installed at the University Campus was under construction, and part of it should be ready when the computer arrived, that is, in January, 1961. Meanwhile, the future analysts and programmers were trained, an engineer, the late Oscar Matiussi, was sent during one year to the University of Manchester in 1960 to acquire experience in maintaining the computer and other engineer, Jonas Paiuk, spent three months in Manchester in Ferranti's laboratories. When the computer began to be installed, Professor Cicely Popplewell (who had worked with Alan Turing, with whom her relationship was never easy, see [8]) came from Manchester to complete the training of the local staff. Soon programmers from several national universities (and also programmers from the Uruguayan University of the Republic, at Montevideo) and from different institutes of research were trained. From then on, and till 1966, the computer was intensely used by the groups of research of the Instituto de Cálculo (in mathematical economy, operations research, statistics, applied mechanics, numerical analysis, programming systems and computational linguistics, groups directed respectively by Oscar Varsavsky, Julián Aráoz, Sigfrido Mazza, Mario Gradowczyk, Pedro Zadunaisky, Wilfred Durán and Eugenia Fisher), by other groups of researchers of the School of Sciences and other universities and scientific institutes and by external users to which fees were charged, thanks to which researches and graduate students could be funded. After the 1966 coup d'état all its staff (around one hundred people) resigned, and the Institute disappeared during more than twenty years.

The concept of "powerful tool" has evolved: Ferranti Mercury II had a memory of 1024 40-bits words, an auxiliary memory initially composed of 16,384 words, data input through punched paper tape, and data output through punched paper tape and teletype; later on, Paiuk constructed a converter from punched cards to punched paper tape, and a facility was connected to graph curves ([2] describes carefully the technical characteristics of this computer and others that were installed in those years). The computer needed also a large room specially prepared and air-conditioned. The comparison with the current standard personal computers seems funny. Moreover, of course a short visit to the web pages of manufacturers - and above all manufacturers of supercomputers - gives us a much more impressive image of the technological advance, without taking into account innumerable options of current computers that the Mercury had not.

The third foundational project on computing in Argentina, also carried on by Sadosky, was the creation of the computer science degree (computador científico), presented to the Directive Council of the School of Sciences in 1962, and approved definitively by the High Council of the University in 1963. The computer science program - the first offered in the country - was shorter than the other traditional ("licenciado") programs (that were five years long); its objective was to educate "scientists assistants": programmers, analysts, etc., that could get integrated into the scientific community. Besides, the computer science degree would be useful in the sense that the large public and private companies - that already had began to install computer equipment for administrative purposes – could hire personnel not necessarily trained by them, with all the flaws that this procedure has.

The computer science curriculum [4] included, as compulsory courses, one-variable calculus, algebra, linear algebra, several variables calculus, probabilities and statistics, complex analysis, programming, introduction to numerical analysis, topics of numerical analysis (errors, interpolation, numerical linear algebra), advanced numerical analysis (numerical solution of ordinary and partial differential equations and integral equations), programming, data processing, operations research, and advanced computational techniques. The students had also to assemble eight credits in elective courses (eight credits usually meant three elective courses). The elective courses included statistics, physics, mathematical economy, advanced programming and others.

The curriculum shows that computer science was not yet understood as an independent science. The graduates in computer science were thought of as qualified auxiliary personnel of the scientists. Anyway, many graduates eventually had very successful professional careers in banks, industries and public administration, what indicates that the general level of the education at the School of Sciences was good, and the students were well trained. Many students, by the way, were students of mathematics and physics that had decided that they did not want to continue an academic career, and that wanted a degree to get a job as professionals in a new and interesting area; besides, the program was shorter than the "licenciado" program. Anyway, before the military coup the authorities were already thinking and working in the creation of the "licenciado" in computer sciences degree. The coup d'état suspended all discussions, and it was necessary to wait until 1982 to have a "licenciado" degree, as in mathematics and the other sciences.

4.   Research at the Instituto de Cálculo

It is interesting to follow the history of some of the former members of the Instituto de Cálculo after their resignations as a consequence of the attack against the universities in 1966, because the histories show both the research done at the Institute and the success and influence that many of its members had later.

Oscar Varsavsky (who, in fact, did not resign after the assault on the universities, but some months before, to go to Caracas to work at the Central University of Venezuela and at the Center for Development Studies, CENDES) continued. On the one hand, his ambitious project of mathematical modeling in social sciences, for which he affirmed that he needed a type of mathematics different from the type of mathematics used as a language for natural sciences, but that used the computer as a basic tool. On these subjects, he had begun to work at the Instituto de Cálculo, see for instance [5], [12], [16]. In 1970 he returned to Argentina after having implemented a series of mathematical models (demographic, educational and economic) in CENDES, that required an intensive use of computing, and his activity had a more and more political bias until his passing away in 1976. He considered that scientists should be qualified professionals involved in a "liberating" political project and, with his openness, perceptiveness and confronting style - that he maintained during all his life - spent a lot of time popularizing this standpoint writing a series of books, to me very arguable, but plenty of interesting ideas. We can specially mention [17] and [18]. In the 1970s his influence in some intellectual circles in Latin America was considerable.

Mario Gradowczyk headed a group on computational fluvial hydraulics and hydrodynamics and continued his research on fluid mechanics in Montevideo, Boston (MIT) and the Argentinean National Agency for Atomic Energy until 1970, when he began his work as a private consultant in mathematical models in fluvial engineering.

Julián Aráoz settled in Venezuela, where he continued his academic career until his retirement, with an intermission when he was in Canada finishing his Ph. D. studies. Both his Ph. D. thesis and his subsequent academic activity were centered in combinatorial optimization. Aráoz collaborated generously with Argentina from the restoration of democracy in 1983 on, fundamentally as invited professor at the Department of Computer Science of the School of Science of the University of Buenos Aires (that was created in 1985, after the restoration of democracy) and at the ESLAI (Latin American College of Informatics).

It is worth mentioning that, when they worked at the Instituto de Cálculo, Aráoz and Varsavsky directed a project on simulation of Andean rivers [1], after an agreement with the Argentine Federal Council of Investments (CFI) and the Economic Commission for Latin America and the Caribbean (ECLAC). This was probably the first contract in Argentina related to applied mathematics, and was similar to - but developed independently of - the Harvard Water Program, world leader in water resources planning. Had the experience of the Instituto de Cálculo not been shattered, Argentina could have now an internationally known academic school in water resources planning - subject particularly important for Argentina.

Pedro Zadunaisky got a position at the San Miguel Observatory and later at the National Agency of Spatial Activities (CONAE). He returned to the Department of Mathematics of the School of Sciences of the University of Buenos Aires after the 1983 restoration of democracy, and is currently professor emeritus. He continues active, working, as usual, in numerical solution of the equations of celestial mechanics (an asteroid has his name).

Sigfrido Mazza emigrated to Brazil, where he was one of the founders of the Brazilian Society of Statistics. Wilfred Durán emigrated, as many others, to Venezuela. While working at the Instituto de Cálculo, Durán, with his collaborators Cristina Zoltan and Clarisa Cortés, had implemented the programming language COMIC, that was friendlier than Autocode for certain researches at the Instituto de Cálculo.

Besides, many young scientists worked at the Instituto de Cálculo, in the different groups, that later stood out individually. We can include among them Víctor Yohai, founder of the school of robust statistics in Argentina, currently professor emeritus at the School of Science of the University of Buenos Aires; Roberto Frenkel and Arturo O'Connell, distinguished economists (O'Connell is currently member of the board of the Argentinean Central Bank and Frenkel was member of the board of the Bank of the Province of Buenos Aires); Alberto Minujin, specialized in sampling in underdeveloped countries; the late Jorge Sabato, sociologist and former Minister of Education of Argentina during the Alfonsín administration, that had prepared, with Oscar Varsavsky, a mathematical model of an Utopian society [12]; Cecilia Berdichevsky, one of the first programmers of Argentina, currently an active member of the Argentinean Society for Informatics and Operations Research; Alberto Rivas, who after the 1966 military coup went to MIT and obtained there a Ph. D. degree in linguistics; Víctor Pereyra, who specialized in numerical analysis and worked in Venezuela and USA (his interesting remembrances may be consulted in [11]); and Hugo Folguera, that created the group of research in applied mathematics at FATE Neumáticos, first group of research in a private firm in Argentina, group that, after the untimely death of Folguera in 1979, could not survive the economic policies of the Videla's dictatorship.

Finally, Manuel Sadosky, after the restoration of democracy in Argentina in 1983 was during all the President Alfonsín administration (1983-1989) his Secretary for Science and Technology, where he contributed to the revival of computer science (see [9]). He died in 2005. Rebeca Guber collaborated with him as Under-Secretary for Operational Coordination, and is currently member of the Board of the Argentinean Agency for Promotion of Science and Technology.

It is remarkable, as may be seen analyzing these histories, how interdisciplinary was the work at the Instituto de Cálculo: its members afterwards oriented themselves to very different areas of research. In particular, it is worth mentioning that Sadosky always insisted in *applied* research and was an extraordinary manager, with a profound insight in and solid knowledge of the problems which could be solved at the Instituto: the Instituto had many clients, and all of them wanted numerical solutions to original and, in many cases, sophisticated mathematical problems in science and engineering. The income from contracts was several times more significant for the Institute than its ordinary budget.

5.   Computer Science Outside Buenos Aires

The previous paragraphs may induce the reader to think that computer science was developing only in Buenos Aires; this is not true, as can be checked describing Jorge Santos project in Bahía Blanca [15]. At the end of 1956, before the brand-new Southern National University was one year old, Santos organized the Seminar on

Computing with senior students of the electrical engineering program, germ of the current Laboratory of Digital Systems of the Department of Electrical Engineering and Computers. When Santos returned from a sojourn in Manchester, UK, between 1959 and 1960 (with a fellowship from the National Council of Science to study logical design of computers) his group began to work in the development of a small computer and to research in multivariate algebras and their electronic implementation. The construction of the computer was suspended when, after President Frondizi was overthrown by the usual military coup d'état in 1962. The grant on which it depended, awarded by the Province of Buenos Aires, was interrupted (in 1976 the former main participants in this group were fired from the University by the military dictatorship, so that the group disappeared until, in 1987, Santos returned to the University and recreated the group, that is currently active).

6.   Conclusions

In the mid-1960s the activity in computer science, both professional and academic, was rapidly developing in Argentina, with a growth characterized by the enthusiasm of people involved, both professionals with other backgrounds, young students, brand-new graduates and even practitioners without degrees, when President Illia was overthrown by General Onganía coup d'état, followed by the revocation of the autonomy of the universities. Although it is perfectly known the damage that this attack on the universities caused to Argentinean higher education and science (for instance, at the University of Buenos Aires more than 1,300 faculty, graduate students and teaching assistants resigned), it is not necessarily known by the general public how this policy was a catastrophe for computer sciences, because it completely destroyed the academic development of the new science in a crucial moment of its development in the world. As an example, let us mention again that *all* the members of the Instituto de Cálculo resigned.

That was the time in which computer sciences began to have significance as autonomous science and technology (let us remember that 1968 was the year of the first curriculum of the ACM) and all that period was lost in our country. In particular, it is worth mentioning that at the School of Science of the University of Buenos Aires the computer, whose replacement was already under study before the military coup, simply disappeared and the degree was offered during fifteen years without computational facilities. The students had to use the IBM 360 computer installed at the University Hospital, or the computer installed at the School of Engineering, where a system analysis degree was created at the beginning of the 1970s on the personal initiative of Emilio Jáuregui.

In short, the balance of the 1966 military coup d'état, regarding informatics, is that it caused the almost total paralysis in research matters, and an abrupt fall in the quality of teaching. The seriousness of this fact and the responsibility of the military and their collaborators increase when we remark that not only informatics is, together with biology, the area of knowledge that developed most in the second half of the twentieth century, but also that, due to its characteristics, its development in Argentina would had permitted the creation of a high-technology software industry like India's, Israel's and Ireland's.

Acknowledgments

The author grateful acknowledges Jorge Santos his valuable commentaries on the Southern National University and Rosita Wachenchauzer her critics and remarks although, of course, he is the only responsible of the opinions here expressed. Besides, he acknowledges Eugenia Kalnay, Jonás Paiuk, Antonio Martese and Rebeca Guber for their lively and interesting remembrances of the Instituto de Cálculo.

References

[1]   Aráoz J, Varsavsky O (1965) Estudio del aprovechamiento hidráulico de ríos andinos por el método de modelos numéricos. Instituto de Cálculo de la Facultad de Ciencias Exactas y Naturales de la Universidad de Buenos Aires, Publicación Nro. 11, Buenos Aires
[2]   Babini N (2003) La Argentina y la computadora: crónica de una frustración. Editorial Dunken, Buenos Aires
[3]   Bunge M, Weinberg G, Martínez T E, Jaim Etcheverry G, Jacovkis P M (2004) Honoris causa. Manuel Sadosky en sus noventa años. Libros del Zorzal, Buenos Aires
[4]   Consejo Superior de la Universidad de Buenos Aires (1963) Resolución Nro. 727
[5]   Domingo C, Varsavsky O (1967) Un modelo matemático de la Utopía de Moro. Desarrollo Económico, 7:3-36. This work had been made at the Instituto de Cálculo
[6]   García R V (2003) La construcción de lo posible. In Rotunno C, Díaz de Guijarro E (eds) La construcción de lo posible. Libros del Zorzal, Buenos Aires, 43-70
[7]   Goldstine H H (1972) The computer from Pascal to von Neumann. Princeton University Press, Princeton
[8]   Hodges A (1992) Alan Turing: the enigma. Vintage, London. First published in 1983 by Burnett Books Ltd in association with Hutchinson Publishing Group
[9]   Jacovkis P M (2004) Reflexiones sobre la historia de la computación en Argentina. Saber y Tiempo, 17:127-146
[10] Morero S, Eidelman A, Lichtman G (1996) La noche de los bastones largos. Biblioteca Página 12, Buenos Aires
[11] Pereyra   V   (1996)   An   annotated   bibliography.   http://www.wai.com/Applied Science/Software/Integra/pereyra-bio.html
[12] Sabato J, Varsavsky O (1966) Experiments with a mathematical model of Utopia. Proceedings of the International Symposium on Mathematics and Human Sciences, Rome, 259-267
[13] Sadosky M (1973) Cálculo numérico y gráfico. Librería del Colegio, 8th   printing, Buenos Aires. First published in 1953

[14] Sadosky M (1972) Cinco años del Instituto de Cálculo de la Universidad de Buenos Aires [interview]. Ciencia Nueva 17:13-18.

[15] Santos J (2002) Personal communication

[16] Varsavsky O (1963) La experimentación numérica. Ciencia e Investigación, 19:340-347

[17] Varsavsky O (1971) Proyectos nacionales. Periferia, Buenos Aires

[18] Varsavsky O (1994) Ciencia, política y cientificismo. 8th printing, with an introduction by M de Asúa and a preliminary study by C Mantegari. Centro Editor de América Latina, Buenos Aires

Some Aspects of the Argentine Reception of the Computer

Nicolás Babini

Av. Córdoba 2540, 1120 Buenos Aires, Argentina
<babini@netex.com.ar>

Abstract. This paper describes activities developed in Argentina between 1956 and 1966 related to the computer and that were coincident with the arrival of the first machines in the country. It deals, particularly, with the work of the mathematician Manuel Sadosky (1914-2005) in the University of Buenos Aires, who was responsible for the first university computer, the first applied mathematics laboratory, the first computer career, and the first professional computer society in Argentina. The construction of experimental computers and the first imported business computers are also mentioned in this paper.

1. Introduction

The computer arrived in Argentina in 1960 and it involved business as well as university environments. The fact that an early attempt to produce computer science preceded and then accompanied its arrival (which had an interruption in 1966), made me consider that the computer created a unique situation in Latin America and even a rare one for the rest of the world.

The Mercury II, an English machine produced by Ferranti Ltd., was among the computers that arrived in the country. The University of Buenos Aires (U.B.A.) received the first Mercury II and it would have been the first *operating* computer in Argentina if it were not for the delay of construction for its location. The achievement was possible thanks to the tireless efforts of the Argentine mathematician, Manuel Sadosky.

Please use the following format when citing this chapter:

Babini, N., 2006, in IFIP International Federation for Information Processing, Volume 215, History of Computing and Education 2 (HCE2), ed. J. Impagliazzo, (Boston: Springer), pp. 193–201.

2.   The Work of Manuel Sadosky

Manuel Sadosky (1914-2005) received his doctorate in the National University of La Plata under the direction of the Spanish mathematician, Esteban Terradas, who had orientated him to applied mathematics. Sadosky traveled to France in 1947 due to a grant awarded by the French government and there, Sadosky heard about computers for the first time. The following year, another grant allowed him to become acquainted with the Instituto Nazionale per l'Applicazioni del Calcolo (INAC), founded by Mario Piccone in 1932. Each sojourn was a decisive event for his visionary future. In 1950, he wrote about computers in *Ciencia y Técnica*, a publication of the engineering students of the University of Buenos Aires [1]. After the university removed him from his teaching post in 1952 because of political reasons, he wrote two mathematics books, which became popular and which were widely known. When the University of Buenos Aires recovered its autonomy in 1955, after the overthrowing of Juan D. Perón dictatorship, it appointed Sadosky as professor and then Director of the Department of Mathematics of the Faculty of Exact Sciences, where he was able to put his innovatory projects into practice.

2.1   The first university computer

An intense training campaign of the people who would operate the Ferranti computer preceded its acquisition. The training included courses about calculations with tabulators and programming seminars given by foreign mathematicians like the Spaniard, Ernesto García Camarero [2] and the Englishwoman Cecile Popplewell. Ferranti Ltd. also undertook the training of two Argentine engineers in its plant who would take charge of the machine maintenance.

The Mercury II was acquired in 1958 thanks to a subsidy given by the National Council of Scientific and Technical Research (currently, the Conicet). Its installation reached a conclusion at the beginning of 1961 in a building of University City, then under construction. The machine, which the University of Manchester had designed, held the features that were characteristic of the first English computers. These features included its large size, its thermo-ionic tubes, and its punched tape operation. The machine used a high-level language (called Autocode), and its operation was more suitable than the other existing computers for doing scientific tasks. It operated intensely until 1966. In addition to the University of Buenos Aires using it, different public organizations gravitated to it including the researchers from the University of the Republic in Montevideo, Uruguay.

Unlike what was happening in the Faculty of Exact Sciences, in the Faculty of Engineering of the same university, Professor Horacio C. Reggini (b. 1933)— another computer science pioneer—could not reconcile that his students and colleagues would accept the computer as an auxiliary to the teaching of engineering. (The universities of Michigan and Houston had discussed that issue during those years [3].) However, such a goal finally became a reality at the Faculty of Engineering of the recently created Argentine Catholic University (U.C.A.), where an IBM 1620 operated until Reggini's resignation in 1966. Reggini also created a Study Group for Computer Applications (GEAC) in the Department of Stability of the U.B.A. In 1966, that Group published a book about Stress, [4] a language that had just appeared at MIT—an institution with which Reggini maintained a close relationship.

2.2 The "Instituto de Cálculo"

It is highly likely that the idea of a computer-based applied mathematics laboratory had been in Sadosky's mind during the very first moments. However, it could only become official in 1962, when the University approved the creation of the "Instituto de Cálculo" [5]. In the meantime, about fifty graduates participated in the organization of working groups. Most of the people were mathematicians and engineers, and later, a great many of them went on to have distinguished careers in Argentina and abroad.

One of those groups developed models related to the Argentine economy, which applied new concepts through its director Oscar Varsavsky. He conceived those models such as "numerical experimentation models", which differed from the ordinary econometric models [6-8]. Another group, directed by Pedro E. Zadunaisky, worked on numerical solution of differential equations and particularly in the trajectory of the Halley comet [9-11]. Zadunaisky in the United States then continued those calculations resulting in dedicating an asteroid in his own name. The group, directed by Mario Gradowczyk, worked on solid and fluid mechanics and structural analysis [12-15]. Another group, under the direction of Julián Aráoz Durán, conducted a study of the hydraulic use of Andean rivers by applying the method of mathematical modeling. He developed that study in the framework of an agreement between the Argentine's Federal Council of Investments (C.F.I.) and the U.N.O. Economic Commission for Latin America (CEPAL) [16]. The same group also worked on linear programming problems and the "Critical Path Method" for public organizations and private companies [17].

The group in charge of the maintenance and development of the Mercury worked on the expansion of the machine, particularly on the construction of a card-tape converter, the installation of magnetic drums, and a line printer, in addition to the construction of an analog-digital converter for a neurology research of the Buenos Aires Children Hospital. The engineer, Jonás Paiuk, developed an outstanding reputation in all those works. He had taken part in the construction of an experimental computer in the Faculty of Engineering—to which I will refer afterwards—and had received training at Ferranti Ltd. itself in Manchester. Paiuk would later become a pioneer of industrial automation in Argentina.

The Programming Group, directed by Wilfred O. Durán, developed a new language called COMIC (Compilador del Instituto de Cálculo) [18] to overcome the limitations of the Mercury's Autocode and to satisfy the economic model demands under development by Varsavsky. The group was also in charge of the programming of a plotter acquired in the United States. The Statistics Group, directed by Sigfrido Mazza, had received the greatest number of assignments from third parties (such as the design of the sample of the National Census of 1960) [19]. The Computer Linguistics Group, directed by Eugenia Fischer, worked on the Russian-Spanish automatic translation.

In the early 1960s, mathematical models and automatic translation were new. Planning and control techniques based on networks—like PERT and CPM—dated back from 1958 and they demonstrated a degree of advancement based upon the works developed at Sadosky's Institute. The Institute itself published many of those works (see references).

2.3   The first computing curriculum

In the Argentine of 1960, the only computing training courses were those offered by the importing companies conducted by their own personnel. That same year, an IBM subsidiary began to train its sales engineers as System Engineers (which included a stay at the head office in the United States). In 1962, Sadosky proposed the creation of the Curriculum of Scientific Computer in the Faculty of Exact Sciences. At first, people viewed it as a minor specialty though it lasted three and a half years. The curriculum included mathematics, programming, numerical analysis, operational research courses, ten obligatory courses, and some other courses that were optional. However, when it became evident that such scientific guidance reduced the labor opportunities of the graduates, they called people from IBM to give courses also. Mathematics and physics graduates from their own faculties (whose studies lasted for five years) mainly nurtured the curriculum. The faculty had already approved a great number of the curriculum courses. For that reason, the computing curriculum had produced its first graduates in 1963.

2.4   The first professional society

In 1960, the Argentine Society of Calculus (S.A.C.) came into existence. Sadosky had driven that undertaking and he assembled the first students, teachers, and professionals of computer science. Between 1961 and 1962, the S.A.C. published the *Boletín de la SAC*, which was the first specialized journal of computing in Argentina. The second one, *Decisiones Gerenciales y Computadoras*, which had also a short life, appeared in 1965. During those two years of the early 1960s, the S.A.C. had an intense activity and in 1962, it became the Argentine member of IFIP. After a period of little activity, it reconstituted in 1972 as the Argentine Society for

Computing (Sociedad Argentina de Computación), which then evolved into a new society after having an essential part in the organization of the First Ibero-American Congress of Informatics (I CIADI) held in Buenos Aires in 1972.

The beneficiary of those efforts was the Argentine Society for Operational Research (Sociedad Argentina de Investigación Operativa, SADIO), founded also in 1960 by a group of teachers of operational research. Until 1977, the SADIO had organized ten conferences (called JAIO) that had a growing participation of computing papers. In 1979, the Society adopted the name of Argentine Society for Informatics and Operational Research (Sociedad Argentina de Informática e Investigación Operativa). In the following year, IFIP recognized it as a replacement of S.A.C.

3. Experimental Computers

While Sadosky lay the foundations of what would be the "Instituto de Cálculo" of the Faculty of Exact Sciences, the engineer Humberto Ciancaglini (b. 1918), who had just been appointed Director of the Department of Electronics, began the development of an experimental computer in the Faculty of Engineering, which shared the building with the Faculty of Exact Sciences. Ciancaglini, who was a civil engineer, had received training in electronics in the laboratories of the Dutch company Philips. The company installed these laboratories in Buenos Aires in 1943 after they had moved them to England during the Nazi invasion of the Netherlands. Ciancaglini was able to see operating computers for the first time in 1956, during a business trip to Europe. He realized that Argentina could not stay behind those advances. Therefore, he decided to build a computer and began the preparatory activities, which extended during a year. Among them was a course consisting of a series of public lectures aimed to interest the entrepreneurs in the field. The course, patronized by the Argentine Center of Engineers, was not successful in convincing these business people that the university was able to achieve that goal. However, it did provide the reason to produce the first book on computers that had appeared in Argentina. Remington Rand Sudamericana published the book in 1958 and reprinted it in 1962 [20].

The machine, called CEFIBA (Electronic Computer of the Faculty of Engineering of Buenos Aires), was built with a great effort between the years 1958 and 1962 [21-23]. The director of the project was the engineer Felipe Tanco (b. 1923), who had just returned from the United States where he had participated in the Radio Corporation of America's role in the Bizmac development. A group of graduates took part in the design and construction of the machine. They include Eduardo T. Ulzurrun, who designed the circuits, and the already mentioned Jonás Paiuk who played an exceptional role in its development. The project had a subsidy from the National Council of Scientific and Technical Research and had the collaboration offered by the National Commission of Atomic Energy Workshops. The Naval Laboratories were also important because of the great shortage of equipment and components at that time.

The CEFIBA had a central processing unit of transistors of intermediate frequency, a memory of magnetic drum (ten thousand characters), a paper tape as input, and a typewriter as output. The programming was in machine language. According Ciancaglini, they did not conceive the CEFIBA as an experimental machine but as an implementation that allowed students to familiarize themselves with that new technology.

Another experimental computer began construction in 1960 at the Southern National University in the harbor city of Bahía Blanca (situated over the Atlantic Ocean, 800 kilometers away from Buenos Aires). In 1956, its designer, the engineer Jorge Santos (b. 1927), had created a "seminar" that became a Laboratory of Computers (which had the participation of the Spaniard mathematician Ernesto García Camarero). In 1959, he received a grant from the University of Manchester, where he worked under the direction of Thomas Kilburn in the design of the Atlas computer. With that experience, he began to construct a machine called the CEUNS (Electronic Computer of the Southern National University) [24]. In accordance with the defined project, the machine would contain a central processing unit of transistors and a main memory, subdivided in a "fixed memory" and a "work memory" of 64 words of 64 bits, consisting in a piece of the ferrite memory from the Manchester's Mark 1 (that had been donated by Kilburn). Secondary memory consisted of a 9,000-word magnetic drum (a loan from Ferranti Ltd.) and punched tapes for input and output. The programming was similar to that of the Ferranti Mercury of the "Instituto de Cálculo" and the programmer was Victoria Bajar, the first graduate of the Specialist of Scientific Computer. The construction reached an impasse in 1962 when the financing stopped because of the fall of the Buenos Aires Province Government, which had given a subsidy to the project.

After that attempt, Santos worked on ternary systems (as an alternative of the binary systems that had then begun to prevail) and with collaborators, wrote several papers about them that appeared in publications in the United States between the years 1964 and 1970 [25-26]. We should recall that in 1959 in the Soviet Union, Nikolai Brusenzov was able to build the ternary computer Stun [27].

Finally, it is worth mentioning the unsuccessful attempt by the Fate Electronics Division of Fate S.A. (an important Argentine tire manufacturer) to produce minicomputers at that time. The development of the minicomputer, called Serie 1000, began in 1970 and it extended to 1979; it became evident that the design had become obsolete and the investments involved had caused a significant financial loss. The adventure put an end to the Division, which during that time had also successfully produced the first electronic calculators of Argentina—from pocket calculators to accounting machines.

4.   Other Imported Computers

Apart from the Ferranti's Mercury II, two public utilities received the other computers that arrived in 1960; they were a railway service (that received two Univac USS 90 machines) and an urban transport service (that received an IBM 305). A second IBM 305 also arrived and IBM installed it in its local headquarters. IBM also displayed the machine to the public at a fair held in Buenos Aires in 1960; there, people would pose questions to it and wait for a response. A similar model of this machine had fulfilled the same functions in the Brussels World's Fair of 1958.

At the end of the 1960s, the number of imported computers reached almost 340, with IBM maintaining a 60% predominance of the market. The main competitors of IBM were the French Bull machines and the NCR and Burroughs computers. We should remember that these machines were very expensive and that they required a significant initial investment. In addition, the expense of the physical set up of its site and the training of the people who would be in charge of the machines was costly. In fact, it was often necessary to make a total rearrangement of the procedures and forms and even of the internal organization of the user company to adapt them to the precision and rigidity of the computer.

The increase of computers went on continuously. In 1980, before the "microcomputer explosion", Argentina had more than 5.700 computers. I think that there were two principal motivations for this. The first "actual" motivation was the replacement of the abundance of accounting machines (known as tabulators or unit record machines) at that time. The other motivation was symbolic; that is, having a computer implied the achievement of a certain business prestige. The combination of these two factors often led to an inefficient use of the computer, which in essence had become a giant typewriter and had caused significant financial losses to its users.

5.   Conclusion

Though Argentina continued receiving computers, the activities related to the computing sciences suffered a considerable delay after 1966. That year, the army overthrew President Illia and universities came under government control. The administrators, teachers, and students of Exact Sciences and Engineering Faculties were repelling the "intervention". The resulting severe repression caused people like Sadosky, Ciancaglini, and Reggini to resign their positions. Curriculum teachers and institution's researchers did also.

The leaders of the scientific and technologic effort of the years from 1955 to 1966 stopped their participation at the university, which had been traditionally the core of the Argentine scientific research. Many of these leaders and their followers went abroad, largely due to the political instability and an atmosphere of intolerance that prevailed in Argentina during the second half of the twentieth century. In this new twenty-first century, the hope is that an atmosphere will come into existence that would allow Argentina to take the path once again that had begun by its computing pioneers.

References

[1]   M. Sadosky, "Progresos recientes y evolución del cálculo mecánico y automático". *Ciencia y Técnica,* No. 580, 1950, pp. 170-186.

[2]   E. García Camarero, *Autocode. Un sistema simplificado para la programación de la computadora Mercury,* Instituto de Cálculo, Buenos Aires, 1961.

[3]   H. C. Reggini, "Aplicación de las computadoras a la enseñanza de la ingeniería". *Ciencia y Técnica,* No. 662, 1963.

[4]   Grupo de Estudio de Aplicación de Computadoras, *Stress. Un lenguaje de computadora para ingeniería estructural,* Universidad de Buenos Aires, Facultad de Ingeniería, Departamento de Estabilidad, Buenos Aires, 1966.

[5]   M. Sadosky, "El Instituto de Cálculo de la Facultad de Ciencias Exactas y Naturales" *Revista de la Universidad de Buenos Aires,* V época, vol. VII, No. 4, 1962, pp. 646-650.

[6]   O. Varsavsky, "La experimentación numérica". *Ciencia e Investigación,* vol. 19, no. 30, 1963.

[7]   O. Varsavsky, *Los modelos matemáticos numéricos como herramientas de decisión en problemas difícilmente cuantificables. El MEIC-0,* Instituto de Cálculo, Buenos Aires, 1965 [mimeo].

[8]   O. Varsavsky, N. Lugo, H. Paulero, R. Frenkel, M. Malajovich, L. Lew y V. Yohai, *Matrices positivas. Propiedades utilizadas en teorías económicas,* Instituto de Cálculo, No. 13, Buenos Aires, 1966 [en prensa; no se publicó]

[9]   P. Zadunaisky, V. Pereyra, *Sobre la convergencia y precisión de un proceso de correcciones diferenciales sucesivas.* Instituto de Cálculo, No. 5, Buenos Aires, 1965 [traducida al inglés en *Proceedings of the International Federation for Information Processing, 1965*].

[10] P. Zadunaisky, V. Pereyra, C. Berdichevsky, G. Oliver, E. Ruspini, G. Galimberti, *Un método para la estimación de errores propagados en la solución numérica de un sistema de ecuaciones ordinarias.* Instituto de Cálculo, No. 1, Buenos Aires, 1964.

[11] P. Zadunaisky, V. Pereyra, C. Berdichevsky, G. Oliver, E. Ruspini, G. Galimberti, *El movimiento del cometa Halley durante el retorno de 1910,* Instituto de Cálculo, Publicación no. 4, Buenos Aires, 1964.

[12] M. H. Gradowczyk, *Una teoría matemática para el estudio de problemas de erosión,* Instituto de Cálculo, No.10, Buenos Aires, 1965.

[13] M. H. Gradowczyk, H. C. Folguera, *Modelo matemático para el estudio de la erosión de lechos móviles.* Instituto de Cálculo, No. 6, Buenos Aires, 1965 [traducida al inglés: *Analysis of scour in open channels by means of mathematical models*].

[14] M. H. Gradowczyk, J. Schujman, H. C. Folguera, E. Risler, A. Rivas, O. Maggiolo, *Tensiones térmicas en cáscaras elásticas,* Instituto de Cálculo, No. 2, Buenos Aires, 1964.

[15] M. H. Gradowczyk, J. Schujman, H. C. Folguera, E. Risler, A. Rivas, O. Maggiolo, *Discusión sobre un modelo matemático para el estudio de los problemas de erosión de lechos móviles,* Instituto de Cálculo, No. 3, Buenos Aires, 1964.

[16] J. A. Aráoz Durán, O. Varsavsky, J. J. C. Riva, R. Carranza, *Estudio del aprovechamiento hidráulico de los ríos andinos por el método matemático*, Instituto de Cálculo, No.11, Buenos Aires, 1965.

[17] J. A. Aráoz Durán, M. Larramendy, N. Sameghini, J. C. Fränkel, *Camino crítico aplicado a la construcción de edificios*, Instituto de Cálculo, No. 12, Buenos Aires, 1966 [en prensa; no se publicó].

[18] W. O. Durand, *Introducción al lenguaje Comic*, Instituto de Cálculo, No. 14, Buenos Aires, 1966 [mimeo]

[19] Instituto Nacional de Tecnología Agropecuaria. *El uso de la computadora Mercury en el análisis de los datos experimentales*, INTA, Buenos Aires, 1963.

[20] *Ciclo de conferencias sobre computadoras dictadas en el Centro Argentino de Ingenieros*. Remington Rand Sudamericana, Buenos Aires, 1958 [2ª ed., 1962].

[21] F. Tanco, La computadora construida en la Facultad de Ingeniería de Buenos Aires. *Boletín de la Sociedad Argentina de Investigación Operativa*, No. 3, Buenos Aires, 1960.

[22] H. A. Ciancaglini, "Computadoras digitales", *Revista Telegráfica Electrónica*, No. 628, Buenos Aires, 1957.

[23] M. Diamand, "Circuitos lógicos", *Revista Telegráfica Electrónica*, No. 639, Buenos Aires, 1957.

[24] J. Santos, "Diseño lógico de una computadora de costo limitado", *Revista Telegráfica Electrónica*, No. 580, Buenos Aires, 1961.

[25] J. Santos, H. Arango, "Base 3 vs. Base 2 Synchronous Arithmetic Units", *IEEE Transactions on Electronic Computers*, 1964.

[26] J. Santos, H. Arango, On the Analysis and Synthesis of Three-valued Digital Systems. *Proceedings of the 1964 Spring Joint Computer Conference*, 1964.

[27] S. V. Klimenko, "Computer Science in Russia: a Personal View", *IEEE Annals of the History of Computing*, vol.21, no.3, 1999, p. 17.

Bibliography

[1] N. Babini, *Tres décadas de SADIO*, Sociedad Argentina de Informática e Investigación Operativa, Buenos Aires, 1990.

[2] N. Babini, *La informática en la Argentina. 1956-1966*, Ediciones Letra Buena, Buenos Aires, 1991.

[3] N. Babini, "Modernización e informática. Argentina 1955-1966", *Quipu*, Vol. 9, No. 1, México, D.F., 1992., pp. 89-109.

[4] N. Babini, "Bibliografía informática argentina 1949-1975". *Anales de la Sociedad Científica Argentina*, Vol. 224, No. 1, Buenos Aires, 1994, pp. 75-114.

[5] N. Babini, "Los primeros trabajos sobre la computadora en la Argentina", *Saber y Tiempo*, Vol. 1, No. 2, Buenos Aires, 1996, pp. 171-188.

[6] N. Babini, "La llegada de la computadora a la Argentina", *Llull*, No. 20, Zaragoza, Esp., 1997, pp. 465-490.

[7] N. Babini, *La Argentina y la computadora. Crónica de una frustración*, Ediciones Dunken, Buenos Aires, 2003.

[8] N. Babini, *Historia de la computación en la Argentina. Informe final*, seminario dictado en SADIO entre el 15 de abril y el 18 de septiembre de 2003 [inédito].

The Beginning of Computer Science in Argentina – Clementina - (1961-1966)
A Personal Experience

Cecilia Berdichevsky

[1] SADIO-Argentine Computing Society-Uruguay 252-Buenos Aires-Argentina
http://www.sadio.org.ar, <cecily48@ciudad.com.ar>
[2] ICDL Argentina (International Computer Driving Licence)-Rincon
326-Buenos Aires-Argentina http://www.icdl.org.ar, <info@icdl.org.ar>

I dedicate this work to the memory of Dr. Manuel Sadosky.

Abstract. 1957 marked the beginning of modern education in computing in Argentina. I was lucky enough to live this part of the history. After issuing an international bid that year, all members of a special commission from the University of Buenos Aires selected the Ferranti Mercury computer to be purchased for the University. Once installed in 1961, an Institute of Calculus[1] was created with the aim of improving the use and professional and technical applications of the machine. Almost at the same time, a new course of study was organized, the Scientific Computist[2]. Those three events, promoted by our teacher and mentor Manuel Sadosky, set the start point of education assisted by computers in our country. The work at the Institute covered three fields: problem solving, research and teaching. Several Working Teams were organized looking to solve "real problems" in different disciplines: Mathematical Economics, Operations Research, Statistics, Linguistics, Applied Mechanics, Numerical Analysis, Electronic Engineering and Programming Systems. The architecture, structure, operation, languages and other characteristics of the machine, quite advanced for the time, determined the specific area of each of the working teams. After the military coup of 1966 disrupted several institutions, the University and several of its working teams, especially our Institute, the Institute stopped all of its operations. The Mercury computer era came to an abrupt end in our country. 90% of the members of the Institute, scientists, professors and highly trained professionals, resigned and many of them left the country taking their knowledge and expertise abroad.

[1] Instituto de Cálculo
[2] Computador Científico

Please use the following format when citing this chapter:

Berdichevsky, C., 2006, in IFIP International Federation for Information Processing, Volume 215, History of Computing and Education 2 (HCE2), ed. J. Impagliazzo, (Boston: Springer), pp. 203–215.

1.   Introduction

In 1956, some leading personalities from several universities in Argentina began to develop the idea of becoming a part of the modern computing world. One of their first steps was the creation of a Calculus Institute in the UBA aiming to promote the development of Applied Mathematics using resources of Electronic Automatic Computing. In 1957, a public international bid was launched by a commission of the UBA, created with the purpose of providing the School of Natural and Exact Sciences with a modern computer. With that purpose a special subsidy was granted by the CONICET (National Council of Scientific and Technological Research). As for the bidding, four companies presented their proposals: IBM, Remington and Philco from USA, and Ferranti from England. After a careful study, and taking into account the technical characteristics and prices, the members of the Committee unanimously recommended the purchase of the Mercury, offered by the English company Ferranti from Manchester. It was in those days a state-of–the-art machine with excellent technical features: speed, different types of memory, and mainly because it used Autocode, a language developed for Mercury by researchers from the University of Manchester

This language was easy to learn, user friendly at that time, and fit to deal with scientific problems. The computer arrived to Buenos Aires in 1960, and the following year, during its installation at the University, a small group working in the UBA (the author included) were immediately attracted by the computer work. From the beginning we named our machine "Clementina", because it was programmed to play the popular American melody "oh my darling Clementine", that was easily recognized even if the machine sounded in a peculiar way. Some time later we programmed it to play opera songs and a well-known tango named La Cumparsita. 1957 to 1961 were devoted to train the first group of analysts and programmers, and also to inform to possible future users, news of the arrival of a modern computer at the University. That was one of the landmark experiences in the development of computing education in the country.

2.   Installation of the Computer at the University of Buenos Aires

The installation of the Mercury was completed by the beginning of 1961. The reason for such delay was that the chosen room to place the computer, being prepared on the second floor of the new building of the School of Exact and Natural Sciences, was not yet ready and did not suit the required [2] strict Ferranti specifications. The members of the staff appointed to work with our Mercury were to be trained in Manchester, at the Ferranti plant. This was one of the factors that favoured the choice for the Mercury computer. Actually, that training began in

Buenos Aires; our teacher was Cicely Popplewell, who had been one of Alan Turing's assistants. Ernesto Garcia Camarero, a Spanish mathematician engaged by the University for the training of future computer users, also participated in the formation of the analysts and programmers of the Institute.

3. The Calculus Institute and its Working Teams

The Institute of Calculus was created by the University at the end of 1962 with the aim of doing research, working with the machine, learning, teaching and using it with different purposes. Additionally, a new course of studies, called Computer Scientist, was developed. Both projects were promoted by our mentor, teacher and leader Manuel Sadosky, who has also been instrumental in the decisions and actions that led to the era of Scientific Computing in Argentina. One of the tasks of the Institute was to tackle "real problems", and thus two lines of work where defined: on one hand, the Institute received and attended problems to be processed and solved, such as those requested by researchers and professors from the different UBA Schools or other national institutions that needed its services. On the other hand, different specialized Working Teams were created to analyse and develop different subjects [8].

3.1 Mathematical economics

That group was the largest one and was a multi-disciplinary team. Members included economists, sociologists, statisticians and professionals from other disciplines.

It was directed by Oscar Varsavsky, and composed by Arturo O'Connell, an important Argentine economist, Jorge Sabato, who became later Minister of Education of Argentina, Victor Yohai, a well known statistician, among others. This team produced two economical models Meic-0 and Meic-1, developing a new technique that used the computer to process statistical data provided by Argentine sources.

3.2 Operation research

This group started to work on a problem of great national relevance: the study of the rivers of the Andes ridge, using numerical models [9]. The project was proposed by a national institution, the Federal Council of Investments (CFI) and the Latin-American CEPAL. An automatic "rolling mill" for the company Siderca, and a human diet for CONADE (The National Council for Development) were also performed. That team was directed by Oscar Varsavsky and Julián Aráoz, with the advice of renowned engineers and teachers from universities, like Roque Carranza, who was a professor in the Department of Mathematics, and became later a Minister and President of the CONADE. The work of this group turned to be one of the first examples in the world of the use of numerical experimental methods in complex dynamical systems. This same group leaded by Julián Aráoz performed the first computer works on Pert, Linear Programming and Critical Path Analysis [1].

3.3   Statistics

One of the main objectives of the Institute was to promote the study and Statistics applications, undeveloped in the country at that time. The Statistics team leaded by Sigfrido Mazza worked in two areas: on one hand, special studies were undertaken about the problems concerning the work of important national institutions like the National Institute for Agricultural Technology (INTA), the National Petroleum Company (YPF), the National Telephone Company, and the National Health Institute, among others. The group also had the responsibility of designing the sample and evaluating the errors of the compiled material of the 1960 Population Census. On the other hand, part of this team centred its activities on permanent collaboration with INTA and published a paper about "The use of Mercury Ferranti computer in the analysis of experimental data", to inform users all over the country on how to normalize the compilation of statistical agricultural material [7].

3.4   Applied mechanics

Mario Gradowczyck led this area with the collaboration of a team mainly composed by engineers like Jaime Schujman and others. That group had two lines of work: solid mechanics and fluid mechanics. Regarding the first one (solid mechanics) they developed and divided their work in 3 different areas: computer calculation of structures, theory of shells and numerical calculation of elasticity problems. Concerning the second one (fluid mechanics), they studied the erosion and transport of ground material in canals and natural ditches and in the not stationary problems in piping [6].

3.5   Numerical analysis

This team was created under the direction of Pedro Zadunaisky, a well known scientist in Planetary Mechanics, with the participation of Victor Pereyra, Enrique Ruspini and others. A team of Numerical Analysis was created, which I was part of. This team had the objective to work in problems of convergence in the numerical solution of differential equations regarding the calculus of planetary orbits, especially the one of the Halley Comet, to which Zadunaisky devoted a great part of his life, spending also some time at the Smithsonian Institute. An asteroid was baptised with his name, as an appreciation for his work ([10] and [11]).

3.6 Computational linguistics

This was a section directed by the engineer Eugenia Fisher, and composed among others by Victoria Bajar, who developed an important career in Mexican universities. The main objective of that team was the automatic translation especially from Russian to Spanish and vice versa, and the Spanish Language Structure in collaboration with the cathedra of Philology of the School of Philosophy and Literature of the UBA, and other institutions. They had a communications area in which Juan Carlos Angio performed different works for ENTEL (the National Telecommunication Company).

3.7 Electronic engineering

This was a very particular team directed by Jonas Paiuk who was trained in Manchester and became the chief of Maintenance of Mercury, and Oscar Matiussi followed in the direction of the team. Their main task was to ensure the proper functioning of the computer, something they accomplished with exceptional efficacy. They also undertook Research and Development tasks to improve the equipment, mainly its input and output, i.e. the construction of a converter from punched cards to punched ribbon, installation of new magnetic drums, a line printer and also an analogical to digital converter whose destination was the analysis of neurological data required by a research group at the Buenos Aires Children Hospital.

3.8 Programming systems team

This team was established under the direction of Wilfred Duran. Its main achievement was the creation of a new language the Compilador del Instituto de Cálculo (COMIC - Compiler of the Calculus Institute). See the details of this project in Section 4.3.6.

4. Working at the Institute of Calculus

4.1 Fields of work

Work in the Institute, covered three fields:

1) Solving problems on demand by scientists and professors of the different UBA Schools, other universities of the country or from abroad, and public and private institutions.

2) Application of the computer to research in the different fields the scientists of the Institute or University worked in.

3) Teaching how to program and use the computer and the languages that it allowed, a task every one of us took part in. Some of us also lectured on different subjects in careers related to computing or to the Institute, especially those enrolled in the new career of Scientific Computist.

4.2   Work at the institute

First, the team was quite small, only 7 or 8 people including, Manuel Sadosky and Rebeca Guber, a mathematician and excellent organizer, also a public relations person, who was Chief of Services during the entire life of the institution, and managed the Institute's every day operation, problems, services and financial concerns. By the time Mercury arrived and the operations began, I had the luck to have in hand a real problem of Physics that, Mercury solved as soon as it was installed. In one of her first mornings in Buenos Aires, Cicely Popplewell gave me a private lesson in which I got instructed on the programming needs of a problem to which I had devoted several months of Nestler Rule calculation without reaching the solution. That afternoon, the problem got solved.

Like my colleagues, I also helped in solving problems that were the everyday worries of different researchers of some universities of the country and other national institutions, like the Departments of Physics, Meteorology, Chemistry, Industries, and others from our UBA Schools, like the School of Engineering of the UBA, the National Universities of La Plata, Cordoba, Rosario, San Juan, the Institute of Physics of Bariloche, the University of Cuyo, and even some Universities of abroad. They were all related to the Institute, as well as the University of Montevideo in Uruguay, University of Chile, and an Institute of Mathematics from Dublin, Ireland.

National institutions like the National Commission of Atomic Energy (CNEA), the Meteorological National Service, the National Company of Communications and others, among some outstanding private companies like Shell, Ducilo, Mellor Goodwin and so on, asked help from the Institute.

4.3   Working with Mercury

Work with Mercury was defined by its resources and its characteristics, structure and operational capabilities, as well as by the languages, routines, stored libraries and facilities that it offered

Characteristics of Mercury: Clementina was an improved version of the Mercury developed in 1955 at Manchester University. It was defined in the Manchester Manual [4] as a Scientific Electronic Digital Computer of Stored Program, Large Size and High Speed, which meant:

Digital computer: Discrete representation, essentially counting arithmetic, direct descendant of the abacus and of counting with hand fingers. Besides counting, it also had to perform functions that were not arithmetic such as: storing, retrieving data or instructions from memory, using intermediate results or organizational tasks. Those functions constituted the "red tape functions".

Stored program computer: To be run, the program and data had to be completely stored in the machines memory and the instructions were executed one by one.

Large size computer: The Mercury could operate at its normal speed only if it had instructions, operators and data stored beforehand in the memory. Therefore, it needed a great space of memory. It also needed space to store the intermediate results, otherwise it could lose speed.

High speed computer: Additions and subtractions, took 180 microseconds each and multiplication 300 microseconds. At that time, that was high speed indeed.

Scientific computer: Mercury was considered a scientific computer unlike data processing or general-purpose machines, because it could perform large and complex numerical calculus of nuclear physics or aeronautic engineering, carry out a numerical integration of complicated functions of more than one variable, play chess, or prove theorems of symmetry logic. Nevertheless, it could also perform the daily routine of book keeping of a bank.

4.3.1 Some features

Mercury was a first generation computer because it worked on valves. Its programming language was Autocode, which was user friendly and that was one of the main factors in favour of this language at the time. It was not necessary to know either the machine language or the structure or details of the "real machine", but the programming language and the running of the "ideal machine", that could understand the instructions.

4.3.2 Operation

The machine's operation had concepts that were developed much further, 10 or 15 years, in other computers. For example, the pagination system was in Mercury by software and gave birth to the idea of pagination by hardware. Mercury was state-of-the-art for the time. Consider: the facility of pagination, selection of rounding or truncate to improve results, the use of sub indexes, cycles with negative steps and more, none of them used by other computers on that time. The machine had a physical structure conceived for scientific tasks, so its capacity of calculus and processing speed was not too bad. Only input and output operations were very slow.

4.3.3 Languages

By the time it was received, Mercury operated three languages

1 - *Absolute* or machine language.
2 - *PIG2*, a symbolic language that was an Assembler.
3 - *Autocode*, a higher level language which was a Compiler, developed by A.Brooker from the University of Manchester and improved in 1957 for the Ferranti Mercury. This was the language used, until COMIC came along.[4] and [5].

Example of a Routine that calculates x^5, and stores it in register of address 832, programmed in Pig2 and in Autocode. This example shows the difference between both languages and how Autocode simplified and shortened programs.

Pig2

173 [B] ← 4	Put the value 4 in counter or register B
174 [A] ← C [700]	Put x contained in register 700 into the accumulator
175 [A] ←C [A] x C [700]	Put x.x in the accumulator
176 [B] ← [B] – 1	Subtract 1 from the counter or register B
177 If C [B] ≠ 0 [IAR] ←175	Conditional jump to 175 (IAR, Instruction Address Register)
178 C [A] →[832]	Put x^5 in register with address 832.

Autocode

	Z = x	Put x in Z
	I = 4	Put 4 in counter I
7)	Z = Z. x	Multiply content of Z by x
	I = I-1	Subtract 1 from counter
	Jump 7, I ≠ 1	Conditional Jump depending on value of counter.

4.3.4 Basic functions

The machine contained a set of basic functions and each step of the programming would be the use of one of them. Mercury could not perform more than one operation at the same time, and they were the three basic arithmetical operations: addition, subtraction, and multiplication. Division was not a basic function: the quotient of a pair of numbers consisted in executing a sequence of the three basic operations: a succession of subtractions, combined with the counting of the quantity of subtractions. In spite of the fact that multiplication was included in the basic operations, a repeated and counted addition could be enough, but being a scientific computer, Mercury had a set of electronic functions, one of which was the multiplication; in that way it took less than half the time than the iterated addition.

4.3.5 Input and output

A photoelectrical reader that read the punched paper ribbon made input, and the program ran instruction by instruction, only one at a time. The output after processing was produced by a paper ribbon perforator and teletype.

4.3.6 COMIC (Compiler of the Calculus Institute)

When the nature of the problems that were analyzed, studied and solved in the Institute became more complex, it became necessary to think of researching in order to create new languages to obtain the maximum potentiality from our equipment.

As it was said above, the team of *Programming Systems* under the direction of Wilfred Duran created the COMIC acronym for Compiler of the Calculus Institute. [5]. It was published in May 1966 and from the first moment it proved suitable for dealing with some of the Institute programming problems. The language was mainly created to satisfy the needs of the Mathematical Economics team directed by Oscar Varsavsky. The requirements of the Economical Models programs exceeded the Autocode capacity. With Comic, the variable identifiers got more length, and the language became more "user friendly". It also had additional operations to manage matrixes and vectors. The use of COMIC had also the purpose that it fulfilled perfectly, of making easier the use of the machine to programmers from different institutions and different disciplines, without them having to be familiar either with the internal structure of the computer or with the machine language. COMIC was constantly improved by adding new capabilities to it. Among those improvements were routines prepared by the students of the Career of Scientific Computist as part of their curriculum. For instance: Cristina Zoltan, one of the first Scientific Computists graduated, later an important authority and professor of the Simon Bolivar University in Venezuela, designed a routine for the use of the Graphic devise that was purchased by the Institute at that time.

5.   My Training Abroad

In 1961, the International Computation Centre with headquarters in Rome offered two fellowships to the UBA. Argentina was a member of the ICC and Dr. Sadosky the Argentine representative.

I received one of the scholarships. The second was not used because at the time nobody filled the required qualifications.

The fellowship consisted of a six-month stay at the Computer Unit of the University of London, the English equivalent of the Argentine Institute of Calculus and another six months at the Centre of Nuclear Studies of Saclay in France, which had an Arithmetic Electronic section. Both institutions had a Ferranti Mercury machine in their equipment.

5.1   Stay at the London University Computer Unit

The issues I worked on in the Unit, whose one and only computer was Mercury, were:

5.1.1 Programming techniques

In the Unit, I became acquainted with a very powerful new method of calculating the eigenvalues of a general matrix, the Francis method, which I studied, programmed and wrote the specifications of, under the guidance of the Unit staff. The program that calculated the eigenvalues of a general matrix up to the order 15x15 was successfully applied.

The second problem, a library routine in which I was working in, was also finished and became the third library routine for the Mercury in the Unit. Thanks to the fact that the London Unit operated as an "open store", i.e. that the persons that knew how to operate it were allowed to use the machine, I could personally carry out all the tests, something that gave me a good background to operate our Mercury back in Buenos Aires.

5.1.2 Lectures and seminars

During my stay in London, a week duration meeting took place in order to analyse and discuss the CHLF 3 compiler, which was a new Input Routine. That seminar was very instructive; it gave me an insight of the structure and characteristics of a compiler. The Routine was finished and put to use at the Unit in April 1962.

I also attended lectures in Numerical Analysis and a course in Matrix Calculus, by Professor Wilkinson. Professor Crank developed the second course in Numerical Analysis and the subject was: Numerical Methods for the solution of Partial Differential Equations allowing me some insights into new unpublished works.

Other English computer centres, such us the computing laboratory of Manchester University and the University of Cambridge were visited with the same purpose of analysing their organizational structure and computer work as I did in the London Unit

5.2   Stay at the Nuclear Studies Centre in Saclay, France

In Saclay, the Nuclear City of France, there was an "Arithmetical Electronic Service" where I spent the second part of my fellowship.

5.2.1 Programming and technical work

The machines in Saclay were: the IBM's 1401, 1620, 704 and 7090 and one Ferranti Mercury. The work system was "closed store", so I could never visit the Computing Centre, nor run my programs in any of their computers.

In view of the equipment they had, a short period of my stay in Saclay was devoted to learn and practice FORTRAN, the high-level language that had been in use in the computing world since 1959 and was useful to programme the IBM machines in use in the Centre.

The subject in Numerical Analysis that the Senior Analyst of the Mathematical staff, (with whom I was assigned to work), suggested, was the study and adjustment of a method in Approximation of Functions.

This part of the fellowship was completed at the Blaise Pascal Institute, where the Francis method for solving matrix eigenvalues subject that I worked in during my stay in the London Unit, was translated by me into FORTRAN, tested and later used by the Institute.

5.2.2 Courses

Two complete courses in Numerical Analysis were attended to during that second part of my fellowship. They took place in the Henry Poincare Institute, and they were:

a) Approximation methods to solve Partial Differential Equations of the elliptic type, lectured by Jacques Louis Lions, a famous French researcher.

b) Matrix Calculus, taught by Jean Louis Rigal- (With the purpose of making possible the use of CHLF in our Institut´s Mercury, a new version, "version B", of the CHLF routine was written and with some adjustments performed by members of the staff of our Institute, and put to use in our Mercury)

6.   End of Clementina's Era

Political changes in our countries always bring important changes in authorities, in educational institutions and in the Universities.

A political event also marked the end of Clementina, but The Mercury computers continued operating in other places of the world. Our Mercury was beginning to be dismantled shortly after the Institute of Calculus had an important change of staff following the military coup [3].

7. Epilogue

In 1966, a military coup and the brutal invasion by the army of some institutions, one of which was the School of Natural and Exact Sciences and our Institute of Calculus, where students and professors were beaten and injured, had disastrous effects.

In our Institute, the 90% of the scientists, professors and staff resigned and took on relevant positions in the country and abroad, working in private and state institutions. Whole teams of great scientific importance emigrated and went to enrich other communities. Most of them left the country and took with them their knowledge and expertise. Those groups were successful in the country and abroad in everything they undertook.

Our mentor, *Manuel Sadosky*, was exiled, first in Venezuela and afterwards in Barcelona, Spain. In Barcelona he took part in the creation of a Science Museum for Children.

In Venezuela a group of scientist from our Institute filled important positions at the Simon Bolivar University and the Central University of Venezuela; where they had successful careers.

Manuel Sadosky, was invited later in Uruguay, where he repeated the experience of the Institute of Calculus, joined the "Universidad de la Republica" of Uruguay and obtained an "Honoris Causa" title in Montevideo.

References

[1] Aráoz Durand Julián. *Camino crítico aplicado a la construcción de edificios*. [Publicación 12 del Instituto de Cálculo].

[2] Babini N. (1997): *La llegada de la computadora a la argentina* Llull.20

[3] Babini N. (2003): *La argentina y la computadora*, [Editorial Dunken]

[4] Broker R.A.,Richards B.,Berg E,,Kerr R.H.:(1961): *Mercury Autocode Manual* [University of Manchester]

[5] Durand, W. O. (1966). *Introducción al lenguaje Comic* [Publicación 14 del Instituto de Cálculo]

[6] Gradowczyk M.H. *Tensiones térmicas en cáscaras elásticas delgadas* [Publicación 2 del Instituto de Cálculo]

[7] INTA- Instituto Nacional de Tecnología Agropecuaria. *El uso de la computadora Ferranti Mercury en el análisis de los datos experimentales* [Buenos Aires – INTA]

[8] Sadosky Manuel. *Cinco años del Instituto de Cálculo de la Universidad de Buenos Aires. 1961-1966*. Ciencia Nueva - No.17

[9] Varsavsky Oscar y Aráoz Julián. *Estudio del aprovechamiento hidráulico de ríos andinos por el método de modelos numéricos*. [Publicación 11 del Instituto de Cálculo].

[10] Zadunaisky, P., V. Pereyra, C. Berdichevsky, G. Oliver, E. Ruspini, G. Galimberti (1964). *Un método para la estimación de errores propagados en la solución numérica de un sistema de ecuaciones ordinarias* [Publicación .1 del Instituto de Cálculo].

[11] Zadunaisky, P., V. Pereyra, C. Berdichevsky, G. Oliver, E. Ruspini, G. Galimberti. *El movimiento del Cometa Halley durante el retorno de 1910* [Publicación 4 del Instituto de Cálculo]

Evolution of Computer Science Degrees at Science School-University of Buenos Aires (FCEN-UBA)

Pablo Factorovich

*1 Sociedad Argentina de Informática e Investigación Operativa, Uruguay 252 piso 2 D,
1015, Buenos Aires, Argentina, http://www.sadio.org.ar
2 University of Buenos Aires, Science School, CS Department, Ciudad Universitaria |
Pabellón I P.B. (C1428EGA), Buenos Aires, Argentina, <pfactoro@dc.uba.ar>,
http://www.dc.uba.ar*

Abstract. This paper shows the evolution of the Computador Científico (Computer Scientist) undergraduate program of the University of Buenos Aires Science School, and how it evolve into Licenciado en Ciencias de la Computación (Computer Science Degree). The original curriculum content is shown, the attempts to modify the program are explained and finally a comparison is made between the early program and the beginnings of the Computer Science Degree from 1983. This evolution is analyzed taken into account the development of new areas in CS and the argentinean political situation in this period.

1. Introduction

In 1956 the University of Buenos Aires (UBA) was reorganized after peronist administrations of 1945-1955. The following period of 1956-1966 was probably the most prolific of this university, particularly its Science School (FCEN). This was due to several reasons, including changes in UBA internal structure, the return of intellectuals that had been forced to leave for political reasons and the creation of the CONICET (an organism to help developing research, similar French CNRS or the NSF in the EEUU) in 1958. This period finished with the General Onganía's coup, followed by the well-known violent intervention of UBA, called "Noche de los bastones largos".

As a result of the Science School reorganization the new "Instituto de Cálculo" (IC, Computing Institute) was created by Manuel Sadosky. It began activities in

---

Please use the following format when citing this chapter:

Factorovich, P., 2006, in IFIP International Federation for Information Processing, Volume 215, History of Computing and Education 2 (HCE2), ed. J. Impagliazzo, (Boston: Springer), pp. 217–226.

1957 giving courses. The next year CONICET bought a Ferranti Mercury II scientific computer (named Clementina) to be used in the IC. The IC had an important production in many research areas like statistics, econometric models, theory of languages, differential equations resolution, fluid mechanics and operations research. The IC also produced high quality wide range applications for industry and government. Because of the intervention of UBA in 1966, most of the IC researchers (who also were professors and assistants) left the FCEN [1].

2.   Computador Científico Undergraduate Program

"Computador Científico" (CC, Computer Scientist) program was created at the end of 1963 and was first taught in 1964 at the Mathematical Department. Manuel Sadosky was the main driver CC for its creation. The main program goals were: systematize the courses that IC already offered and to educate professionals fundamental skills, allowing them and not to depend on proprietary training by hardware providers companies like IBM or Borroughs. The graduate goal was to be assistant of scientists and engineers looking for massive computing [1]. The name of the program was chosen because of the use of *scientific computers* (as opposed to *commercial computers*, used for administrative systems).

During its first years, the relationship between CC people and the IC was crucial. Most of the teachers (professors and its assistants) were researchers at the IC; many students helped with research projects, and used the same computer the researchers used for work for their homework. So, the excellent and prolific production of the IC worked as a very good influence for generating a CC degree of great quality.

The CC program was three year and a half (seven periods) long. The courses to be taken were:
- six courses shared with mathematical students: *probability and statistics, algebra, geometry* (linear algebra) and *calculus I, II* and *III* ;
- four core courses of computer science: *data processing systems, operations research* and *numerical analysis I* and *II* ;
- plus 8 credits in three or four elective courses.

The core courses covered the followed subject:
- *Data processing systems*: comprised architecture and organization of a computer system, namely logical internal components (like ALU and CU), input output system, file organization, compilers and primitive operative systems(OS).
- *Numerical analysis I*: included FORTRAN programming bases, numeration system error propagation and methods for solving common problems like equation roots finding, interpolation, integration, curve fitting, resolution of linear equations systems, eigenvalues computing, etc.
- *Numerical analysis II*: comprised differential equations resolution methods.

- *Operations research*: included linear and integer linear programming with applications to problems of assignment of resources, flow, etc; game theory was also taught in the early courses.

2.1   Elective courses

In this section, we will cover the relevant elective courses for CC that were given from 1964 to 1981. In tables 1 and 2 we can see the list of all classes given and the year of its appearance.

In the second semester of 1964, the first elective courses, operations research II, curve fitting and programming complements, were first taught. The former included some embryonic topics (in 1964): stochastic simulation, queues theory, graph theory and later dynamic programming.

The subject of the latter was assembler language and its relationship with the OS. In 1965, a course that dealt with low-level hardware was taught a single time: logic of digital computers. This topic has never been approached again in that school[1].

From that year to 1967 some courses related do Varsavsky's econometric group were given: mathematical economy, macroeconomic, econometrics and economic models and econometric models. Probably, since Varsavsky's group left FCEN motivated by Onganía's intervention, this line of research was abandoned and so were its classes too.

At the end of 1960's, looking at the curriculum and considering that few elective courses were been given, we can infer that a graduate could choose between two mayor subjects: numerical analysis and operations research (including everything related to optimization of resources). This can also be noticed by looking at the names of the only argentinean graduate associations in 1960's: "Sociedad Argentina de Cálculo" (Computing Argentine Society) and "Sociedad Argentina de Informática e Investigación" (Operations Research Society).

However, in the following years, many of the techniques involved in operations research(OR) constituted its own courses as a reflex of its "emancipation" process. New courses related to "Systems" were added to the program and also some specific subjects "emancipated" from applied mathematics and electronic engineering. Alone with this process a shift of the focus from continuum disciplines to discrete ones can be observed (table 1 to table 2). This is similar the pure mathematics shift of subjects since beginnings of the twentieth century.

---

[1] This sort of subject was mainly developed at Engineering School of UBA

Table 1. Courses started between 1964 and 1970

Year	Systems	Operations research	Programming	CS new areas	Numerical analysis & app
1964	Programming complements	Operations research II			Curve fitting
1965	Digital computers logic	Stochastic sequences; Math economy			Experiments design
1966		Stochastic phenomena; Macroeconomic; Econometrics and economic models			Statistical inference
1967	Introduction to OS	Variations & optimization computing; Variations computing II; Simulations; Econometric models	Programming languages		
1968	Remote information processing	Optimum control theory	Computing exercises		
1969		Stochastic processes	Programming	Languages & compilers	
1970	Timesharing languages; Simulation & design of systems		Programming II	Introduction to sequential machines	

In the context of the "Systems" area, operative systems and remote information processing appeared. The latter included topics like communication network, timeshare systems and real-time systems, began to be used for flight reservations in 1970's. In 1979, that subject was revisited in a modern way by teleprocessing.

In 1967 programming languages focused on APL and PL/I, in 1969 programming on FORTRAN and Assembler, and in 1970 programming II on COBOL and administrative systems. But in 1974, programming had a big improvement moving its subject to modular and structured programming following Dijkstra's theory, and providing some functional programming concepts, which is very similar to the way programming is being taught today in FCEN. The first approach to functional programming was in 1972 with Lists programming which focused on Lisp.

Table 2. Courses started between 1972 and 1981

Year	Systems	Operations research	Programming	CS new areas	Numerical analysis & app
1972			Lists processing; Information structure	Math seminar; Compilers design	Integrals equations
1973			Adm. systems	Math, computability & complexity seminar; Information retrieval	Numerical process error bounding; Finite elements methods
1974		Graph theory			
1975	Systems simulation seminar	Dynamic programming			Biomath; Biomath seminar; Computing errors & CS theory seminar
1976		Matroids introduction			Mechanics for CS
1977			Programming III		Analogical-digital simulation
1978		Differential games		Databases	
1979	Teleprocessing			Computer graphics	
1980				Artificial intelligence	
1981	Data processing system eval.		Pascal & Ada languages.	Math. theory of comp; Logic & auto. inference	

In 1972 information structure taught the main mathematical containers (sets, maps, Cartesian products, etc.), some of its implementations (lists, balanced trees, hash tables, etc) and some applications too. In the following years, the last topic became more important leading the course to applications in databases.

In 1969 languages and compilers had been included using some primitive formalisms that were improved in the next year when "introduction to sequential machines" appeared. This course introduced the Halting Problem representing the first appearance of theoretical CS topics in the curriculum. Since 1975 biomathematics and biomathematics seminar started to study application of maths and computing to circulatory system, biological systems and environment, using a large variety of techniques like graph theory, image patter recognition, simulation, differential equations resolution, curve fitting, etc.

In 1976 the so called "Proceso de Reorganzación" dictatorship begun. Many FCEN professors had to leave Argentina or were killed[2] and some recent improvements were rolled back. As an example of this, programming course left Dijkstra's theory and functional programming moving back to Assembler. For more examples see sect. 2.2

Though databases subject had been presented previously in information structure and data processing systems the database course started to be taught in 1978 and 1980 had very similar topics to current ones (for instance, relational database or distributed systems).

Data processing system evaluation taught established formal parameters and computational methods to evaluate systems giving birth of a software engineering area. Finally, logic and automatic inference focused on Prolog and its use to prove theorems.

2.2   Evolution of elective courses and politics

In this section we will try to analyze the influence of political changes on the development of new elective courses.

As a first remark, we can see a fall in the number of elective courses in the years related to changes of administration: 1966, 1971, 1975, and 1976-77. The only exception to this observation is the year 1973, and it was likely due to the return of democracy after 1966-1973 military administrations (see figure I).

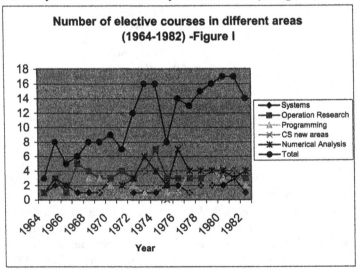

² Actually, this process started one year before at the end of peronist administration

As a second remark, the proportion of new Operation Research courses grew in the years of *coup d'etats* (1966 and 1976) and in 1975, when the peronist administration in Argentina turn to the right. In addition, the proportion of new "Systems" courses was not altered in those years (see figure II). We will mention, as a possible explanation for these facts, that operation research area in Argentina was traditionally related to the army (in particular CITEFA, the research army institute) and "Systems" area were more related to business (less influenced by politics).

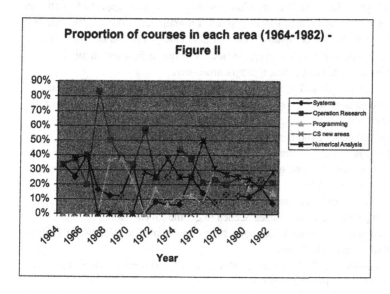

As a final remark, the fall of "Numerical Analysis" courses in 1966 shown the impact of IC researchers quits.

2.3   1973-1974: The failed creation of a Licenciatura en Computación

This section summarizes a process that is not known by the community, even in the FCEN. Since the middle of 1960's some problems of the curriculum were detected.

- The lack of training to work in business environment since it was a scientific degree. Companies had started to need professionals and there were no systems engineering degree in Argentina to supply the demand.
- Giving the huge evolution of CS, training was becoming insufficient to per form research activities.

Prior to the "Noche de los bastones largos", some discussion including professors and students had begun trying to find a curriculum for a Licenciatura (five years degree) similar to others in Science School like mathematics, physics or chemistry. The project was delayed because of the already explained consequences of the intervention in UBA.

In May of 1973 elected president Cámpora assigned new authorities for UBA that quickly approved making of Calculus III and Numerical Analysis II elective courses for those considering working in industry[3].

A year later, with some of the people that had left FCEN in 1966 back, the four and a half year Licenciatura en Computación plan was approved, with an intermediate degree after the first two years: Programmer. The goal of the last degree was to supply the companies needs of personnel, while the the first one was created thinking in scientists and project leaders working in business in mind.

The courses needed to become a programmer were:

- two courses shared with mathematical students: calculus I and algebra;
- introduction to CS, giving a first approach to several subjects of the program;
- programming I and II : following topics explained in sect. 2.1;
- systems I and II : the former related to hardware and the latter to batch processes, compilers, generation of computers, loaders, file systems, etc;
- programming lab;
- numerical applications: similar to Numerical Analysis;

The following were the extra courses needed to get the Licenciatura.

- improve mathematical concepts by complements on calculus, probability and statistics and logic;
- programming III : combinatorial algorithms and formalization of concepts presented in previous courses;
- operations research;
- introduction to compilers;
- another courses of system area: operative systems, system architectures and systems lab;
- three elective courses of certain area.

However, and as a result of the lack of policies followed by different argentinean administrations, Licenciatura was dissolved few month after its creation by new authorities in FCEN[4] and the program rolled back to CC degree. The reasons that authorities gave for taking that decision was that school had very few professors or assistants and with not enough formation to teach the degree.

Also, they argued that with this set of scholastics was not possible to educate researchers and that the goal of this school was not to form businessmen. Finally

---

[3] About 85% of students considered that option as record by a poll

[4] In 1974 a new peronist government, more rightist than the previous one, assumed in Argentina

the authorities suggested to form people in foreign countries or to hire experts to teach in FCEN in order to create a Licenciatura in the future.

Probably the reason for the lack of professors was due to massive resignations for political reasons, and it was intentionally left out of the considerations given by the authorities. As a prove of this massive resignations, the number of elective courses went down from 16 to 8 from the first months of 1974 to the beginning of 1975. This shows that the number of professors was reduced dramatically.

3.   Beginning of Licenciatura en Computación: 1982 Curriculum

With the restoration of democracy in Argentina, in 1982, the need for a change in the undergraduate program became clear since it had been created to train programmers in numerical analysis and operation research, assistants for scientific of other disciplines. A Licenciatura had to be created since a new science had arisen and the new political situation made it possible.

The core of new curriculum included five mathematical courses (algebra I, geometry, probability and statistics, calculus I and II), numerical analysis I and II, introduction to CS, programming I and II (this one oriented to software engineering), two of systems (data processing systems and operative systems), operations research, artificial intelligence, programming languages theory and databases. Also, 15 credits in elective courses had to be accomplished to get the degree. The new curriculum was designed using the core courses of Computador Científico, plus some of its elective classes and introduction to CS.

Besides, this curriculum was similar to the ACM recommended one for CS in 1986[4], but considering the elective courses proposed by ACM as part of the core[5]. Some differences could be found in the number of numerical analysis courses and the approach to programming, that actually was more similar to the curriculum suggested by ACM in 1978[3].

4.   Conclusion

In the 20 years analyzed it can be observed the large evolution that CS experienced, both in developing new areas and in teaching its subjects. However, the coming and goings of argentinean politics made the changes slower than they should have been, delaying the development of CS in Argentina and missing the chance given by the IC.

---

[5] This is as a fair approximation since a bachelor degree is 3 years long and a licenciatura is 5 years long

References

[1] Babini N, La informática en la Argentina (1956-1966) (Letra Buena, Buenos Aires, 1991).

[2] Babini N, La Argentina y la computadora. Crónica de una frustración. Dunken, Buenos Aires, 2003).

[3] Austin R, Barnes B, Bonnette D, Engel G, Stokes G, Curriculum '78: recommendations for the undergraduate program in computer science a report of the ACM curriculum committee on computer science from Communications of the ACM 22(3), 144-166 (1979).

[4] Gibbs N, Tucker A, A model curriculum for a liberal arts degree in computer science from Communications of the ACM 29(3), 202-166 (1986)